Best Wishes!
Frances Patton Statham

Mountain Legacy

Mountain Legacy

A Story of Rabun Gap-Nacoochee School
With Emphasis on the Junior College Years

Frances Patton Statham

Cherokee Publishing Company
Atlanta, Georgia
1999

Library of Congress Cataloging-in-Publication Data
Statham, Frances Patton.
  Mountain legacy : a story of Rabun Gap-Nacoochee School with
emphasis on the junior college years / Frances Patton Statham. –
1st ed.
    p.   cm.
  Includes bibliographical references (p.) and index.
  ISBN 0-87797-282-6
  1. Rabun Gap-Nacoochee School–History–20th century.   I. Title.
LD7501.R23S73   1999
378.758.123–dc21   99-28287
                                                              CIP

This book is printed on acid-free paper which conforms to the American
National Standard Z39.48-1984 *Permanence of Paper for Printed Library
Materials.* Paper that conforms to this standard's requirements for pH, alkaline
reserve and freedom from ground wood is anticipated to last several hundred
years without significant deterioration under normal library use and storage
conditions. ∞

Manufactured in the United States of America
First Edition
ISBN: 0-87797-282-6
03 02 01 00 99   10 9 8 7 6 5 4 3 2 1
Design by Kenneth W. Boyd and Nancy Hutchison Prentice
Cover illustration by William J.J. Chase

 Cherokee Publishing Company
P O Box 1730, Marietta, Ga 30061

"...I would address one admonition to all; that they consider what are the true ends of knowledge, and that they seek it not either for pleasure of the mind, or for contention, or for superiority to others, or for profit, or fame, or power, or any of these inferior things; but for the benefit of life; and that they perfect and govern it in charity."

Francis Bacon, *Instauratio Magna*

Contents

PART THREE
POST WORLD WAR II

Introduction

This book is a celebration of spirit, of times past in the history of a community, a state, a nation – a story whose significance might have vanished as easily as rain forests before an encroaching civilization, except for the farsightedness of one group of people, who approached me to record their stories.

As the author of other historical works, I have often seen how interpreters of history, in choosing what is considered important for that day, have overlooked the events that assume much greater relevance to new generations. And only when the information becomes irretrievable, does one mourn for what might have provided important insights into an era.

This story of Rabun Gap-Nacoochee School traces the path of faith, strong ethics, and hunger for knowledge that began with Andrew Jackson Ritchie and his wife Addie Corn, who gave up their own promising futures to return to the isolated valley of their youth.

Divided by feuds, illiteracy, and poverty, the people of the valley were persuaded to come together as one community, to share in the Ritchies' dream — the establishment of a school that they could proudly claim as their own.

Mountain Legacy is not intended to be a definitive history of the school in its centennial year. Rather, its emphasis is on a unique time period, encompassing the years 1934-45, when the junior college was in existence.

History and biography are interchangeable. And the role of an author concerned with both is not only to show historical milestones, but as Samuel Johnson pointed out, "to lead the thoughts into domestic privacies and display the minute details of daily life."

And so, in Part Two, in the profiles and reminiscences of the school's junior college alumni, who later became educators, doctors, war heroes, and outstanding citizens, I have tried to capture the essence of those remarkable years.

But as our nation changed, Rabun Gap-Nacoochee School changed, as well. Old priorities and struggles gave way to new challenges and to new visions for the future. This change is reflected in Part Three, in the chronicled events that occurred after World War II and the dissolution of the junior college department.

To each reader, I hope you will enjoy this picture of a mountain school and especially the events that shaped those who walked the hills and valleys of north Georgia in times past.

Frances Patton Statham

Part One

The Early Years

DR. ANDREW JACKSON RITCHIE

Mrs. Addie Corn Ritchie

Chapter One
ESTABLISHMENT OF RABUN GAP INDUSTRIAL SCHOOL

HODGSON HALL

n a valley surrounded by the majestic Blue Ridge Mountains in the northeast corner of Georgia, a unique school thrives—one that had its inception nearly one hundred years ago, with the goal of making a better life for the isolated mountain people.

Today, the influence of the Rabun Gap-Nacoochee School reaches far beyond the dreams of its founders. Despite devastating fires, wars, the Great Depression, and other adversities, the school survived, while the indomitable spirit of its earlier students has manifested itself into a mountain legacy that flourishes in the lives of continuing generations.

Yet, after the Civil War, no region of the United States seemed less destined to achieve success for its inhabitants than this Appalachian valley, hemmed in by surrounding peaks—Rabun Bald, Pickens Nose, and Massengale Mountain.

In those early years, if anyone asked for directions to this northernmost county of Georgia, the answer would more likely have been, "Go one day by railroad, one day by horse and buggy, a third on horseback, a day on foot, and then on all fours until you climbed a tree. And when you fell out, you'd be in Rabun County."

In 1895, a young man of the valley by the name of Andrew Jackson Ritchie was equally at a disadvantage when he chose to leave the county for the fourth time to continue his education. A former student of W.A. Curtis, a Civil War soldier who had opened a log cabin school in the area, he still had a burning desire to learn — to get beyond Noah Webster's Blue-Back Speller and McGuffey's Reader that he had studied in the Curtis School and later in Hiawassee. He was older than most students — twenty-seven — when he left for Harvard College. In fits and starts, he had already gone to school at Emory at Oxford, stopped and worked, then spent a year at Baylor University in Texas, before his money again ran out.

Each time he came back home, penniless, his neighbor, Uncle Roland Coffee, would always ask his father if he had graduated. When told, "Not yet," the mountain man would shake his head and say, "I hain't never been to no college. And I don't know nothin' about it. But there must be a heap to larn in a college, or else Andy must larn mighty slow."

ANDREW J. RITCHIE AS A YOUNG MAN

In his book, *Sketches of Rabun County History*, Ritchie described those dark days and his despondency in having his collegiate education interrupted so many times because of the lack of money. But in the Baylor library, he had found a pamphlet that gave him new hope, for it spoke of an opportunity for a few students to work their way through Harvard, although the college was well-known as a rich man's school.

Coming back from Texas on a rail pass, Ritchie, with this final hope spurring him on, worked hard during that summer on the family farm, while his mother sewed new shirts and knitted socks to pack in the battered trunk that he would take with him that fall.

After the war that impoverished the South, Andy Ritchie's father, Riley Bunton Ritchie, had purchased four hundred acres of mountain land from the other Ritchie heirs. On it, he had settled down to farm and raise a family. Content, he could not understand why this particular son was eager to leave, to pursue more education. Yet, as a young man, Riley had also pursued a distant goal—traveling to California twice, first by ship and then by wagon across the prairie—to find the gold that he had used to purchase the farm.

Reconciled at his son's course of action, Riley shared a portion of the money made in cash crops that season to help pay his tuition. So, with his application mailed to Harvard, Ritchie headed toward Atlanta in a circuitous route that would eventually take him North. Finally catching a freight train ride in the cinder box engine with the fireman and engineer, he changed short line trains several times. Five days later, he arrived at the terminal in Atlanta. There he "bought a scalper's ticket" for thirteen dollars to Boston.

When he presented himself in President Eliot's office, Ritchie received disheartening news. "Did you not get my letter?" the president asked. "I told you not to come. There's no room for you here."

Nevertheless, Dr. Eliot relented when he heard Andy Ritchie's story. If he could find a room in a private house where he could work for his board, then the young Georgia man would be admitted as a student. So Ritchie, dressed in the one suit he owned, began knocking at doors. Up and down the residential streets of Cambridge he went until, at last, a kind lady of the house told him that he could live in an attic room in exchange for shoveling snow and keeping the furnace running.

Elated, he returned to the campus and paid his tuition. But

when he tried to find his lodgings again, he could not. He had failed to note the name of the street and the number on the brownstone house. In the city, all the houses looked alike to him. So he not only lost his lodgings, but the trunk containing his clothes, as well.

By the next day, Ritchie found a job in a restaurant, which would earn him enough money to pay room and board. Unfortunately, the restaurant was a mile away, with no trolley line running toward the school. So that first year, he walked back and forth to classes in snow and sleet.

Ritchie succumbed to the cold of that New England winter. Despite his earning a scholarship for that next year, he returned South to get well, and he did not go back to Harvard for two years.

In the meantime, he enrolled at the University of Georgia. As a recipient of the Joe Brown Loan Fund, he was able to finish the work towards an A.B. degree, with a year of law school. Awarded an LL.B degree also, he was fully qualified to practice law. But his heart had been set on college teaching.

Once more, he found himself at Harvard, to prepare for teaching college English composition and literature. His work scholarship in the dining room and his private tutoring helped to take care of his expenses, while he earned his A.B. degree in that discipline, graduating in the class of 1899. In 1901, he received the A.M degree from Harvard, which also awarded him an honorary A.M degree in 1924 — followed by an honorary Ped.D degree in 1926 from the University of Georgia.

Earlier in Ritchie's student career, the school at Hiawassee, Georgia had played an important part in his life. There, he had first met the teacher and minister, George Truett, who later became a trustee at Baylor University in Texas. And it was there, also, that he and another student from the valley, diminutive, red-headed Addie Corn, had come to an understanding. Each shared the same dream — to get a college degree and then to marry and spend a lifetime of service together. Addie, five years younger, had done as her future husband had done—working her way through college in increments—going to school, then teaching, then returning to school, so that, by the time Andy came home from Harvard in 1899, she had also graduated—from Georgia State College for Women.

Now, the prospects looked bright for both of these young people, who had worked so hard to achieve success. Alerted by George Truett of the vacancy of the English Department Head at Baylor, Ritchie applied for the position and was hired. He and Addie were married on August 19, 1900 and left for Texas. Their future in higher education seemed assured, with Addie also finding a place—in the Home Economics Department.

For several years they remained at Baylor, returning to the mountains of Georgia only during summer vacations. By the third summer, their small daughter Ruth accompanied them.

Nothing had changed in the valley. The area was just as isolated and poverty-stricken as it had ever been. That beautiful land, with its mountain feuds, moonshine stills, and barefoot, illiterate children, seemed frozen in time. According to the 1900 census, over thirty percent of Georgia's voters could neither read nor write. The percentage of illiteracy was even higher in Rabun County.

Addie Corn and Andy Ritchie looked at each other, as if to say, "What are we doing, so far away from the valley, when our own people need us so desperately?"

Their ensuing decision was met with alarm by the elder Ritchie. "I know these mountain people," he said. "They won't support you, and you'll never be successful in starting a school for them here in the valley. You will wear out your life in old rocky Rabun County, and have nothing to show for it." But again, his mother, Sarah Ann Martin Ritchie, must have seen the determination in Andy's eyes. If this were what he wanted to do, then he should be encouraged to do it.

With that said, both father and mother gave him full support, despite misgivings. How hard it must have been to see this son, who had worked so diligently, resign from his college position at Baylor and begin to look for land upon which to build his fragile dream.

With one dollar and a personal note, Professor Andrew Ritchie chose the school site—the first five acres set upon a magnificent hill, surrounded by mountains in the distance and overlooking the countryside. For the next two years, Andy and Addie sent out letters of subscription to the community and to other would-be contributors. If it were to be a school to benefit the community children, then the members of the community were asked to support it. During that first summer, many of the people in Rabun County gave pledges according to their means, from one hundred dollars to one dollar. And those who had no cash to give pledged so many hours of manual labor to work on the project. Soon, the young couple had raised five thousand dollars in pledges within the county.

Judge Logan E. Bleckley, who was a native of Rabun County and a friend of the Ritchie family, had been impressed enough to go the bond for loans and introduce Andrew Ritchie to friends in Atlanta, as well as write a testimonial for him to present in his fund raising.

Dated January 4, 1904, a year after Ritchie had first introduced the idea of the school to him, the judge wrote in part: "....There is no school above elementary grades within the limits of the county." He went on to show the need for the numerous poor children to be given a chance, since "many of them have as bright minds as can be found on Earth."

In tribute to the young man he had known all his life, Bleckley said of Ritchie, "He is devoting his time and energies to this noble work as a labor of love, and without hope of other reward than the good which others may derive from it in years to come."

All his life, Ritchie treasured this testimonial that carried such weight in his Georgia fund raising.

Yet another show of faith from Judge Bleckley enriched those beginnings. Commissioned by the judge, his son, Haralson Bleckley, an Atlanta architect, designed the main building. With the blueprints in hand, for the two-story building with basement, the newly elected board of trustees could begin construction.

The men who had pledged manual labor began clearing the building site and hauling granite from the nearby mountain. At two dollars a day, two local stone masons began to construct the walls of the basement.

It was not long before the building committee realized that it would take ten thousand dollars to build this main building. To complicate matters, few of those who had pledged a hundred dollars each could come up with the cash at that time.

The naysayers, who had suggested from the start that the project was doomed to failure, shook their heads and decided that the only recourse was to abandon this scheme.

The pessimists had not counted on Ritchie's remarkable resilience in the face of adversity. He would not give up. More money could be raised, he thought, but it would have to come from benefactors outside the county.

MR. PRINCE HODGSON

On a trip to the University of Georgia, Ritchie sought out the chancellor of the university, who seemed uninterested in the idea of a remote mountain school. But he gave him the name of Mr. Edward R. "Prince" Hodgson, an Athens businessman.

Listening to his story, Mr. Hodgson said he would look into the matter, once he got some of his pressing obligations out of the way. And if he felt it a worthy cause, then he might be able to help.

Ritchie returned to Rabun County where the work continued, until one Saturday afternoon when the workers were paid with the last money left in the fund.

As Ritchie and the building superintendent, David Rickman, stood on the hillside and discussed what course to take, a horse and buggy suddenly appeared on the dirt road below.

Prince Hodgson had sent his son Ned to assess the situation. The ensuing conversation brought the project back to life. On the next day, a Sunday, instead of a church service in the little church in the Tennessee Valley, the people gathered to hear the message that Hodgson would give one thousand dollars to the building fund if the people could raise fifteen hundred to match it. The people accepted the challenge and the construction continued.

But just as Ritchie had been forced to stop his education each time his money had run out, so the construction of the building stopped until more money came in.

By 1905, two years from the time the land was purchased, the main building, named Hodgson Hall, was completed, with dormitory space for boarding students who lived too far away to walk to school.

Hiring college trained teachers, the school opened to both mountain boys and girls, who were given the opportunity to work and study for an education beyond the three-to-five month term of the nearest rural school.

The school land, with abundant rainfall, was lush with vegetation—fields waiting to be plowed; gardens to be hoed; cows to be milked; corn to be harvested; and sorghum syrup to be made. The students worked two days each week during the school session and went to classes for four. And Addie and Andy Ritchie worked tirelessly to nourish these students as carefully as the land, so that they would gain self-confidence, self-esteem, and lose some of the shyness that isolated children throughout all rural areas seem to possess in great quantity.

STUDENTS CHURNING BUTTER (CA.1908)

More land was purchased; more buildings were erected, while the first benefactor of the school, Prince Hodgson, who had continued to give generously, oversaw activities from his small clapboard summer cottage across the road. This was the same rustic house in which Rabun County's first teacher, W.A. Curtis, had once lived and also the future home of the Ritchies.

Without Addie Ritchie, the school would not have run so smoothly. She seemed to be everywhere—tending to the office, putting her arms around a homesick student, and taking over completely when her husband Andy traveled to find funds for work scholarships and the unending expenses incurred in a school without an endowment.

A large test of faith came for them both when, in 1914, World War I began in Europe, just at the height of a major fund raising campaign for the school. Overnight, the shipping of cotton, lumber, and other goods that Georgia exported to Europe was curtailed, and the fiscal future of Georgia seemed to be jeopardized. For the next two years, the school received few donations, and the necessary operating expenses began plunging the school into debt.

During the crisis of those war years, when Ritchie was attempting to save the school and its educational program, and the older students who had been the work force on the school farm were leaving the campus to join the American Expeditionary Forces, a letter from his wife Addie must have given him tremendous encouragement.

"If I saw I was going to fail in Atlanta," she wrote, "I'd borrow money from Mr. Parrott (another generous contributor) and go straight to Boston and fight for life to raise the $50,000.... It could be done there. We can run things here for a year all right. We can take care of the farm and the school. Just leave things to us, and go.

"...If those rich men won't help you, go to President Eliot.... The Lord will surely take care of us. Affectionately, Addie."

Andy took his wife's advice. Armed with a unique plan to present to the Carnegie Foundation and the moneyed members of his Harvard class, he went north, to Boston and New York.

Trustees Powell, A. Grist, Addie Ritchie, and Bob Ritchie (ca. 1914)

FARM FAMILY HARVESTING SORGHUM CANE

Chapter Two
FARM FAMILY SETTLEMENT PROGRAM

DR. RITCHIE INTERVIEWING MOUNTAIN FARMER

've never heard of that kind of school before—a farm school for whole families," Dr. Pritchett, president of the Carnegie Foundation, said when Ritchie presented his unique plan.

Earlier, during the acquisition of farm property surrounding the school, Ritchie had allowed the tenant farmers to remain in the cottages and their children to attend the school. The tenants had helped to supplement the labor lost when the young men students had left for military service.

Now, Ritchie had a much broader vision. With an expansion of three hundred acres, he could develop the Farm Family Settlement Program—building other cottages, selecting outstanding, hardworking tenants, who could be educated the same time as their children. With a definite length of residence—no more than five years—the men would be taught classes in agriculture, dairying, and related industries, while their wives received classes in homemaking and health care. Once the residency term was up, then the families would return to their communities, with a better knowledge of running a productive farm and enjoying a more educated way of life.

Impressed with this unusual idea, Dr. Pritchett sent an agent to Rabun Gap to investigate. "To bring together a colony of mountain families with their children," he later wrote, "and make them part of the school, and then send them out in the neighborhood with a whole crop of new ideas and habits—while another group comes in— if such a scheme can be made to work... the problem of the isolated rural community is solved."

The Carnegie Corporation became a benefactor to the school, donating twenty thousand dollars for the purchase of the three hundred additional acres, and several years later another twenty thousand dollars for the building of farm homes and a new community school, provided that matching funds could be raised by January 1, 1921—in less than two months.

A fellow classmate of Ritchie's at Harvard was Henry James (the nephew of the famous novelist), whom he had not seen in twenty years. At that time, James was devoting himself to the gentlemanly pursuits of writing and overseeing various philanthropies, including the Rockefeller Foundation. So Ritchie, with little time to raise the additional twenty thousand dollars, went to New York to see him. James immediately arranged for Ritchie to speak at a luncheon of former classmates. In the group were James F. Curtis, a past assistant treasurer of the United States, and then counsel to the Federal Reserve Board; Roger Wolcott, whose father had been a governor of Massachusetts; and Henry Thompson, a Boston banker. These four men would become the nucleus of Ritchie's support in the North.

On Christmas Eve, after one of the men present at the luncheon had been brave enough to approach Mr. John D. Rockefeller for his approval, the Foundation announced that it would give ten thousand dollars to the school as a Christmas gift. That left only a few days for Ritchie to find the additional ten thousand, or he would risk losing the twenty thousand from the Carnegie Foundation.

He returned to Georgia, back to his original base of supporters.

In 1893, two years before Andrew Ritchie left for Harvard, Ernest Woodruff, with his wife, the former Emily Winship, had moved from Columbus to Atlanta, to begin building a financial empire that would include the Trust Company of Georgia and the Coca-Cola Company. One man, impressed with his phenomenal success, declared that Mr. Woodruff had brought Wall Street to Atlanta.

As patriarch of a philanthropic family, that included his sons George, Henry, and Robert, he was already familiar with the mountain school.

Earlier, Andrew Ritchie had gone from door to door in an exclusive Atlanta neighborhood – Inman Park – where he had called upon the residents for donations to his school. At one home, the lady of the house had been so touched, that she gave Ritchie part of her household money. It was through her interest that her husband, Ernest Woodruff, became involved with the school.

On January 1, in Mr. Woodruff's office at Trust Company of Georgia, ten men agreed to donate a thousand dollars each to the school's project, thus saving, at the twelfth hour, the Carnegie Foundation grant.

Andrew Ritchie now had the necessary funds, and the expansion of the Farm Family program could go forward.

The Georgia Chapter of the United Daughters of the Confederacy also played a part in the plan's success. On one hundred and fifteen acres of adjacent land which it owned, the UDC built three complete cottage units.

Mr. Esco Pitts, the first family farm supervisor, helped in the construction of fourteen additional farm houses, along with barns, poultry houses, and a few silos. By 1931, Dean Henry L. Fry became administrator of the program and remained in that capacity until his retirement in 1959. His daughter, Frances Fry Deal, in the profiles of outstanding alumni, gives an intimate account of the Fry household in those years and the high esteem in which her parents, Henry and "Ma" Fry, as her mother was affectionately called by the students, were held.

During those earlier years of the settlement program, prior to 1931, Andrew Ritchie owned a Model-T Ford, but he had never taken the time to learn to drive. On campus, his wife Addie was the one seen in the driver's seat and, at certain times, as the car maneuvered the muddy ruts of the mountain back country, Esco Pitts shared driving duties while the search for prospective farm families took place.

With missionary zeal, rural families with a number of children were interviewed. After the high standards of citizenship, industry, and economy were explained, each family was invited to fill out an application to become a part of the settlement program. According to Pitts, "there was only one family that was asked to leave after the first crops were in."

With a house and barn, the families were also given space for a garden and a one-acre truck patch, a pasture suitable for two milk cows, and firewood for cooking and heating. They were required to maintain the property, attend classes—both children and adults—go to church on Sunday, and keep accurate accounts, so that by the time they returned to their communities, they would know how to handle money and perhaps have enough saved to purchase their own farms.

Each year, the harvested crops were shared equally; half going to the school; the other half to the farm family. Those who excelled were given additional incentives of bonuses and prizes.

Ritchie considered each acre of land, each kitchen, cornfield, or barn as an educational opportunity, a part of the total picture of an extended family that worked for the common good.

In such a close-knit community, where social activities on a Saturday night brought the young people together, where whole families attended church on Sundays, and adults visited on Sunday afternoons, lifelong friendships were forged. A number of these young people, "door-neighbors" to each other, later married and formed successful households of their own.

By 1926, all the programs of the school were thriving – the community school for younger children, the high school for older students, and the unique educational opportunities for the adults in the Farm Settlement program. Yet the constant search for funding had not lessened. The spectre of financial insolvency was omnipresent.

On the wintry cold morning of February 18 of that year, life on campus started no differently from the others. At Hodgson Hall, the administration building that also housed the teachers and the young women students, one of the first priorities was to start the fires that would take away the mountain chill that swept down into the valley on a blustery wind.

The carrying of wood up to the teachers' quarters was one of the morning chores assigned to the boys. When they had completed their work, all, with the exception of one boy, left for classes. A short while later, he too left the building.

The fire started insidiously, supposedly from the kitchen where sparks from a loose stovepipe escaped. But Esco Pitts had another story – of a troublemaker who had run away from school several times. He was the one who had lingered; he was the one who later told friends in his community back home what had actually happened.

Within a short time, as flames spread from the bell tower downward, the school records in the office, the living quarters, the library, and the classrooms were all destroyed. No one could save the building, or the nearby dairy barn and work rooms. When the fire had finally subsided, two sewing machines and a transit were all that remained of Addie and Andy Ritchie's dream of a mountain school that had been made manifest because of their years of faith and hard work.

Devastated at the loss, Ritchie wondered whether he would ever be able to rebuild. But he had to try. Even though the central core of the campus was gone, his faith had not been destroyed with the buildings.

The Graduating Class of 1921

MRS. REBECCA GALLOWAY COIT

Dr. John Knox Coit

NACOOCHEE INSTITUTE DORMITORY

Chapter Three
ESTABLISHMENT OF NACOOCHEE INSTITUTE

NACOOCHEE INSTITUTE 1903

n the valley of Nacoochee, west of Rabun Gap, a simi-
lar work school had opened in 1903 for underprivileged
boys and girls. Under the auspices of the Presbyterian
Church—particularly the Athens and Augusta
Presbyteries—the Nacoochee Institute began as a two-
teacher, one-room school, with the Reverend Joel T. Wade as its
first president and Miss Minnie Asbury as his assistant.

Until the late eighteen thirties, this area of Georgia that lay
between Yonah and Lynch mountains had been Cherokee land,
with place names still reflecting its Native American heritage, along
with burial mounds of an even earlier, unknown Indian civilization.
In the Cherokee language, the name Nacoochee meant "Evening
Star."

The pristine Chattahoochee River flowing through the valley
provided a plentiful water supply to the surrounding pastures and
fertile farm land, now tilled by descendants of the land lottery.

At its beginning, even though the institute was to receive
benevolent offerings from the church, the amount was meager—in

relationship to the small numbers of Presbyterians in an area settled mainly by Baptists and Methodists. So with few funds, the school did not thrive, and its doors were closed within a short time.

By 1908, the Athens Presbytery, realizing that the educational need still existed, decided to reopen the school, with the Reverend John Knox Coit to assume the presidency. Leaving a pastorate in Rock Hill, South Carolina, he arrived with his wife to find a sheriff's notice nailed to the school door. "This Property for Sale."

Upon seeing it, Dr. Coit is said to have removed the sign immediately, preferring to deal at a later date with the back taxes that had been assessed because the property in the interim had ceased being used for religious purposes.

In biographical material provided by John Knox Coit, Jr., Ph.D., the picture of two dedicated people becomes quite clear.

Born on February 12, 1872, in Charlotte, North Carolina, John Knox Coit, Sr. was the son of Julius Thornwell and Dovey Knox Coit. Prior to the Civil War, the male line on his father's side were all graduates of Harvard and Yale. By the time the son was born, educational opportunities had become limited. When he was eight years old, his father died, and his mother and three siblings moved to Salisbury, North Carolina to live with relatives.

When Coit finished public schools that ended at the ninth grade, he first went to work in a tobacco factory to support his family, since he was the eldest child. Soon thereafter, his uncle gave him a job in a cotton mill where he rose to management positions. From an early age, he was religious and seemed to connect with people. His work in churches, his traveling throughout the mountains of North Carolina to establish mission schools, and his apprenticeship with Dr. Robert Campbell, a minister in Asheville, North Carolina, finally steered him to seek more religious training at Dr. White's Bible School, now Biblical Seminary in New York.

There he met a young visitor to the school, Rebecca Galloway of Toronto, Canada, who had gone to the University of Toronto for a year and then to Moody Bible Institute in Chicago. Her father, a businessman, was also a part-time religious worker, a "licensed exhorter" in the Wesleyan Methodist Church.

When Coit was ordained and given a pastorate in South Carolina, he made a trip to Canada to claim the woman "with the deepest blue eyes" for his wife. He now had a helpmate, equally dedicated to Christian service. And when the call came for her husband to reestablish Nacoochee Institute in the mountains he loved, she willingly packed their belongings and accompanied him.

Under Dr. Coit's stewardship, the school took on new life. But much of his energy had to be devoted to visiting the various Presbyterian churches, since the suggested percentage of benevolences was not always forthcoming. Occasionally, in good weather, the entire school of teachers and the sixty or so students would walk the several miles to the railway station, choosing to accompany the surrey sent to meet the Coits returning from one of their trips. Later, another form of transportation was also used on official visits—the Coit's Model-T Ford with the name "Nacoochee" emblazoned in large white letters on its upright windshield.

In those years, the institute grew into a complex that included a boys' dormitory, a girls' dormitory, a domestic science building, and classrooms. The educational institution became a boarding school for students from both rural and urban areas—such as Atlanta and Savannah—and a public school for the students of White County.

Also under the supervision of the institute was a children's home of twenty little girls, aged two to twelve. Two babies, nine months old, were also cared for.

In an article for *Presbyterian Survey*, Dr. Coit wrote, "Think what it means to train even one child, developing the well-rounded four-fold life, through the years from childhood to graduation from high school. Think of the number dependent upon Nacoochee for food, shelter, clothing, education, and in many cases, even medical and dental bills....Then, you can better realize Nacoochee's responsibility."

At the beginning, since there were no arbitrary standards set in Georgia, the first teachers of the school ranged from "genteel young ladies of independent means who wished to do missionary work," to extremely well-educated college graduates. In reminiscing about those earlier days, the younger Coit provided a particularly vivid view regarding one of the more unusual educational events that took place on campus—a biology class taught by Mary Belle Taylor of Canandaigua, New York.

"It was a shock to me," he said, "to observe this lady-like creature cutting up dogs, cats, frogs, and earthworms. The one thing for which I never quite forgave her was the result of a commission she gave to some of the older boys to obtain the skeleton of a stray dog for laboratory use.

"The boys saw no reason for asking the first dog they encountered for his credentials. They simply picked a little black mongrel up, boiled it for a while, and delivered the skeleton to Miss Taylor. The dog was mine.

"He was not pedigreed and not very attractive. But he was my dog. He probably served a nobler purpose in death than in life, but advancing learning was not high upon my agenda at the time, and I resented the loss of my dog. Happily, all the skeletons which Miss Taylor needed when teaching history were metaphorical, and I liked history."

Clearly inheriting the wit that the senior Coit was noted for, the son also had a wry view of his mother's dealings with new students and the missionary barrels that arrived at various times at the school.

For his mother, in the hierarchy of graces, the social graces were only slightly lower than divine grace, and she firmly took new students in hand the moment each set foot on campus. Seven at the time, she invited them to her home for a crash course in manners before she began her "Monday Talks" in the central dining hall.

Greeting them at the door, she would introduce the students to each other and, after a few minutes of conversation, they were invited to the dining table, where the lessons began in earnest. Besides teaching them to give a firm handshake in greeting, the boys learned how to seat a lady properly, while the young women also received instructions as to how to be seated. The proper way to sit was also emphasized—no less than three inches separating the guest from the table, with the same distance between the person and the back of the chair while he or she was dining.

Such caveats as "Never talk while chewing," or "Always bring the food to your mouth, never the other way," or "Do not attack your meat as if it were alive and trying to escape," were considered well worth knowing. As the year progressed, finer social graces were introduced in the dining hall once a week, with Mrs. Coit walking among the tables to observe the students' improvements.

As the younger Coit commented, "Happily, one could 'be saved' without knowing good table manners, but one of the first things to be learned in heaven would surely be how to eat correctly."

Because of Mrs. Coit's Monday Talks, those students at Nacoochee Institute must have had an edge when they eventually met St. Peter.

As to the missionary barrels sent from various churches, they were welcomed most of the time, since the contents played an important part in the dealings of the school. Some of the poorer students were outfitted from them and, at times, their contents were also used to barter with the mountain people for much-needed home grown food for the kitchen. The farm and gardens which the school owned were small and did not provide an abundance.

One of the less useful barrels contained old hymn books that had gotten soaking wet in transit. Despite Mrs. Coit's attempt to dry them out in the attic, they were ruined. Never one to throw anything out, she decided the illegible pages might be used to start the morning fires. But the woman who had sent them arrived on an unexpected visit and became incensed at this cavalier treatment of her gift.

Perhaps the greatest gift to the school was one of the teachers, Miss Aline Clayton of Atlanta, who became principal. In a tribute to her, the younger Coit remarked, "The one great lady whose memory I revere, and to whom both Nacoochee and Rabun Gap owe a tremendous debt, was Miss Clayton.... She was utterly charming, personable, and unbelievably hardworking. She was in charge of the entire academic program throughout her tenure at the school. This released my father for general administrative work and fund raising. Later, when the Carnegie Foundation recommended

MISS ALINE CLAYTON AND MISS ANNA LEE JONES

her for further academic study, she pursued degrees at the University of Georgia.... When the state of Georgia finally came to pensioning public school teachers, it was Miss Clayton who received the first check from the hands of the governor at the State Capitol in Atlanta."

Over the years at Nacoochee Institute, the wooden buildings on campus seemed to be plagued by fires—resulting from overheated stoves to lightning striking during a violent electrical storm. At various times the boys' dormitory, the domestic science building, a pump, a winter's supply of wood, and a "pest house" where contagious students were quarantined, were destroyed. Coupled with this propensity for all buildings heated by fire to be at risk, there was the added risk of inadequate firefighting equipment in all rural areas at the time.

Dr. Coit was aware of the tragedy that had occurred in February of that year to the Rabun Gap Industrial School. He had met Andrew Ritchie in 1925, when Mrs. Coit was in Atlanta for surgery, and a troubled Ritchie had come to Atlanta to see if he could raise much needed funds. A mutual friend, Judge Kontz, had suggested that the two men meet, since their problems were similar. Perhaps they could gain sustenance from each other. At the hospital, the two men, in charge of similar schools with all their inherent problems, had gotten down on their knees to pray together and ask for the Lord's guidance. Judge Kontz, in remembering this event, remarked that "there are no accidents." In light of what was to come, the meeting of the two, he felt, was preordained.

Now, on April first of 1926, two months after the disaster at Rabun Gap, the boarding students and faculty at the Nacoochee Institute were in the dining hall, enjoying their midday meal, while outside, a menacing high wind ripped through the campus.

"The schoolhouse is on fire," a voice shouted, as some of the day students rushed into the dining hall to tell the news. Despite the water stored in the wooden tank on the hill, and the great effort by faculty and students, the fire became uncontrollable, demolishing the main building and spreading to other buildings. Only the volumes in the library were saved—and the principal's desk. Everything else went up in flames. No cause could be found, although arson was suspected.

The fine group of teachers were left without classrooms, while over the mountain lay a campus getting ready to rebuild.

Through adversity, the two schools would merge, each bringing its strengths to the other, to become the Rabun Gap-Nacoochee School.

RABUN GAP-NACOOCHEE SCHOOL (C. 1928)

Chapter Four
The Merger of Two Schools

The New Hodgson Hall

n September 5, 1928, the rebuilt Rabun Gap-Nacoochee School opened its doors to students at Rabun Gap. The merger of the two schools was a *fait accompli*, with the financial, logistical, and administrative problems worked out in the previous two years.

Dr. Coit, at first co-president and then vice-president, had brought to the merger the support of the Presbyterian Church, most of the faculty members from Nacoochee, and the library that had been saved from the fire.

It had been decided that trustees of both schools would be equally represented on the new board of trustees, with John Bulow Campbell elected as chairman. While the church would provide yearly operating expenses of $25,000, Rabun Gap would raise $150,000 for a new main building and two dormitories, all to be fireproof.

So from 1926 to 1928, Dr. Ritchie, president, had risen to this overwhelming challenge. Through his friend, Henry James, who wrote the prospectus for fund raising in the North, Ritchie received a subscription of $50,000 from Mr. John D. Rockefeller, Jr., and in the South, another $50,000 from Mr. Ernest Woodruff and his associates at the Coca-Cola Company in Atlanta. Mr. Woodruff also became a member of the merged board of trustees of the school.

Another gift came from the Community Church Council of New York. To accommodate the number of Presbyterians moving from Nacoochee to a valley with no Presbyterian church, the Council helped to fund a third of the cost to build a community church to be shared by the several denominations, while the community raised the rest of the needed funds. "I know of no other school or community," Ritchie wrote, "where church buildings for three different denominations have been built with money raised in a single campaign."

DEAN HENRY LEE FRY

In 1931, two important events took place—the arrival of the beloved Henry Lee Fry as dean of the school, professor of agriculture, and head of the Farm Family Settlement Program; and the forming of the Rabun Gap-Nacoochee Guild in Atlanta, a women's organization whose sole purpose is to raise money for the school. With a club and junior guild formed later, the members have, over the years, raised more than a half million dollars for needed equipment and scholarships, and have provided seed money for new buildings. A guild also was formed in Athens.

The remarkable story of this era in the '30s is the school's survival in a time of economic crisis in the United States. The Great Depression had closed banks for a "holiday," some permanently. Foreclosures on farms were happening with unceasing regularity, while the price of farm goods had plummeted in the market. The average citizen had little money to spend for necessities, and unemployment in the general population was rampant.

To alleviate some of these problems, Franklin D. Roosevelt, who took office as President of the United States in 1933, removed the nation from the gold standard; established public works projects that put people to work building roads and highways, and established the Civilian Conservation Corps, better know by its initials — CCC camps — to provide work for the youth of the country.

By 1934, one of the benefits of these programs was the improvement of roads in Rabun County. With a number of roads built so that school buses could now provide transportation from isolated areas, consolidated public schools, with their free tuition and books, began to take the place of small rural schools, such as Scat-away and Scuffletown, where Addie and Andy Ritchie had first taught.

With this progress and the new educational opportunities also came the sudden diminishing of the number of high school boarding students attending Rabun Gap. Ritchie's initial goal of reaching as many students as possible in the county and surrounding areas was now tremendously successful. But that very success had brought a new problem to the boarding school.

To address that problem, the Carnegie Corporation spearheaded a study to survey the needs of the young people in the mountain area. Experts arrived on campus and remained for several weeks. When the report was written, a recommendation was made as to the future of the school. Since many of the students interviewed wished to continue their education beyond the high school level, it was recommended that the school should establish a junior college department.

Seeing the value of this apparent solution, Ritchie and the trustees received a charter for this new department, which also brought new problems of funding and building additional living space. Yet, foremost was the need for an advanced curriculum that heralded a new era in the life of the school that had been founded thirty years previously.

In the educational mix were a community school up to the ninth grade, the boarding school composed of the final two years of high school– the tenth and eleventh grades – the adult education program of the farm families, and now the junior college.

The junior college courses were designed to concentrate on agriculture, home economics, and teacher training, those areas of greatest need. With a two-year provisional certificate, graduates could be certified by the state of Georgia to teach. This training would help to elevate the quality of faculty in many small, isolated elementary schools, where pupils were still being taught by those who barely had a high school education.

Freshman junior college courses included Social Science, English, Mathematics, Chemistry, Botany, Bible, Agriculture (for boys), and Home Economics (for girls).

Required sophomore classes were similar, with the addition of Biology. Elective courses were in advanced units offered in all these subjects, with further courses including Education, Rural Sociology, and American Government. Foreign languages were missing from the curriculum, for the society was a rural one and the emphasis, of necessity, was promulgated on the idea that the students were to be given the tools to lead a successful, Christian life when they returned to their own rural communities.

Mr. Berry Floyd, who was brought in to head the Department of Education, established an excellent program, with emphasis on aims and objectives of education, psychology, and the teaching and management in an elementary school. Choosing the grade in the Community School he or she wished to teach, the student teacher under his guidance became proficient in a classroom setting, blending ideals with pragmatism.

"Public education in Rabun County certainly benefited from the work of that fine man," one former junior college graduate commented, of the man who later became Superintendent of

Education for Rabun County.

In 1936, the first graduating class of the junior college received certificates. And for the next ten years, until World War II intervened, some of the most outstanding men and women in the country, those who, Judge Bleckley had earlier said, had some of the "brightest minds on Earth," passed through those doors, first opened by co-founders Andrew Jackson and Addie Corn Ritchie.

Their determination and hunger to receive an education, despite odds that would deter less dedicated persons, are reflected in their own stories of survival and success.

For each person profiled in Part Two, there are numerous others equally worthy to have had their stories told, such as the dynasty of Nix brothers—Claude, Clinton, Victor and Goodwin; the Dillard family, synonymous with the valley—Earl, Louise (Coldren), John, and Henry. Then there are the professionals, such as Sherman Wilson, D.D.S., James Ogletree, D.V.M., Fayette McElhannon and Elmer Lee Fry, M.D.'s, and two outstanding elementary educators— Rebecca Minor, for whom a school was named, and Ruth McPherson Yates, selected as the Outstanding Elementary Teacher in America.

From the golden years of the junior college marched over six hundred Appalachian men and women, to rural and urban communities, and to other continents, to inspire a new generation in the inherent values of work, study, worship, and responsibility.

All deserve admiration.

Part Two

Profiles From
The Junior College Years

Men's Basketball Team

Chapter Five

JACK KNOX ACREE
EDUCATOR AND BUSINESSMAN

 shall always be grateful for the God-given privilege of being able to continue my work with young people," the ebullient eighty-five-year-old Jack Knox Acree said, in speaking of his long years as a teacher, consultant, administrator, and advocate in the educational field.

The only living teacher of those junior college years at Rabun Gap-Nacoochee School, Acree is an honorary member, advisor, and friend of the organization made up of the men and women he taught over a half century ago.

A legend in Southern education, he shows no signs of slowing down. But that is to be expected of a man who, through the years, has been called: Cactus Jack; a tough nut to crack; Olympic champion in education; a Fourth of July firecracker.

Yet, at the time of his birth on July 4, 1913 in Stephens County in north Georgia, there was little indication that he would ever be able to get an education himself, much less become the champion of every school child in Georgia.

His mother, Annie Andrews Acree, had been one of twenty-eight children, and his father, Henry L. Acree, a tenant farmer, had been hard-pressed to provide more than food and shelter for his four children.

When Acree was five years old, his mother died of influenza. That tragedy split the family apart. In the custom of the day, Jack, his brother Joe, and sister Mozelle went to live with one set of grandparents—the Acrees—while his younger brother James was sent to the Andrews.

Jack recalled one of those years with his Acree grandfather, whom he described as a hard taskmaster.

"When my grandmother died, my grandfather and I carried on with everything. He'd have me up by four or five o'clock. I'd feed the horses, milk the cow, do the churning, and then pick a sack or two of cotton in the fall before I went to school."

That rural school of six grades was Canon Academy, where his beloved "Uncle Dub" had first taught.

"Uncle Dub, my mother's brother—W.J. Andrews—came to play a major role in my life," Jack commented. "He was so personable, and I remember when he came to live with us during his first year of teaching at the academy. He was a bachelor then, and he used to get down on the floor with me and play games."

When Acree finished at the academy, Uncle Dub, who by that time was married and had five children, invited Jack to come and live with him in Toccoa, seven miles away, to attend the high school there.

"I did a lot of pinning on of diapers and milking cows, and other chores. I earned my way, but he more or less adopted me into his family. Uncle Dub was the father figure for me and he treated me like a son. For twenty-six years he was school superintendent in Stephens County. I really looked up to him. His personality and influence directed me into education, too.

"After my first year at Toccoa, my father remarried and moved to south Georgia, to Worth County. He then began to round up his family. So we left the mountains for the Georgia flat lands. But I almost died of malaria, and I really missed my friends and the cool mountain air. I despaired of ever getting back because we were needed to work on the farm.

"But then something unexpected happened. The man who had leased land to my father was very impressed with how hardworking he was. This man reportedly owned over half the county and had a huge farm property with plenty of workers. He offered the position of overseer to my father, and suddenly Joe and I were no longer needed.

"One day my father casually mentioned that some of the Farmer boys with whom we'd grown up in Stephens County were going to Rabun Gap-Nacoochee School. Until that time, I'd never heard of the school. But with the chance to go back to north Georgia and be with our buddies again, my brother Joe and I would not cease insisting that my father take us up there."

Without informing the school, Mr. Acree started out with his two sons and their belongings. When they arrived on campus, a surprised Dr. Ritchie, founder and president of the school, said, "I'm sorry. We don't have dormitory space for them. All rooms are committed." But then after talking with them, Dr. Ritchie relented. "Mr. Acree, they seem like good boys, so we'll find space for them somewhere."

Jack acquitted himself well. He was a natural athlete. "From the time I first went to school, I loved to play ball. In the early years, we'd play 'cat ball'—a semblance of baseball. We'd wind up some yarn or thread into a ball and hit it with a stick. In high school, the only sport that we could organize and participate in with other schools was basketball. Our industrial arts teacher, Mr. Brand, was a fanatic in basketball. He developed an outdoor court and erected lights so that we could play at night. You can imagine the mountains in December and January and how cold it was in our flimsy shorts and shirts. We had a game one time with the high school from Highlands, North Carolina. It snowed, but we played anyway."

Because of his boundless energy, Jack was described as a restless student. But he was also an extremely bright student, graduating in 1931 as valedictorian of his high school class. Yet, his dreams of going to college seemed unattainable. He could not afford the cost of tuition. Knowing that he was hardworking and personable, Dr. Ritchie hired him as a supervisor in the school's farm work program.

After a year, his Uncle Dub, who had come to his graduation ceremony, entered the picture again. "Jack," he said, "I know you want to go on to college. And I also know that you don't have the money. I tell you what I'll do. If you'll go down to Piedmont College for the first six weeks of summer school, I'll get you a permit to teach. Then, I'll give you a position for the second six weeks back at your home school, Canon Academy. A young lady is teaching all six grades. You can assist her by taking the first three grades for her."

As Acree explained, in those early days of education in rural Georgia, one could get a teacher's permit with only six weeks training. So following his uncle's advice, he enrolled at Piedmont and soon found himself back in his home territory as a teacher, earning ten dollars a week.

"That was an unusual experience at Canon Academy. During that term, I lived out of a suitcase. I went home with a different student every night for my room and board, although I had a headquarters for the weekends.

"During the Great Depression, people in those rural areas were hard up, but it was my community, so they treated me royally. If they had only two chickens, they'd fry one of them for dinner that night. I lived on a steady diet of fried chicken.

"One family took me on a coon hunt. I also went to camp meetings and on hayrides in a wagon."

After that term, he returned to Piedmont College where he worked his way through in three years. He was a leader on campus and graduated with honors.

Armed with his degree in education, Acree began looking for a teaching job. Times were tough and jobs were scarce, but a friend had told him about a vacancy in Troup County. So he hitchhiked down to LaGrange and sought out the superintendent.

At that time in Georgia education, each militia district was a separate educational entity, with a local board of trustees that ran the school, with the superintendent writing the checks for the teachers and providing the meager transportation system.

Acree doesn't remember how he got to that rural community seven miles away to see the trustees. But he found the first trustee, a Mr. Bassett, working in his garden. He was leaning on his hoe and chewing tobacco.

Mr. Bassett looked him up and down. "Can you teach Latin?" he asked. "I have a daughter who's going to be a nurse, and she needs to study Latin."

"The good Lord must have guided me," Jack acknowledged. "I had taken two years of Latin in high school.

"Yes, sir."

"Then go over to see Mr. Freeman, the chairman of the board."

Marveling that he had asked only one question, Jack next went to find Mr. Freeman. He was a country store keeper, described by Acree as "a real Southern gentleman, dressed in a suit, bow tie, and straw hat." He explained that if Jack were hired for the ten-grade school, he would be responsible for teaching general science in the sixth and seventh grades, and everything else in the upper grades. They chatted for a while, and then Mr. Freeman finally said, "Do you have a car?"

"No, sir."

"Can you get one?"

Jack swallowed hard. But with innate faith, he said, "Yes, sir."

At that moment, he had no idea how he was going to get a car. But if he had not answered in the affirmative, he would not have gotten the job. "I had to live in the home of one of the young lady teachers, where the other teacher, also a young lady, boarded. And I was required to transport them back and forth to the school."

Jack's father, up to that time, had never been able to provide much support for his son. But when he'd become overseer, he'd sold his own stock and mules and, using that money, he was able to help buy a car for Jack.

At the beginning of the school year, Principal Jack Acree proudly drove his Model-A Ford, with the two lady teachers seated in the back. He had been told that, for propriety's sake, neither one could sit beside him in the front seat. "They were two of the loveliest young ladies I've ever known, and I have to confess that I kind of fell for one of them." He also confessed that after the sun went down, when community eyes could no longer see, one of them sometimes rode beside him.

And as for the Latin, the course worked out well for his one student. He had studied Latin all summer, boning up on conjugations and declensions, and "all Gaul divided into three parts."

Along in the year, Acree heard that there was a vacancy across the county in a six-teacher school of eleven grades. He had also heard that the chairman of the board of trustees, who had run the school with an iron fist for years and who had the only other key to the school, beside the principal, had been soundly defeated as chairman by a lady in the community.

"You don't want to get mixed up in all this. You certainly don't want to work for any woman," he was advised. But he took no heed. He applied for the position. Yet again, he was asked a leading question. "Can you teach French?"

Acree had taken French his last two years at Piedmont. For the second time in his early teaching career, a foreign language made the difference. He was hired as principal, coach, and janitor, with a raise in salary from eighty-five dollars to one hundred and fifteen dollars a month for the eight months.

Uncle Dub had been watching his nephew's career with a benevolent eye. By 1938, with a recommendation from him, Jack was offered, and accepted, the principalship of a twenty-two teacher junior high school in Thomaston, Georgia. In late August, with the school year only a short time away, Dr. Ritchie, who had received a charter to establish a junior college at Rabun Gap-Nacoochee School four years previously, asked Jack to come back to the school as athletic director and coach, assistant dean of men, and full-time instructor in the junior college.

He was given an honorable release from his previous contract, and he returned to the school that had meant so much to him during his high school years and would mean even more to him throughout his adult life.

During his second year as a member of the faculty, he met a young woman named Ruby Nell Taylor.

In 1933, while Jack Acree was a student at Piedmont College, A.C. Taylor, a trustee in the Rock Branch community of Elbert County, Georgia, enrolled his eldest daughter, Ruby Nell, in the high school at Rabun Gap-Nacoochee. The ethics of the school reflected the Taylors' own and although it was a hardship, the family was determined that their bright, conscientious daughter would have the opportunity

RUBY NELL TAYLOR ACREE

of a good education. By the time she graduated from high school, the junior college was already in place. So she remained for two more years. Then in 1937, she became a student at Georgia State

College for Women in Milledgeville, where she graduated in 1939, with a B.S. degree in home economics and education.

In her childhood, Ruby Nell had taken care of her younger siblings, a prelude to her later career. She was the one who cooked for them when her mother was busy working on the farm. Her sister, Johnnie Sue, also a Rabun Gap-Nacoochee student, recalled that Nell's biscuits were a specialty. She'd begun making them at the age of four. And if she ruined or burned anything, Nell would hurriedly bury the evidence in the yard, so that her mother would not get angry.

Like Jack, Nell also returned to her alma mater as a teacher. That first school year, she taught the farm family children in the elementary grades, but by the second year, she had moved on to the high school and junior college levels.

"In those two years, Nell and I became friends," Jack confided, "and then fell in love." But with the war clouds on the horizon, he fully expected to be drafted. So that was no time to be making plans for the future. Acree resigned his teaching position to take effect at the end of the school year.

In the meantime, he received a call from a friend. "Jack, Mr. LeTourneau wants to see you."

"I had never met the owner of the LeTourneau Company at Toccoa," Jack said, "but I was aware of who he was. 'What about?' I asked."

"He's developing an apprentice machinist school program. He's got about thirty to forty boys over at the new hotel on Lake Louise, and they're tearing the place up. He's looking for somebody to take them in hand."

"Well, I jumped at it, for it was classified as a war industry since the company made casings for shells," Acree said. "It would put off going to the battlefront immediately, and then Nell and I could get married."

The wedding ceremony, with Johnnie Sue serving as bridesmaid, took place on May 29, 1941 at the Head of Tennessee Baptist Church across the river from the school, and Nell and Jack spent their honeymoon, getting settled in their apartment at one end of the dormitory at the LeTourneau Machinist School. "I became everything to those boys—from mother, priest, athletic coach, and teacher of shop math."

Nell was not the only one to go with him. About five of his athletes and a few other students also went to work in the war industry and to be a member of Jack's athletics teams.

After a year, with the Pearl Harbor tragedy signaling a patriotic response, Jack volunteered for the U.S. Navy. Because of his background, he led a physical fitness program for recruits.

During his stateside assignments, Nell was able to be with him. In 1945, their first daughter, Jackie, was born.

Once the war ended, Jack entered a graduate program in education at the University of Georgia and soon after he received his degree, he began his long, uninterrupted career in school administration.

From Manchester and Elberton, where Gay, the second daughter, was born in 1950, Acree moved into a veritable hornet's nest in Cartersville, where he was hired and fired three different times as superintendent, because of the political situation. "Being in Cartersville was the best job of my career. I got the community involved, but evidently cheap labor in the community was more important to some than quality education for the young people," Jack alleged. A false charge of misappropriating school funds in postage stamps, which Acree was supposed to have used in his statewide activities in YMCA and Kiwanis Club, was quickly disproved. Since he was not given due process of law, he was reinstated by the courts. Soon thereafter, the Southern Association of Colleges and Schools took away the school's accreditation for a year. Eventually, things in Cartersville worked out for Jack. When he was ready to leave the school system, his arch political enemy admitted that Acree had made the best superintendent Cartersville had ever had.

It was during these tumultuous years that Jack became known as a "tough nut to crack." His perseverance to make sure that this trumped-up charge did not remain on his record, and his insistence that every schoolchild should receive a quality education brought respect and praise from the community, and an amendment to the city charter.

In 1961, Acree went to Atlanta to serve as CEO of the Georgia School Board Association, for which his Uncle Dub had laid the groundwork. "It was easier to work for one hundred and eighty-seven school boards than it was, working for one," Jack jokingly said. So he stayed for eighteen years.

In reminiscing about the improvements in Georgia education, Jack gave credit to Mr. Robert Cousins, who at that time was in charge of Negro education in the state. "He was one of the greatest educators in Georgia. I was aware of the work he did. He was discreet and able. Mr. Bob went down to Daytona Beach each summer for a Southern states workshop, where they discussed innovative ideas. It was in '65 or '66 that he came back and told me about his intense interest in Georgia's developing a kindergarten program. Over and over, he would say, 'Something ought to be done.' So I asked him to meet with my GSBA board of directors. The board heard him, and they were very impressed. The board named a committee to go with me to present the idea to the state school superintendent. He was not interested. In spite of this, we kept on. This was the fragile beginning of the statewide kindergarten program."

During Governor Carl Sanders' administration, a school board member, who had been the governor's campaign manager, recommended that a Blue Ribbon Study Commission be appointed to study and update the minimum education foundation program, which had been passed in 1949 and implemented in 1951 under Governor Herman Talmadge, when the three percent sales tax came into being. The senate approved it, and the appointed study commission went to work, actually next door to Jack's office.

"I got the idea that it would be great if, when the committee completed its report the following spring, the school board association could stage a conference for a representative group of Georgians to hear and react to the report."

So Acree presented his plan to the governor, who was enthusiastic. He had only a few words of caution. There was no money for it in the budget. But if Acree could get it off the ground, with a maximum number of legislators and leading citizens attending, without charge, then he had the green light.

"Of course we didn't have the money either," Jack admitted. But with a number of school superintendents underwriting the cost, a successful two-day conference was held, and Acree worked with the Governor's Conference on Education for a number of years. Governor Maddox, in a later tribute, said, "Jack Acree is an innovator. He has a 'tiger in his tank' for education." And Governor Zell Miller called Jack "an Olympic champion in education."

In 1978, Acree retired from the Georgia School Board Association. A year later, after working all his life, he was restless. That's when he became an unpaid executive with a professional organization called PAGE—a non-union alternative to the Georgia Educators Association.

In 1980, Jack's beloved Nell died of cancer.

For thirty-nine years, she had been at his side, always supporting him with her own talents and continually adapting to new surroundings. She had thought nothing of driving cross-country in the war years, to find housing for them and to supplement his military stipend by teaching in her adopted community. Over the ensuing years, she returned to the classroom, when Jack, because of a teacher shortage, could not find a suitable teacher at the last minute. During the Cartersville years, she provided a safe, secure haven for her family, despite threatening letters from Jack's political enemies.

Their daughter, Jackie Walsh, remembers her mother putting her arms around her and sweeping away her tears, after she was chased home by children throwing stones at her and calling her bad names, because of the political upheaval. But she also remembers the time that her two-year-old sister, Gay Nell, disappeared, and when Jack was not available, the principal of the high school suspended classes so that the students could search for her on campus, where the superintendent's house was located. Much to Nell's chagrin, the two-year-old was found later, sound asleep under a skirted vanity at home.

Nell Taylor Acree was a three-star alumna of Rabun Gap-Nacoochee School—high school graduate, junior college graduate, and teacher. Her love for the school was well-known. One of her former students spoke of how she was also loved by the students because of her care and concern for them. Nell returned time and again to the campus for reunions.

Grief-stricken at her death, Jack found solace in working untiringly for PAGE—pouring his energies into that organization, so that he saw it swell rapidly from a membership of eight hundred members to twenty thousand, with the executive position becoming a paid one. Today, PAGE—Professional Association of Georgia Educators—claims over forty-four thousand members.

When the Acrees had moved to Atlanta, another Jackie and her husband were compatible next door neighbors. Jackie Shartle was a CPA on a year's maternity leave at the time and, being extremely energetic, according to Jack, she helped him in the GSBA organization during her leave. She was so capable that, when he opened up an office near the Capitol, he asked her to become a staff member. She declined, preferring to go back instead to her own profession.

Through the ensuing years, the two couples—the Acrees and the Shartles—found themselves occasionally at the same neighborhood parties. When Nell died, Jack and Nell's daughter Gay was already engaged to be married and had begun making wedding plans. Later, unknown to Jack, Gay asked her next door neighbor, Jackie, who had lost her husband several years previously, to coordinate her wedding.

It was late at the wedding reception when Jack asked Jackie Shartle to dance. But as soon as they reached the dance floor, the band stopped playing for the night. The reception was over. Jack mentioned a rain check, which did not occur until a year later. Two years after that first date, they were married. Speaking of Jackie's daughter, Gretchen, Jack said, "She is as dear to me as if she were my own."

Since their marriage, Jackie, owner of her own CPA business, has never missed going with Jack on his meetings all over the state and nation.

"She was a godsend," he said. "She has meant so much to me."

Acree's many contributions to civic, community, religious, and educational affairs have resulted in his being honored time and again on a local, state, and national level. He has been recognized as "Outstanding Executive in the State of Georgia," inducted into the Georgia Educational Hall of Fame, the Piedmont College Athletic Hall of Fame, and has been called by his peers, Georgia's Champion Educator.

Jack's legendary rise in the field of education has within it the milestones of education in the South: professional standards for teachers, students, schools, and school boards.

When asked what his proudest achievement in life has been so far, he answered, "Two things—my perseverance in the face of adversity in Cartersville, and my role in the Professional Association of Georgia Educators to keep the union out of the classrooms.

"I just didn't feel that any child should ever be denied one minute of educational opportunity because a teacher walked out on strike."

Acree's second wife, Jackie, and his two daughters—Gay Nell Little, a mortgage banker, and Jackie Walsh, a professional educator—are also honorary members of the Rabun Gap-Nacoochee Junior College Alumni. Jack has been instrumental in bringing to fruition many of the projects of the alumni group. And he continues to touch the lives of his former students.

Carrying the work, worship, and study ethic of Rabun Gap-Nacoochee School into the arena of life, Jack Knox Acree is a shining example of the type of man Dr. Ritchie had in mind when he founded the school.

How lucky for education in the South that over seventy years ago, Dr. Ritchie made a place for "Mr. Acree's boys!"

Chapter Six

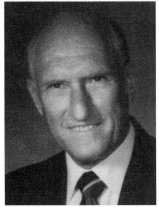

DR. CHARLES EDWIN BISHOP
UNIVERSITY PRESIDENT, ECONOMIST

n 1966, during President Lyndon Johnson's administration, the brilliant University of Chicago economist, Dr. Charles Edwin Bishop, received a call from the White House. President Johnson had selected him as the expert to come to Washington to direct the National Advisory Commission on Rural Poverty.

At that time, Bishop was Head of the Economics Department at North Carolina State University and the William Neal Reynolds Distinguished Professor in Agricultural Economics. Less than twenty-four hours previously, he had turned down a vice-presidency offered him by President Friday of the University of North Carolina System. If he accepted the White House appointment, Bishop would not only have to move to Washington for a period of a year or so, but also would have to seek a leave of absence from President Friday, whom he had told that he would prefer to remain where he was, since he was building a very able faculty and was getting a challenge out of doing that particular work.

So he sought the advice of his local administrator, the chancellor of North Carolina State.

"Ed, you must do this," the chancellor urged him. "You're better qualified than anyone else in the country. But if you want to come back to North Carolina State afterwards," he cautioned, "you'll have to get permission from President Friday."

Bishop immediately called the university president and asked for an appointment. Once more, he drove from Raleigh to Chapel Hill, where he explained his situation. "I talked with the chancellor about it, and he thinks it's something I should do. And I'd like to do it," he added. "But I understand, in order to get a leave, I'll have to have your permission. Would you be willing to give me a leave?"

President Friday hesitated only a moment. He then smiled and said, "I'll be glad to, Ed, on one condition. When you return, you'll become my vice-president."

Dr. Bishop kept his bargain. After he and his wife Dorothy returned from Washington, he worked with President Friday for four years. But once the national report was published, institutions from all over the country began seeking him out, offering him the position of university president, himself.

In a deep, resonant voice, Bishop spoke of his humble beginnings in the small Southern town of Campobello, South Carolina. He dissected certain syllables with the precision of a scalpel, but as with many self-assured men, he also allowed himself to lapse into a more colloquial drawl, when telling stories of his early years.

"It was in 1939, when my brother Elbert and I graduated from the local high school," he began. "I had been sick for a year, so he caught up with me. We were in the top four of the graduating class, and we both wanted to go on to college. But that was during the Depression, when money was hard to come by.

"A man came through Campobello—supposedly representing a North Carolina institution. He told us that, with our good grades, he could admit us to this particular school, but he would need a down payment. It was twenty dollars, a lot of money in those days.

"My father borrowed the money and paid the man. As the time got closer, and we had heard nothing further, we contacted the school. No one had any knowledge of our enrollment. The man had been an imposter."

The Bishop brothers swallowed their disappointment. But in the back of their minds, they still did not lose hope that they might find some way to continue their education.

No one in their family had ever gone to college. Their father was a mechanic, their mother, a housewife. Yet, it was their mother who still nourished the dream, for she knew that if they did not go on to college, her sons would always have a ceiling over their heads. She realized that there was little in Campobello for them to do. And in later years, she was proven correct, for from the time they left in 1939 to the present day, the small town went the way of numerous other small towns in the South, with few industries left to support the remaining population.

In talking about his mother and the influence she exerted on his life, Bishop said, "My mother had graduated from high school which, in those days, was something. My father had not. He grew up in a family where it was the belief that young men should go to work when they became physically able. It was a time when the market rewarded your physique rather than your brain."

So the two boys went to work, picking peaches, thinning cotton, and anything else that might bring in a little money.

Then, through their minister, who had a son attending Rabun Gap-Nacoochee School, the Bishop family discovered that there was a junior college in the north Georgia mountains, where students could work for their tuition. The minister drove the two boys to meet Dr. Ritchie, the president of the school.

"I shall always remember meeting him," Bishop said. "He was coming out of the dining hall. And when we were introduced to him, I stuck out my hand to shake hands with him. He rubbed his fingers across my palm and said, "I don't find too many calluses there, but maybe you'll do."

Both boys did much better than that.

"Dr. Ritchie put us to work during the summer. And once school started, we worked two days a week during the school session, too. I did just about everything you can think of," Ed recalled. "I started out on the farm. As an extra chore, I fired the furnaces in the administration building at night, and then later got an assistantship which paid a little more—feeding the beef cattle." With a laugh, he said, "I had some mighty pretty beef cattle."

Then, he grew more serious. "Rabun Gap was a family program. You did just about everything you needed to do to support the family. I remember so many people working—the girls doing the cooking, the laundry. And the boys with the farm and dairy."

The two teachers that Ed remembered best were Mr. Fry, the head of the Farm.Family program and the dean of men- "we all knew and admired him—" and Jack Acree, the enthusiastic athletic coach. "I played a little baseball and basketball, but I wouldn't call myself a star—the way I was in high school.

"Rabun Gap, as a college, prior to World War II, had the dominant philosophy of providing an opportunity for young people who needed financial assistance. But if you didn't want to work, then you were urged to pack your duds and go home." As simple as that.

"I have thought a lot about Dr. Ritchie's philosophy," Bishop said. "In a very real sense, it was the same as that of the people who developed the G.I. Bill. The G.I. Bill was promulgated under the notion that all people could learn, given the opportunity—if lack of income or wealth did not stand in the way of getting an education. That's how Dr. Ritchie felt—that people in that region (Appalachian) deserved an opportunity to go to school and learn, irrespective of their financial status. That was the thing, I think, that stuck with me."

When Ed and his brother Elbert graduated from the junior college in 1941, the two worked during the summer, earning the necessary one hundred dollars to enroll at a four-year college. Here the educational path divided, with Ed choosing Berea College in Kentucky, while Elbert enrolled at Berry College in Rome, Georgia. But their goals of becoming outstanding educators were the same.

"Berea College was a work school, similar to Rabun Gap," Bishop said. "But only students from the Appalachian region were admitted. I was lucky that the county in South Carolina where I grew up was considered in that area. My main job at Berea, as I recall, was working in the creamery. I'd get up at 4:30 A.M. each morning to receive the milk that was brought in, and we pasteurized it. Berea sold milk throughout that region.

"I majored in agricultural economics, and that I attribute almost entirely to Rabun Gap because of getting a better understanding of rural values and what went on in rural areas. I did not have that, prior to going to Rabun Gap."

But Bishop was not to get his degree until 1946, because of World War II. In the summer of 1942, he volunteered for the air force. "When I volunteered, I was not alone," he said. "There were a lot of us who wanted to serve our country, but we also wanted to complete our degrees. We were told that if we volunteered, we'd be put in the reserves and, after getting our degrees, we'd go on to active duty."

Ed had met "a lovely young lady," Dorothy Anderkin from Kentucky. And on February 13, 1943, they were married. Upon their return from a brief honeymoon, orders for Ed to report to active duty immediately were waiting for him. So much for any leisurely settling down to married life.

Bishop packed his belongings and reported to Fort Hayes in Ohio for induction, and then went to Biloxi for basic training.

Chosen for pilot's training, he was put into a program that sent him back to college to learn the basics of flying. He was shipped to Transylvania in Lexington, Kentucky, only forty miles from his wife's home. "I could not have been more fortunate," he commented.

Bishop was thrilled with the idea of flying. Given preliminary flight training, he remained at Transylvania for a semester. Because of limited dining facilities, the cadets were marched across town to eat their meals at the University of Kentucky. As they sang their cadet songs, the people in the town lined the streets and cheered them on. To Ed, it was a memorable experience.

Pre-flight training in Camden, South Carolina; basic training in Augusta, Georgia; twin-engine training at Valdosta, Georgia—where Ed received his wings—and then on to Nashville to fly B-24s, commonly known as the "widow-makers," occupied his days and nights.

Once he was commissioned, Dorothy followed him to the various assignments. "She was unbelievable," he commented, showing his admiration for Dorothy who made a home for them in less than ideal circumstances.

When the war in Europe ended, the air force had more pilots than it needed. But Ed declined when asked if he would like to be discharged. He had joined the U.S. Air Force with the idea of going overseas, and since the war with Japan was ongoing, he elected to remain in service. But the battles in the Pacific, too, were over before he had a chance to go overseas.

After the war, Ed went back to Berea to finish work on his B.S. degree in agricultural education. However, his priorities had changed. He no longer wanted to teach vocational agriculture. More interested in agricultural economics, he went on to the University of Kentucky where he received a master's degree in that discipline in 1948.

Recognizing his outstanding abilities, the university offered him a job. "Stay here and work for us for a while," he was told. "And then you should go on to graduate school."

Not long after that, the telephone rang, and the voice at the end of the line inquired, "Is this Ed Bishop?"

"This is he."

The caller said, "This is T.W. Shultz from the University of Chicago. I'm calling to offer you a scholarship to study for a Ph.D. at the University of Chicago."

In remembering that event, Ed interjected, "I guess the head of the department had called my department to ask if there were any promising young men or women who might come to Chicago to study economics."

Shultz continued. "There's just one problem. I'll have to know by tomorrow if you'll take it. I'm leaving the next day for Europe on a special assignment for the government."

Ed assured him that he would let him know. But an offer like that was a rare opportunity and Ed knew it.

"I went home and told my dear wife of the offer," he said. "She asked if it were something that I wanted to do, and I said yes. So we took off for Chicago — we had one child by then — and stayed for two years."

With a Ph.D. in economics, and minors in agricultural economics and political science, Dr. Bishop returned South in 1950 as an assistant professor, and then full professor at North Carolina State University. "I shall always be grateful to the people of North Carolina and the state university for giving me a real start in the profession."

Bishop's rise was rapid. He became Department Head of Agricultural Economics, Department Head of Economics, Distinguished Professor, Director of Agricultural Policy Institute at the university, and served as consultant and a member of various advisory committees for the United States Departments of Labor;

Agriculture; Health, Education and Welfare.

Then, in 1966, the call came from the White House for Bishop to serve as executive director of President Johnson's National Advisory Commission on Rural Poverty.

"President Johnson was a complex person, sometimes a little difficult to understand," Ed said. "He had grown up in a rural area on the Brazos River in Texas. And I think that he felt that something was wrong when millions of people were leaving the rural areas and going into the cities—ill-prepared for productive work—and finding nothing that would fulfill their expectations and, consequently, being piled up into these enclaves of poverty. He felt that maybe we could do more to keep these people in rural areas and, in the process, cut down on the urban problems.

"But I don't think he understood what was happening in the rural areas. Because of the extensive mechanization to enhance productivity, there was a restructuring in the agricultural communities. We had begun to substitute machine power for manpower, and we'd lost the capacity to employ large numbers of people in producing farm products and in supplying goods and services to farms.

"The day of forty acres and a mule—if it ever existed—was gone. Another industrial revolution had taken place."

Bishop, in the report which he called *The People Left Behind* focused on the restructuring, the deplorable schooling in rural areas, the welfare program, and the commodity food distribution programs that were abused by local people to force certain people off their land.

"I shall always remember one of the commission members who was from the Navajo Reservation. He was quite adamant that the report would read that every Indian child should have a seat in school. He said, 'We cannot get seats for them. And we want to make it clear that they need a seat.'

"In the report, we pointed out very clearly that the Social

Security program, while it had good intentions, also had inherent weaknesses, which were going to be tremendously costly. Now, that's come to pass.

"Also included were warnings that the welfare program was destroying the social fabric of the country. At that time, if a family were to draw welfare payments, then the man had to move out of the home. Belatedly, people have come to realize the error in that policy.

"And people who lacked an education needed training to perform effectively in the kinds of jobs that were being created. The commission called on the government to provide that kind of training. This recommendation has also been implemented."

Bishop returned to North Carolina where he became Vice-President for Research and Public Service for the University of North Carolina General Administration—remaining there for four years, from 1966-1970.

He continued with his public service activities, begun before he had left for Washington. He had already served as consultant to President Kennedy's Task Force on Vocational Education, the Organization for Economic Cooperation and Development in Paris, U.S. Chamber of Commerce, U.S. Department of Labor, and Office of Economic Opportunity.

Then, when the report, *The People Left Behind*, was published, Bishop's telephone began to ring, with offers from various colleges and universities.

He left North Carolina to become Chancellor and Professor of Economics at the University of Maryland. "I was head of the College Park campus of thirty-seven thousand students. That's a pretty good baptism for a young person. This was a time of ferment all across the country, because it was the era of Vietnam. I got along well with the students, but we had sit-ins throughout the whole period. The most frustrating thing about that time was that I wanted to be an educator, not a policeman. I wanted to give people an opportunity to learn. My focus was on building a great university. But my time was occupied in putting out brush fires, and keeping Kent State from happening all over again, politically. Finally, I grew weary of it, and I decided that I was going somewhere where I would have a better opportunity of rearing my son and for devoting more attention to academic matters."

In 1974, Bishop became President and Professor of Economics at the University of Arkansas, where he remained for six years. "When I got to Arkansas, the board of trustees had created a five-campus system, and I was to head the system. But I also had the dual role of serving as administrative head of the Fayetteville campus. On each of the other four campuses, I had a chancellor who reported to me.

"I've never been to any place where the people loved their educational institutions as much as the people of Arkansas," Bishop commented. "That surprises people when I say that. Unfortunately, they loved their athletic programs more than their academic programs. But they had the best board system I've ever worked under.

"Board members were appointed in classes of one for ten years. So you had a board member for a long time. The board members got to know what a university was like, and learned the inner workings. It was not where a governor appoints a board member and says, 'Go fire the president.' That happens a lot in the Southern states. I got along well with the board. My only problem was that Arkansas was a relatively poor state and did not have the money to implement some of the programs."

The most famous members of his law faculty at the time were Bill and Hillary Rodham Clinton. Bishop, who knew them well, spoke highly of both as faculty members.

"Bill Clinton was a good teacher. I think his intellectual capacity, his ability to understand things, is equal to any United States

President we've ever had, that I know of, including Jack Kennedy. And he understands international things, too. He was very close to Senator Fulbright of Arkansas, of course."

And as to Hillary Clinton, Bishop said, "She's a very vital woman. I'd put her in the class with Eleanor (Roosevelt). She's very articulate, and an extremely intelligent woman, which is part of the problem. Some people resent that women are capable of thinking, too."

In 1980, Bishop became President and Professor of Economics of the University of Houston System, remaining there until his retirement in 1986, when he was made President-Emeritus. Money in that rich state was no problem. Bishop was able to launch unique programs that were fully funded. He particularly enjoyed the emphasis on the arts, and he became an integral part of the Houston community, serving on the boards of directors of the Houston Chamber of Commerce and Houston Industries, and on the executive committee of the Houston Economic Development Council.

In 1986, Bishop returned to Chapel Hill, North Carolina, where he was not allowed to retire from active service. He became special assistant to the provost. He maintains an office as a Senior Fellow at MDC, a nonprofit research corporation in Chapel Hill.

Confidant to presidents from Kennedy, Johnson, Nixon, and Carter; on boards of directors, such as the Winthrop Rockefeller Foundation and Rural Economic Development Center, and President of Southern University Conference, Dr. Charles Edwin Bishop has been a powerful force in education and public service commitment during the last half of the twentieth century.

His farsightedness was made plain in *Urban America in the Eighties*, the commission report for a national agenda, established by President Carter, underlining future policies and prospects for metropolitan and nonmetropolitan America.

"It has always been for me not to become involved with the politics of it, but to lay out the economics of it," Bishop said. "For Mr. Carter, we pointed out the implications of the industrial restructuring of business in this country, and how manufacturing was shifting. We pointed out that certain cities were too heavily dependent on manufacturing.

"I shall never forget that we pointed out that New York City, the world's financial center, was overemphasizing the manufacture of goods, when it should emphasize its ability to compete in providing services.

"Mayor Koch, who was mayor of New York City at that time, was incensed, and Senator Moynihan wrote me one of the nastiest letters I've ever received in my life. But in view of what's happened in the interim—from 1980-98—New York City has shifted. Virtually in every major city in the United States, the shift has been made from manufacturing to service-based industries."

Dr. Bishop is the father of three children, Susan Thompkins, Catherine Thorne, and Charles E. Bishop, Jr. Recognized by professional organizations and listed in *Who's Who in Science*, *Dictionary of International Biography*, and numerous other biographical works, Bishop commented that his childhood and his experience at Rabun Gap had given him a new perspective that has remained with him during his entire life.

Catapulting him to a place of prominence in the academic world were two strong forces—his concern for the nation's poor, and his realization that education is the avenue of escape from poverty.

Rabun Gap-Nacoochee School has reason to be proud of this outstanding alumnus.

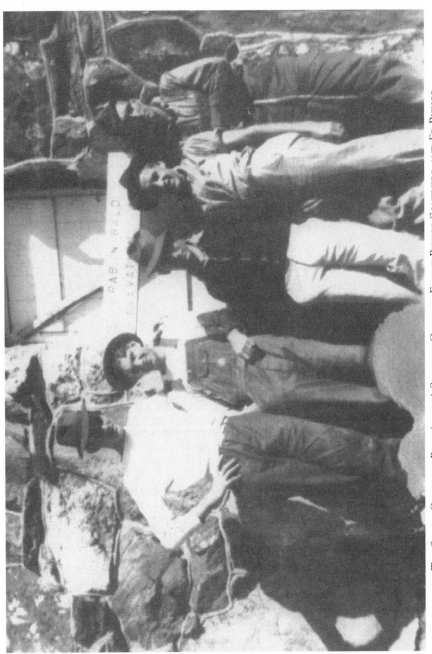

The South Carolina Boys (l to r) Stegall, Gosnell, Elbert Bishop, Southers, and Ed Bishop

LUCY MASHBURN BLACKWELL
WEDDING DRESS MADE FROM WORLD WAR II SILK PARACHUTE

Chapter Seven

Lucy Mashburn Blackwell
Mathematician and Computer Programmer for Space Program

ife is a gift to be cherished, not in a vault—sodden, mildewed; nor on a shelf—glittering, useless—but growing, active, proud of its scars won with courage and valor, learning from the mistakes and failures, radiating out the knowledge that others may succeed where you failed.... Such is the passing of the torch of life. When the flame is low, nourish it; when the flame is high, carry it like a banner.

Life is yours to live, to expend, explore, enrich, savor and, ultimately, to relinquish."

From *Little Earthling* by Lucy Mashburn Blackwell

From the time that her father first cut pine torches so that she might have light to study in a home too poor to afford oil for lamps, to the later flashes of Mercury, Gemini, and Apollo rockets taking off into a space trajectory, Lucy Mashburn Blackwell has had a long tradition of nourishing the flame.

Born on an isolated, two-hundred-acre farm near Franklin, North Carolina on November 30, 1924, Lucy was the third child in a family of seven children. The amenities were few. The Mashburns had no running water, no electricity, and no radio.

Frank and Fay Moses Mashburn started their precocious daughter to school at the age of four, and by the time Lucy was eleven, she entered the local high school.

"Even though I was that young, I got up at four o'clock each morning, so that I could catch the bus to school," she recalled. "I walked alone the four miles down a dirt road to the nearest bus stop—oftentimes seeing shooting stars in the sky. And of course, by the time I got home on the last bus, the sun had set and dark was approaching."

With her father sitting beside her and holding a lighted torch, Lucy did her homework each evening. "My grades were not that outstanding," she confessed, "because I had so little time to study. The only outstanding thing about me was that I graduated from high school when I was fifteen and had the highest IQ in my graduating class.

"I desperately wanted to go on to college. Sometimes, I'd read in the local newspaper about some of my classmates going off to college, and I was envious. But we were far too poor for me to realize my dream of becoming a schoolteacher."

Then, one day in the fall, after her graduation, her former home economics teacher drove Lucy and her mother the twenty miles to Rabun Gap-Nacoochee School. Neither adult had told her beforehand where she was being taken. But after she arrived on campus, Lucy found out that here was a school—a junior college—where she could gain an education by working.

"I thought the campus was beautiful, with the brick buildings and all the green grass. I still think so after all these years."

Lucy went home again, packed her suitcase, and returned to Rabun Gap. Except for a brief visit to a cousin's house in Murphy, North Carolina when she was around six, she had never been that far from home.

Since the fall term had already started, she worked full-time for the rest of that term, acquiring enough points to cover her tuition for the winter quarter. She did a myriad of tasks, such as washing dishes and working in the laundry—ironing the girls' uniforms.

"Our summer uniforms were blue cotton dresses. We wore white dresses on Sunday, with a red scarf tied around the neck. And in the winter time, we wore navy blue skirts and shirts during the week, and a navy blue dress with the same red scarf on Sundays.

"The material for the uniforms was sold at a store in Dillard, which was within walking distance of the school.

"My first year at Rabun Gap, I was more interested in the social life than in the classes," she said. Every day to Lucy was an adventure. She had never been on a picnic; had never eaten a hot dog. "I think the first picnic we went on, I must have eaten about seven hot dogs." There were so many new things to explore, see, and do.

By the second year, the young Lucy settled down and took classes more seriously. In particular, she remembers her physics class during the summer term. The classrooms were not air conditioned, and the laboratory was especially hot, but she was so interested, that she always stayed late, until she had worked out every experiment. Evidently, her extra hours paid off. At the end of the quarter, she had a final grade of 98.

As for the teachers, she recalls how interested they were in all the students. "They seemed to have a special, caring attitude.

"Miss Lennon was my Bible teacher; Miss Tewkesberry taught English, and Miss Davis was my home economics teacher. Miss Miller was in charge of the laundry and my supervisor, and Mrs. Walker had charge of the girl's dormitory.

"I remember that I gave Mrs. Walker quite a start one morning shortly after spring holidays my first year there. My roommate took one look at me and said I'd better go and see Mrs. Walker. So I went downstairs and knocked on her door. She took one look at me and let out a rather shocking exclamation.

"I had measles. She confined me to my room, which was an end room upstairs. Many of the girls went out on the adjoining balcony and peered through the window at me. But I had a light case and recuperated rapidly.

"The work/study program was a disciplined, busy time which kept us out of mischief, for the most part. The brief socializing time was usually on Saturday nights, when we would have planned activities, and on Sunday afternoons, after we had all gone to church. The boys who were dating would come over to the girls' dormitory and sit around outside on the lawn chairs with their dates, or in the living room. And although I rarely had a date that first year, I enjoyed the folk dancing instruction, roller skating and tennis, and visiting with other girls in the dorm on a Sunday afternoon. One of the highlights that year was the surprise visit my older sister made to see me one Sunday afternoon.

"By my second year, I began to date two of the high school boys who lived on campus. They were closer to my own age. I remember that there were chaperones all around, but they did not intrude.

"In general, most of the days were happy ones, but the saddest day of all was December 8, 1941, one day after Pearl Harbor. We were all gathered in the dining hall for the noon meal, listening to President Roosevelt address the nation on radio. I wondered why Miss Clayton was crying. I thought the war would be over in a short while and could not possibly affect us in such a remote part of Georgia.

"How wrong can one be? The men, caught up in the draft, started disappearing from the campus overnight and, without the boys to work on the farm, the school as we knew it changed irrevocably.

"Shortly after my eighteenth birthday, I graduated from the junior college. I'm listed in the class of 1943, although I finished in

December 1942. Dr. Bellingrath, who was president of the school at that time, wrote that I ranked third in my class.

"My mother, who always seemed to find out what was going on in the world, got me into a radio school in Asheville, North Carolina, and the entire class was sent to Philadelphia to the Bureau of Aeronautics for further training. Then, we were distributed out to various aircraft locations. In Allentown, Pennsylvania, I went to work as an aircraft and electronics inspector. A new plane was on the drawing boards when I arrived, and my main duties consisted of filing blueprints.

"As soon as I turned twenty, I enlisted in the U.S. Navy. My father had died in August of that year. With my mother's permission, I joined the WAVES."

Lucy was sent to boot camp in the Bronx, New York in January 1945. She had signed up for the duration. She remembers lying in her bunk one night with silent tears streaming down her face, for in the dark, at that moment, she had no clear picture of her future. Everything seemed so uncertain.

She survived boot camp and was sent to Atlanta to the Link Instrument Flight Training School. And from there, went to the Naval Air Station in Norfolk, Virginia, where she trained navy pilots, all men, in Link. The Link trainers were ground-based instrument flight simulators, but she flew with the pilots at every opportunity on a number of cross-country runs, and once went on torpedo runs in the gunner's seat of an SB2C.

Lucy was promoted rapidly and in two years was Petty Officer, second class, and leading petty officer at the Link building.

She made an excellent instructor and, combined with her petite, blonde good looks, she maintained an excellent rapport with her students. So much so, that she later married one of the navy pilots in her class, Ensign LeRoy E. Blackwell, Jr. of Miami, Florida.

They were married in March of 1948, one month before Lucy

got out of service. Since he was discharged first, he enrolled at Duke University, with a major in electrical engineering.

In 1947, with the war over, and with so many military people going home, there was a shortage of airway traffic controllers. After a short period of on-the-job training, Lucy was assigned as an ATC at Norfolk.

One sunny day, when numerous military planes were flying, and Lucy was on the telephone, talking with another naval air station, heavy objects began hitting the side of the building. The control room was on the ground floor at the front of the building, and to her it sounded as if they were being bombed. While everyone else, including the duty officer, ran outside, Lucy pulled the telephone down under a table and kept on talking. It turned out that one of the fighter planes had taxied through a car in the parking lot. "The propeller on the plane was like a large can opener," she said.

But the event that Lucy remembers most of all happened on the midnight to eight A.M. shift, when a blizzard hit Norfolk, and she was the only ATC on duty. No one could get through the snow to relieve her.

A plane had taken off from another station and had gotten lost. Norfolk was alerted and so they warmed up GCA, the Ground Controlled Approach, to talk him down. But they could not contact him on any frequency, though they were tracking him on radar. The plane circled back and forth for hours. It was Lucy's duty to inform other stations of his position. Finally, with only ten minutes of gasoline left, the plane flew due east, out to sea. "I was grateful to the duty officer when he took the phone," she said, "and gave the final message."

Lucy remained as an air traffic controller until April of 1948. Her total time spent in the U.S. Navy was three years and three months.

Lucy joined her husband at Duke University, where they both

went to school on the G.I. Bill. "I shall always be grateful to Dr. Bellingrath, who helped me get into Duke with his wonderful letter of recommendation."

The couple lived off campus. Lucy studied hard, but when their first daughter was born in June 1948, she stayed out of school for a year. Later, she was a full-time student, as well as a full-time mother, full-time housewife, and she graded homework papers for a math professor, on the side.

In 1952, when both she and her husband graduated, they walked down the aisle together for the second time. Majoring in mathematics, Lucy had made dean's list, despite all of her obligations.

With her husband beginning work as an engineer in Charlotte, North Carolina, Lucy became a full-time housewife and a new mother with the birth of a second daughter. But the marriage did not work out, so in December 1957, Lucy was granted a divorce in Miami, Florida.

Thus began a new chapter in her life—her entry into the space program.

"I answered a newspaper ad," Blackwell confided. "The space program was just beginning to build up, and they had many openings at Cape Canaveral. Just days after my interview and acceptance in January 1958, I reported to work with thirty-five other people, who were being matriculated on that same day."

Once again, Lucy received on-the-job training. She started out in post-flight data reduction. In a surprisingly short time, she was promoted to assistant team leader. She no longer read the film, but found herself doing the mathematical part, the paperwork and computer runs, using computer programs to get test results on the missiles.

"We had Atlas, Thor, Jupiter, Snark, and others. Their flights were recorded first. If you see a picture of a launch pad up close, there are cameras around the pad," she explained. "Those are fixed cameras that take pictures of the first part of the flight. And then, there are– which you don't see, but sometimes hear about–the tracking cameras that track the second part of the flight, and then radar tracks the remainder of the flight.

"The radar tracking system is now world-wide, but at that time we only had it down range, but it was extended–radar data–and on those shots, we had ballistic cameras that, on night launches, photographed against the stars on glass plates, which was our most accurate system.

"But radar was no good near the ground because of noise interference, so we had cameras and radar and ballistic cameras, and sometimes, infra-red data. On all flights, this data was collected and reduced and gotten out within seventy-two hours. Sometimes, we didn't have that long, because the engineers were too interested in seeing the flight results on film. So many times, you'd see the flight ending in an explosion of the missile.

"When I started work at the Cape, the U.S. had put up exactly one satellite, and Russia–two. Working so closely together everyday, we developed a camaraderie among us. When we put up the second U.S. satellite, we teased one of the men at lunchtime that he had to report aboard the satellite, and we would work out all his problems. He said he was quitting at five o'clock, and his carpool would have to meet him, wherever he was. We had to 'invent' a car that would meet him and get him home on time.

"When we launched the first Polaris missile, which is a submarine missile, we had to have a position in order to reduce the data. But there was no way that the navy was going to tell us where the submarine was located. So we went over to the wall map of the world and looked up the coordinates of Moscow and Red Square and put that in, sent it to the computer, and went home.

"The next day when we came in, the shift leader growled at us and said, 'The next time you don't know where it is, put it on Pad Three.' But all they wanted was velocity and acceleration, so it didn't matter."

Blackwell, with another promotion, moved into math analysis and assisted the engineers in their mathematical models for the various tracking instrumentation systems. She worked primarily with the photogrammetrists, but also with some of the radar engineers.

"I used a Monroe calculator. It took me six weeks to calculate one point of position, velocity, and acceleration. So you see how important computers are today. We had computers. However, we were creating newer and better methods, and I had to test out on the calculator that we had the right math – to give a checkpoint for when we put it on the computer.

"Also at this time, I received on-the-job training as a computer programmer. So I used both the calculator and the computer to get the right numbers.

"About three and a half years from the time I started there, I was promoted to Supervisor of the Scientific Research Computer, which could be used by anyone in any department working at Cape Canaveral. This assignment required diplomacy as well as technical expertise. Each morning, the line outside my door would stretch down the hall. The role of supervisor required all the math and education courses I ever took.

"This was a strenuous time at the Cape. While I was supervisor, the Mercury program began.

"The most thrilling space shot for me was the first American manned flight. This was a Project Mercury flight that occurred on May 5, 1961, with Astronaut Navy Lt. Commander Alan B. Shepard, Jr. I had worked at Cape Canaveral since January 1958, and had seen the films of explosions on the pad, explosions when staging, explosions by range safety when they veered off course, and other failures through the years.

"I worked at the Tech Lab twenty miles south of the launching pads. At T-10 minutes, we were notified that all systems were go. We streamed out of the Tech Lab across Highway A1A, to the beach. A few people had transistor radios with them. We heard, 'We have lift-off!'

"I was leaning so far, looking toward the launch pads, that I almost fell headfirst down the embankment. Then, we saw it rising in the sky. A few minutes into the mission, Astronaut Alan Shepard looked at Earth from his viewpoint and said, 'Oh, how beautiful! How beautiful it is!' The flight was only fifteen minutes down range. We had not known about re-entry blackout. This gave us some very anxious moments before we got the news of a successful splash-down.

"When the Mercury program ended and the Manned Spacecraft Center opened up in Houston, many of our top people left for Houston. I was asked to go along and in March of 1964, I moved to Houston, where I began working on the Apollo math.

"Because the math has a long lead time, I worked on that until the summer of '65.

"The highlight of this phase of my career was assisting with the math for the Lunar Excursion Module (LEM) liftoff from the moon and rendezvous with the orbiting mother ship.

"In August 1965, I switched to programming and started supporting Gemini missions in the Real Time Control Center (RTCC) in Houston, since Gemini was flying. For the next eight months after that, I only had Christmas Day off. I worked an eight-hour day, plus going to the computer around midnight, usually each night. Saturdays and Sundays I would try to get computer time twice a day. I worked on nine of the twelve Gemini missions.

"*Gemini 12*, the final flight of Gemini, splashed down in November 1966, and my company transferred me off the space program in December 1966, and assigned me to other contracts.

"On January 27, 1967, a little over a month after I left the space program, the Apollo fire occurred, which killed three astronauts. I was devastated, although there was nothing that I could have done to prevent the fire or the fatalities. The fire delayed the Apollo program for two years.

"While working on the space program, I was always a contractor," she said, "—never a member of NASA. Contractors did the actual work, while NASA was more in an oversight role. I always wanted the hands-on experience.

"I was off the space program for almost three years, while working on other projects. But when Apollo was flying again, I wanted to get back on the space program.

"Since I could not get back on the Apollo program immediately, I went to work on the Viking project, which was the first unmanned Mars landing.

"I was working on the Viking project, when *Apollo 13* flew its near disastrous mission. But I remembered the first successful moon landing on July 20, 1969. That was *Apollo 11*. Air Force Lt. Col. Michael Collins remained aboard the mother ship, while Air Force Col. Edwin E. Aldrin, Jr. and civilian Neil Armstrong descended to the surface of the moon.

"In January 1971, I did get back to supporting Apollo missions at Goodard Space Flight Center in Greenbelt, Maryland. I had the privilege and challenge of assisting in the support of *Apollo 14* and *Apollo 15* missions.

"After these missions, I left the space program a second time and went to work on a contract at the National Science Foundation in Washington, D.C. However, I returned once again to the space program in May 1975."

By that time, with no manned flights going on in the space program, Lucy's priorities changed. She wanted to be close to her family, so she asked for a transfer to Norfolk, where a brother and sister were living. She started working on military projects for the army and navy until she retired in 1988.

"The U.S. Navy wrote me military orders, even though I was a civilian, and sent me to overseas bases to install some new systems," she said. "I traveled on military flights, as well as civilian ones. It worked wonders at customs to be traveling under military orders."

Blackwell now lives in Cornelia, Georgia, close to family, in an apartment filled with her own oil paintings, with titles such as: *Flying Saucer; Deep Space; Fire in the Sky*. She is the author of a science fiction novel, entitled *Little Earthling*. Her oldest daughter, Janet, is deceased. But her other daughter, Rebekah, is realizing Lucy's first dream of being a schoolteacher.

"I think the thing I'm proudest of in my career is the Apollo math– the lift off to the moon and the rendezvous with the mother ship," she said. "The computer program, that I wrote, printed out all the formulas and substituted the actual values, even as it went through. You iterate and minimize on either time or fuel, and decide which orbit you're going to rendezvous on. It was a very thoroughly done piece of work."

Lucy Mashburn Blackwell, in reminiscing about her journey from Rabun Gap to the moon, said, "I feel like Cinderella. I can hardly believe that the barefoot girl from Appalachia could have done what I have done in my lifetime.

"I have not found the right words to express how important the junior college and its work program was to me, for it was the critical first step toward a career that I can look back on with a sense of pride and accomplishment."

Aware of the support of her family in all her undertakings, Blackwell added, "But I have never understood why my parents made such sacrifices on my behalf."

Chapter Eight

BLANCHE TRUELOVE AND L.G. BOWEN, JR.
FARM AND DAIRY OWNERS, CIVIC LEADERS

n October 1945, U.S. Naval Water Tender, 3rd class, L.G. Bowen, Jr. pulled into the harbor at Pusan, Korea on his assigned LST – the large, slow-moving, flat-bottomed boat that had transported tanks, troops, and cargo onto the landing beaches of Saipan, Guam, New Caledonia, and Okinawa. The war in the Pacific was finally over, and he had survived, despite the odds.

Foremost on his mind that day was his wife, Blanche Truelove, and their first child, due to have been born several weeks previously. Like all sailors when coming ashore after a long bout at sea, he eagerly awaited the mail pouch that might provide a letter from Blanche, giving him the news that he was, indeed, a father.

Instead, a cablegram, forwarded by the Red Cross, was received by the ship's communications officer shortly before the LST landed. A son had been born, but neither the baby nor Blanche was expected to live.

Devastated by the news, L.G. applied for emergency leave to return home to Cornelia, Georgia.

An impressively tall, strapping fellow, Bowen had been given the nickname of "Tiny" by his fellow sailors. And as he left the LST, the yeoman handed over all his records and his traveling orders, with the warning, "Tiny, if something happens to you, Uncle Sam will never know that you existed. You've got all your records on your person. You're to take them when you report to the Charleston Naval Station after your leave."

A naval lieutenant due for discharge left the ship at the same time, and the two caught a ride on a mail plane to Taegu, where they hoped to arrange transportation back to the States. There the officer and the enlisted man parted.

By the next morning, a loud speaker in the military barracks announced that no naval personnel would be allowed to ride outgoing mail planes without specific permission from the commander of the Seventh Fleet, who was in Hong Kong at the time.

Realizing how difficult that would be for an enlisted man, L.G. sought out any ship that might be returning to the West Coast. Four times, L.G. was stopped by guards. Stranded for ten days, he was able to get on the fifth ship, an amphibious personnel destroyer headed for San Diego, with an overnight stopover in Guam. No message waited for him in Guam.

Finally, on December 10, two months from the time he had received the message from the Red Cross, Bowen arrived in San Diego. As soon as he checked in at Camp Davis, he found the busy communications room where all the telephone booths were located. By that time, it was almost midnight, but he immediately put in a call to Cornelia, Georgia.

The telephone operator informed him that there would be a delay of several hours. He told the operator that he would be waiting. But approximately thirty minutes later, a voice announced that the call to Cornelia was coming through in Booth Three.

"To hear Blanche's voice, to be able to talk with her, after two months of not knowing whether she was alive—And that the baby was all right, too—" In recalling the event that had taken place over fifty years ago, the tall, white-haired man sat in an easy chair in his living room, and his voice was filled with emotion.

But the story had not yet ended. For in San Diego, he was still separated from wife and child by some three thousand miles. The next day, he boarded the bus that took personnel from Camp Davis to the San Diego train depot. "The depot was so crowded," Bowen recalled. "Everybody was pushing and shoving and trying to get on the train. Finally the conductor said, 'All of you traveling under military orders, hold them up. The others of you, please step back and let them have priority.' Well, I took out my orders and held them as high as I could. I made it. I got on the train."

But yet another obstacle lay ahead for Bowen. It was the dead of winter, with snow piling up around the tracks, and a bitter, cold wind blowing across the deserted flats of Arizona. Suddenly, the passenger train slowed and then came to a halt, for up ahead, lay the wreckage of a freight train, blocking the tracks.

For twenty-four hours, the eastern-bound passenger train remained at a standstill, while a crew cleared the tracks of the wrecked locomotive and the boxcars with their cargo of citrus fruit from California. Over to the side lay one boxcar that had broken open, scattering oranges, tangerines, and grapes. With nothing else to eat for the next twenty-four hours, the passengers availed themselves of the fruit. And once the tracks were cleared, the passenger train continued its journey east.

Seven days later, L.G. arrived home—having experienced a modern day odyssey of a man, blown off course, yet determined to get home to his wife and son, who had been named Denver, in honor of Blanche's heroic brother—killed in action earlier in the war.

A lifetime of devotion to family, church, and community sets

Blanche Truelove Bowen and Luther G. Bowen, Jr. apart as a very special couple.

In recalling the major events in their lives, the two spoke in tandem, with one taking up the story when the other left off.

Blanche Truelove was born in Cleveland, Georgia on February 6, 1917, and later moved to Clermont in Hall County where the Truelove family were farm neighbors to the Bowens.

"I had my eyes on Blanche from the beginning," L.G. admitted. "It was love at first sight. I don't know whether you know the Bible story where Jesse sent Saul to look for his asses. They'd gotten out. Well, our mules had gotten out. They'd been found over at my uncle's place. They'd corralled them, so my brother and I—I wasn't old enough then to drive—were going over there in an old '28 enclosed Chevrolet. Blanche had just recently moved across the creek from where we lived. She was going to another school, and was walking along the road. Since we were going in the same direction, my brother said, 'You want to stop and ask her if she wants to ride?' I said yeah.

"Well, as it happened, the rearview mirror was focused on the back seat, where I could glance in the mirror at her. I was very shy and bashful, but I did steal a glance, and I thought I'd kinda like to date that little girl. But I didn't make any overtures. I found out later that she had a boyfriend, and he had a car. Sometimes, I'd be out in the field hoeing when they'd drive by. And I'd say, 'Lord, I don't know whether my chance to date her will ever come'."

In 1933, L.G. graduated from Chattahoochee High School at Clermont and started to junior college in St. Petersburg, Florida, where he lived with an older brother, who worked at Sears, Roebuck Company. But with the death of his mother in October, he was needed at home, to help take care of his baby brother and to do the cooking and the necessary housekeeping.

By May of 1934, things were a bit easier. Another brother, Price, who was principal of White County High School came by the farm and said, "L.G., I've heard of a place that you might be interested in, to go to college."

That was the year that Dr. Andrew Jackson Ritchie had organized the junior college level of the Rabun Gap-Nacoochee School. So Price took L.G. to visit the school. They met with the dean, a Mr. Harrell, and arranged for L.G. to become a student.

In the meantime, Blanche had graduated as valedictorian of her high school class. "We were very poor," Blanche said, "and all I wanted to do was to go to work and make some money. But Mama, having heard about the school from Price, said, 'Blanche, I want you to go to that school, too.' So she made a trip to Rabun Gap and met with Mrs. Nicholson, who was housemother for the boys' dormitory.

"Mama just fell in love with the school, so she told me I was going. That was in June, only three weeks after I'd graduated from high school."

Blanche's father took both his daughter and his neighbor, L.G. Bowen, Jr. to Rabun Gap, so they could work through the summer to help pay their tuition.

"My parents paid sixty-five dollars the first year," Blanche recalled, "and seventy-five dollars the second year. I felt it was a great opportunity and a cherished privilege to be able to work for my education. The work activities were easy, and I enjoyed the fellowship as I worked with my classmates."

Cataloguing the list of chores during those two years, Blanche said, "I cooked. I was a waitress, and I cleaned the girls' dorm bathrooms. I also did laundry, washed, and helped to iron. The only electric iron was in the home economics department, so we ironed with a flat iron that was heated on the cookstove or in the fireplace.

"In the garden, I gathered wheelbarrows of cabbage and took them to the kitchen to cut them up and make kraut. The canning of vegetables and applesauce was also done in the kitchen. Later on, the students went to the cannery in Dillard.

READY FOR DINNER

"One time, I worked as a dairy maid, to clean the dairy barn and sterilize all the equipment. We separated milk and sold it to the CCC camp. And sometimes, we'd be assigned to watch the cattle on the hill as they grazed. Once they settled down, we would sit in the shade of the trees and study."

Blanche still bears the scar of a dairy accident, the breaking of a milk bottle in the vat, which cut one of her fingers to the bone. But it healed, without infection. A less serious accident, but an embarrassing one, happened that first summer when she was on cooking duty.

"My partner and I had been given the recipe for making corn bread. At that time, we had not studied home economics. And since it took such a long time to measure each teaspoon of baking soda, we decided to convert the measurement to tablespoons. But we erroneously assumed that two teaspoons equaled one table-spoon. The bread came out yellow, and our faces were red. After the second day of yellow bread, the supervisor intervened and told us that three teaspoons made one tablespoon. The bread was better after that."

Because of his size and strength, L.G. worked on the eighteen-hundred-acre farm, helping to plow, harvest, and cut timber.

"I remember very well the first time we ever tried to lay off rows to plant in," L.G. said. "Mr. Shields was the first director of the boys' work when I got there. He sent me out to the field one morning with Old Bob, the stubbornest mule we had. The field was between the girls' dorm and School Farm Road. A beautiful flat field. Nothing in the way, but just to run a straight row. But when I looked back, the row was nothing but wobble, wobble, and more wobble. I laid off about two rows like that when Mr. Shields said, 'You need to pick out an object at the far end. When you start, keep your eyes on it. Don't look back. Then, when you get to the other end, you can look back to see how straight the row is.' "

That lesson, learned well, has remained with Bowen throughout his life. His eyes have been on goals in the distance, and he never seemed to have wavered. From an early age, he knew he wanted to go into agricultural work and own a farm.

Soon after he arrived at Rabun Gap-Nacoochee School, L.G. received another lesson that he never forgot—that some of the older students, specifically Paul Raby and Hollis Epps, and more than likely John Stephens and Archie Crowe, by his account, enjoyed playing pranks on the newer students.

The most famous prank was the invitation secretly passed to new arrivals to attend "Fannie's Party." Fannie, a community girl, was supposedly throwing a party to introduce the newcomers to the young ladies living in the community. Having had little opportunity to socialize with young ladies, the farm boys were eager to attend, although they were not allowed to go off campus without permission.

At twilight, L.G. and fellow student Lanky Jones slipped off campus to attend the party with the others. "We walked from the dorm out by Professor Fry's residence, across a creek, and turned right onto a private drive to a house that looked vacant.

"We could hear some conversation, but we couldn't see any lights. From the doorway, a deep male voice asked, 'What are you boys doing here?'

"Paul answered, 'Some of the boys at Rabun Gap-Nacoochee School heard that Fannie is having a party. We've come to meet her and be introduced to the other community girls.'

"The man with the deep voice said, 'Fannie isn't seeing anyone tonight.'

"A student spokesman pleaded with the man to let us at least talk to Fannie since we were already there.

"'There will be no party here tonight,' the man yelled. 'You get the hell out of here.' And then there were loud bangs, sounding like the rapid fire of a 12-gauge shotgun.

"Lanky and I took off," L.G. confessed, "racing each other back to the dorm. Lanky said that I was running so fast that he could have played a game of marbles on my shirttail.

"When we reached the dorm, we removed our shoes and tried to slip into our room so that Mr. Nick would not find out that we had been gone. He never confronted us about leaving the campus without permission, although I'm sure that he knew about the prank. He was a psychologist, and he probably assumed that we had learned our lesson."

L.G. also quickly learned the difference between stacking wheat and oats on the family farm from stacking rye on a hayrack on the school farm.

"Rye is longer," he explained, "and the secret is to pitch it to the center so it won't be sticking out on the sides."

L.G., with a work crew, had been sent to the rye fields to do just that. "We used a stack pole to stack it out in the field and then the threshers came in August to thresh it. All they had to do was drive to the stack pole and pitch it on the threshing machine.

"We got what I thought was a load on the wagon and started out. We got about three-quarters of the way to the stack pole when the whole load slid off. So we had to reload."

Rye bread or corn bread was the standard fare on the weekday menu at the school. Only on Sundays did the students have rolls made from white flour, since that had to be purchased.

During the Depression, nearly all the food for the students was produced on the school farm. Many people were hungry during those lean years, but Dr. Ritchie, the founder, fed his students well. As a result, he became known as "Uncle Fed" on campus. According to Blanche, this name was always spoken with warm, thankful feelings for "this great man."

Because the school was self-sustaining, only those students who were willing to work for their education were allowed to remain.

Some, like L.G., took on extra jobs, as well. "I also got up at four o'clock every morning and fired the boiler to get up steam to sterilize the milk bottles. On a job like that, they paid us ten cents an hour, or gave us credit.

"We used hardwood for heating the school and the dorms, so some of us also went to the woods to cut timber."

"We had hot air from the furnaces in the dorm," Blanche added. "We also had electric lights in each room, but it was just one ceiling light. Since I had eyestrain from studying so much, Mama got me a reading lamp for the second year.

"But when classes started that first fall, I was so homesick that I thought I'd have to go home. I knew I wasn't social and I didn't have any intelligence. History was called Social Intelligence and Professor Harrell, the dean, was going to teach it, and I just knew I couldn't pass it.

"Mama came to see me and I wanted to go home with her, but she promised me that if I would stay until Christmas, that she'd let me come home. But by that time, I would have cried my eyes out if I couldn't have gone back."

"I wasn't valedictorian of my high school class, like Blanche," L.G. admitted, "but I made it through all right. My grades in junior college were actually better than in high school. Except for one course—Poetry, the Interpretation of Life." With a twinkle in his eye, Bowen said, "I never did know how to interpret life."

Thus began the reminiscing of the teachers who had influenced their lives.

Blanche said, "Our Gap teachers were dedicated professionals who instilled values for living, and I stood in awe of them. Miss Lennon, Miss Clayton, and Miss Jones lived on our ground floor hall on the end with the Walkers, the houseparents. Dr. and Mrs. Andrew Ritchie lived in the little white wooden cottage near the back of the old wooden dining hall, but across the road from it. Dr. and Mrs. John Knox Coit and Mrs. Coit's father, who was our chaplain, lived in the brick house not far from our dorm. I felt that the Coits were very spiritual and genteel."

According to L.G., Mr. Nicholson, or "Mr. Nick" as he was called, was the teacher that everyone grew to love, despite his sometimes abrasive manner. He was also a houseparent in the boys' dormitory.

"He'd given us a problem in forestry—about a log so many inches in diameter at one end and so many at the other end. In our dorm room one night, I was discussing that problem with my roommate, and when I figured out the answer, I got excited and pretty loud when I started explaining it to him.

"Mr. Nick turned that knob and bounced into our room before you could say 'Scat!' to see what all the noise was about. Then when I told him, he said, 'Aah God, you don't have to holler.'

"We all thought he was a little peculiar, but by the time we left Rabun Gap, everybody loved him."

On a beautiful spring day when Blanche was a sophomore, it was Mr. Nick who joined her on her walk from the dining hall to Hodgson Hall, the main building.

He taught psychology as well as forestry, and Blanche remembers that he challenged her to set goals and become a contributing member of society. With his guidance, her self-confidence and sense of self-worth vastly improved.

On that momentous walk, he turned to her and said, "Blanche, I know that you and L.G. are in love. If you expect to become his wife, you will need a college education too. Have you thought about that?"

"I accepted his challenge, and I shall always be grateful to him," she said.

By that time, L.G. had transferred to the University of Georgia.

"All of my brothers – the ones who went to college – had gone to Mercer," L.G. said. "Then I came along and I wanted to be an agriculturalist.

"At the end of the winter quarter of my sophomore year, my brother Price came to me to discuss my future. He had recently changed jobs, from high school principal in White County, where he made eighty-five dollars a month, to educational director of the CCC camp, with an increase in salary to one hundred and thirty-six dollars a month.

"He had a wife and a daughter, but he said that with his increase in salary, he would be able to help me. And that if I planned to go on to get a degree, I should transfer then, since the junior college had just started and all the credits might not be transferred."

Taking his brother's advice, Bowen transferred for the spring quarter. But caught in red tape, Bowen, as his brother had surmised, had to retake some of his former courses for credit at the university.

In the meantime, with her excellent grades, Blanche enrolled with a scholarship at Piedmont College, where she majored in Home Economics. Given credit for her earlier courses, Blanche graduated magna cum laude, finishing a year before L.G.

She found a teaching job at Lula in Hall County, in the school where she had attended the eighth and ninth grades. "I had stayed with an aunt during those years, since my family lived so far out in the country," she explained.

Making dean's list regularly at the University of Georgia, Bowen was able to take extra courses each quarter. His last requirement was practice teaching vocational agriculture at Snellville in Gwinnett County, and then he received his degree in June of 1939.

On June 14, 1939, the day after graduation, Blanche and L.G. were married. Since married couples were not hired in Gwinnett County at that time, Blanche took courses at the University of Georgia. Then, an opening in Hiawassee became available for L.G, with the possibility of a position for Blanche the following year.

During that year, Blanche taught again in Lula, and when the position in the home economics department became available in Hiawassee, it was a great relief to the couple who would no longer have to commute between two towns.

After four years at Hiawassee, they were faced with a vastly different separation, because of World War II. Knowing that Bowen would be going into the service, they left Hiawassee. When L.G. went overseas, Blanche returned to Cornelia, Georgia, to the family-owned home where she waited for the birth of their first child.

L.G. will always remember that first meal at home, upon his return. For months in the navy, he had lived on canned mess food—especially sauerkraut and wieners, and he hoped never to see that fare on his plate again. That evening, when Blanche said, "I think I'll fix some sauerkraut and wieners," L.G. quickly convinced her otherwise.

After the war, Bowen went back into the teaching field, from working with the vocational agricultural programs with the Veterans Administration, to various high school programs in Madison and Clarkesville, Georgia.

In 1950, the Bowens bought a three-hundred-acre farm in Hall County, and later opened a successful dairy.

Pillars of the community, Blanche and L.G. were selected by the FHA as the Farm Family of the Year. And their contributions in business, religious, and community endeavors have been significant.

They helped to organize Pine Grove Baptist Church in Gillsville, Georgia, and retiring again to Cornelia, they became active in the projects of the First Baptist Church there. A deacon since he was in his 30's, L.G. and his wife Blanche have been involved for over sixty years in teaching, training, witnessing, and supporting missions. As an extension of the church programs, L.G. and Blanche taught Sunday School at a nursing home until 1996, and for two years, L.G. served as Moderator of the Chattahoochee Baptist Association.

During Bowen's eight-year-tenure on the Hall County Board of Education, the board was instrumental in establishing Gainesville College and the Lanier Area Technical School. He also helped organize the Towns County Lions Club, which now operates the Georgia Mountain Fair. He has served as a director of the local Farmers Mutual Exchange, and a director and officer of Better Maid Dairy Products Co-op in Athens, Georgia. Other civic involvements include helping to organize the North Oconee River Watershed Association for Jackson and Hall Counties, and the VFW Post in Cornelia.

Equally busy, both at home and in the community, Blanche became the outstanding partner that Mr. Nick predicted. Besides the many business chores involved in the operation of a farm and dairy, and successfully rearing their two children, Denver, and a daughter Valeria to become outstanding citizens, Blanche has volunteered her time to teach others in the church and community to prepare their income tax returns. For twenty years, she served as secretary of the Junior College Alumni Association. And for the past number of years, she has been involved with the literacy program to help immigrants and drop-outs to prepare in taking the GED.

As a tribute to her caring, one of her Laotian students wrote a poem about her, calling her "our Mrs. Bowen."

In the tradition set by their parents, the Bowens' son, Denver, and their daughter Valeria, have found places of service in their own lives.

Recently retired as Superintendent of the Pribilof School District in St. Paul, Alaska, Denver Bowen has served in his church as chorister, organist, pianist, and deacon.

Valeria Partain, their daughter, has also been active in the teaching profession. Studying early childhood education in places like China, Israel, and the Scandinavian countries, Valeria has tutored in Egypt and taught in a private American school in Yemen Arab Republic. Also musical, she has been pianist and a leader in her church.

Now that sense of responsibility has passed on to a third generation. Their one grandchild, Linka Bowen Burdette, is an educator too.

L.G. summed up the family philosophy, with a tribute to Rabun Gap-Nacoochee School. "At Rabun Gap, you were given responsibility. And you learned to take it."

Those lessons, learned so long ago in the Blue Ridge Mountains, have followed Blanche Truelove and L.G. Bowen, Jr. throughout their lives. And everyone whose lives they have touched has become richer for it.

Chapter Nine

JOSEPH HARDING CAIN
ENGINEER, REGIONAL MANAGER

 oseph Harding Cain of Lumpkin County, Georgia, arrived at Rabun Gap-Nacoochee School in the summer of 1938. That first week, it rained every day, and he admits that he has never been so homesick in his life.

Going early, as so many others, to acquire tuition credit for the fall quarter of junior college, Harding was immediately put to work, shucking corn. That chore lasted as long as the rain.

Then, when the sun came out, he was given another task. He duly reported his new work assignment in a letter home to his mother. "I've been busy this week, broadcasting," he wrote.

Harding explained that it was the heyday of radio, and his mother was suitably impressed. "Maybe my son is going to amount to something, after all," she said.

But on his next trip home, Harding had to explain to her that he was not involved in radio at all. He had been broadcasting *manure* from the back of a two-horse wagon.

—Or so he tells the story.

Joseph Harding Cain was born January 29, 1921 to John C. and

Martha T. Cain. He was one of six children, four boys and two girls. He spent his grammar school days in Clermont and Brookton, Georgia, and graduated from Lumpkin County High School in Dahlonega, the town noted for its gold strike and United States mint in its earlier days.

At the age of eleven, he first showed his mechanical and engineering ability. Harding and his thirteen-year-old brother, Ernest, purchased a 1925 Model-T Ford for ten dollars and began to get it into shape. They had earned that sum by cutting pulp wood and selling it in north Georgia, near Clermont. Working on the car during the week, the two would take a ride in it on weekends, if they could come up with gas money. At that time, during the Depression, drivers' licenses were the least of their worries in the isolated mountains.

At the age of seventeen, Harding and his friend, fellow high school graduate Irwin Dyer, became roommates in the Annex at Rabun Gap, along with Claude Lester, Eugene Bryant, John Naglich, and Harold Buffington, who was given the duty of ringing the bell when it was time to march to church on Sundays, and for other events. Supervisor of the Annex was teacher Jack Acree, whom Harding described as a "sharp young man who was physically fit and kept us straight."

One of the assigned tasks that Cain later enjoyed was keeping the furnaces going, for with that, he was given the privilege of driving the school's '38 Ford pickup truck to haul the wood and coal.

The self-ordained barbers of the school, according to Harding, were Fayette McElhannon, who later became a physician, and J.T. Alexander. "I believe we would pay them something like a dime for a haircut. That would leave us a nickel to purchase a pack of chewing gum that we could share on a Sunday afternoon date at the girls' dorm."

That left no money for transportation home. So on the few

weekends, when they were allowed to leave the campus, both Cain and Dyer hitchhiked home together. Each time, they managed to arrive back on campus before the Sunday evening bells rang.

"We also played a lot of tennis together," he recalled, "when we were at the Gap."

With the give and take of growing up on a farm with energetic brothers, and parents who were not averse to correcting their children when they needed it, Cain responded well to the discipline of working together for the common good, which was a hallmark of the junior college. Even today, he gives credit to the teachers for reinforcing the cornerstones of work, worship, and study that have undergirded his life for more than a half century. "The school was a springboard of things to come," he said, "and I'll always be grateful for the opportunity the junior college gave me."

Included in his list of memorable teachers is Professor Nick (Nicholson) whom he described as "a sharp and sly old fox. When you met him in the morning and said to him, 'Good morning,' chances are that he'd look up at you and say, 'What's good about it?' I always wanted to reply, 'It's better than none at all.' But I never got up enough nerve to say it."

His first impressive encounter with Professor Shotts, who taught chemistry and mathematics, was in Hodgson Hall. "As I walked into the room, he called me by name although I had never seen him before. Evidently he had recognized me from a photograph that accompanied my application.

"Mr. Walker, the shop supervisor, was a good man and we worked on many woodworks projects in his class. Probably my best recollection was in helping to build a desk that was later used in the library in Hodgson Hall. I thought we did a pretty good job in building that desk."

Graduating in 1940, with a teacher's certificate, Cain found a job with the Lumpkin County School Board. His assignment was in a one-room schoolhouse about ten or fifteen miles north of his home in Dahlonega. Boarding with a family who lived nearby, he drove home on weekends in his Model A Ford.

That year, one of his duties was to register young men for the upcoming draft, since the threat of war was evident. And although he was not yet old enough himself to register, he began to think of service to his country.

Not waiting to be drafted, since he wanted to choose his branch of service, Cain volunteered on November 9, 1940, and soon found himself undergoing basic training at Fort Benning, Georgia. He was then assigned to the Corps of Engineers, with the responsibility of mapmaking.

"I remember very well that Sunday, December 7, 1941, when the Japanese struck Pearl Harbor. I was pulling K.P. duty at Benning, and shortly thereafter, we were packing up to leave. We took a long troop train to the West Coast, but there we were delayed when the news came in from the Philippines, which fell shortly thereafter. We never knew our original destination, but I feel sure it was the Philippines.

"After that, we were loaded on a ship from San Francisco, and wound up in Oahu, Hawaii, where we did our mapmaking to support the troops and the bombing in the South Pacific.

"By that time, I had advanced up through the ranks to Master Sergeant, which is the top grade for enlisted men. I had a platoon of surveyors, and we later joked that we had fought the 'Battle of Waikiki Beach.'"

But the occupation of mapmaking throughout history has been a hazardous one, filled with intrigue and danger. In earlier days of conquest, mapmakers were closely guarded by rulers, kidnapped and murdered, for to know the terrain is to win the battle.

In World War II, the Allies would be facing the enemy on uncharted Pacific islands, a distinct disadvantage. Admiral Nimitz,

Commander in Chief of the Pacific Fleet, who was temporarily lost while on his way to see Guadalcanal from the air, summed it up best in a letter to General Hap Arnold: "There are no railroad tracks to follow out here."

So Cain and his surveyors began the tedious mission of providing troops with the lay of the land.

On one occasion, as Cain recalled, "I took a small group of surveyors down to Christmas Island, which at the time belonged to Great Britain. There, I obtained ground control for mapping out the island."

Master Sergeant Cain spent Christmas Day on Christmas Island, a fact that he later realized would have qualified him for an appearance on a popular television show of the fifties: "I've Got a Secret".

After several years in the Pacific, he was recommended for Officers Candidate School at the Army Engineer School in Fort Belvoir, Virginia. So he found himself back in the States. Out of one hundred and fifty candidates, only fifty graduated, and Second Lieutenant Joseph Harding Cain was one of them. In a self-deprecating way, he called himself a "ninety-day wonder," but with his background, he was far from being an unseasoned soldier.

Lt. Cain continued with his schooling in a heavy equipment course. And then, he received orders to go to Europe. Landing at Le Havre shortly after the Battle of the Bulge, he was assigned to the Combat Engineers, the unit that took him on the march through France, the southern part of Germany, and then on to the Steyr River in Austria, where they met up with the Russians.

Once the war in Europe was over, Cain fully expected to return to the Pacific. But the dropping of the atomic bomb on Japan suddenly changed the final ending of the war. Shortly afterwards, Cain returned home.

He had served his country with honor, and at that time, his

thoughts turned to what he would do with his life. The summer before he entered the University of Georgia, he worked with the Soil Conservation Service in Gainesville, Georgia. By fall, he began his work towards a BSA degree.

On March 22,1947, he married Myrtice Roberts of Chestnut Mountain, Georgia. They settled onto a small farm outside Athens and then later moved into a pre-fab house on campus.

While Cain worked towards his degree, he also worked with a local civil engineer, surveying pipelines, subdivisions, and drawing up plats.

Despite the extra work, he received scholastic honors. He was voted into the university's National Honor Society, Phi Kappa Phi, and Kappa Delta Pi. He also served as president of the university chapter of Georgia Future Farmers of America.

After he graduated, Cain taught for a short time with the Veterans "On the Farm" Program in Cumming, and then went to work in the Quality Control Department of the GM Assembly plant in Doraville. But education beckoned him again, so he returned to the University of Georgia for a master's degree in education. Remaining in the Reserves after World War II, Cain, upon graduation, was recalled into service because of the Korean conflict. But this time, his tour of duty was in the States.

Resuming his civilian career, Cain joined the John Deere Company, one of the oldest companies in the United States—begun when John Deere gave the world a steel plow in 1837. For twenty-six years, Cain was Territory Manager in the Southeast.

As the representative of the company, he traveled in Georgia, Florida, North and South Carolina, Virginia, and parts of Alabama and Tennessee, where his duties consisted of contracting with local dealers for orders and arranging shipping, assisting the dealers in sales training, auditing records, and promoting sales programs that would assure the dealers of a fair share of the equipment business.

He and his family lived in a number of cities in his territory during those twenty-six years. "Consistent with our style of moving about, our membership in churches went with us," Cain said. "Like so many families and individuals in the Southeast, we are of the Baptist faith—as were our ancestors."

Harding retired in 1979. But he avows that he really needs to go back to work to get some rest, for his retirement years have kept him busier than ever.

Harding and Myrtice, who live in Chestnut Mountain, Georgia, directly across the road from the house where Myrtice grew up, have two daughters, Barbara and Sandra, two grandsons and a granddaughter.

Water skiing, and what he refers to as "barnyard golf," or pitching horseshoes, are some of his activities. And of course, his interest in fine-tuning cars is as strong now as it was when he was eleven.

Active on the executive board of the Rabun Gap-Nacoochee Junior College Alumni Association, Joseph Harding Cain commented that the Rabun Gap experience occupies a large portion in the whole picture of his life.

"I will always be thankful for the excellent opportunity that came my way."

STUDENTS WALKING TO CHURCH

Chapter Ten

MARLAR LAFAYETTE CARPENTER
PHARMACIST AND REAL ESTATE DEVELOPER

n a recent Gallup survey on twenty-six occupations rated for professional honesty and ethics by the public, the community druggist/pharmacist captured the "most trusted" title, beating out clergy, teachers, physicians, and dentists.

This high regard by the public becomes quite clear in the life story of Marlar Carpenter, retired pharmacist and member of the junior college class of 1942 from Rabun Gap-Nacoochee School.

"In a fifty-year practice of pharmacy," Carpenter said, "I tried to base every action on what would be best for my patient and customer."

Working alone as the only pharmacist for the first twelve years, he kept Carpenter's Pharmacy in Chatsworth, Georgia open seven days a week—closing only on Thanksgiving and Christmas. Even then, he confessed that he seldom spent a night without returning to the pharmacy to fill a prescription. And during times of epidemics, he often made seven or eight trips.

"Community meant much to me while growing up at Rabun

Gap and attending the schools there," he said, attributing his own work ethic and community concerns to the lessons he learned by the family hearth and at "the school on the hill" during those years of great economic depression.

But on a hot summer day in 1940, as he was working in one of the fields of his family's mountain farm in the Kelly Creek community, his future seemed uncertain. He had recently graduated as valedictorian from the high school portion of Rabun Gap-Nacoochee School, which, at that time, also served as a public school for the local community.

For the boy nicknamed "Kip" it would have been natural for him to continue his education in the junior college of that same institution. Except for one problem—As the youngest of ten children of James David and Ida Kell Carpenter, he did not have the money for tuition.

While he was turning this dilemma over in his mind, he saw a car coming down the road. It stopped and a man got out and began to walk toward him. Kip immediately recognized one of his favorite high school teachers, H.L. Fry, who was also dean of the junior college.

"Words cannot express my feelings," Carpenter said, "when, after asking about my plans to go to college and finding that I had none, he offered me a scholarship to cover tuition and fees as a day student for the freshman year. This was a great, unexpected opportunity and the answer to a prayer."

By that fall, Marlar Carpenter became a freshman in the junior college. "The academic load was much greater than in high school," he said, "and the professors were much more demanding of excellence." Although he was not required to participate, as a day student, in the work program, he voluntarily spent a number of hours in the school shop, helping to repair farm equipment and keep the tools in good order. His only mishap at that time he attributed to his own carelessness—when the table saw and the fingers on his left hand made contact. Fortunately, no permanent damage was done, and the expertise in handling the various equipment was to come in handy years later.

Once his freshman year was over, Carpenter had to locate a summer job that would provide him with tuition for the second school year. This he found on a work crew, building the road from Clayton to Hiawassee.

The work day was eleven and a half hours long, in summer heat and rain. The pay was thirty cents an hour, and if any complained about the conditions of working continuously with picks, shovels, and sixteen-pound hammers for such a long time, the foreman always reminded the crew that five men were waiting to replace each one on the job. Years later, Carpenter was able to look back and see the benefits of this labor. He not only earned enough to pay tuition for his sophomore year, but gained much self-confidence, as well.

Despite being a day student, the personable Carpenter formed many friendships with faculty and boarding students that have lasted to this day. And his memories of those two years are sharp and clear, although he admitted that he tended to remember the happy times more than the few sad experiences that are a part of teenage life.

Rabbit hunts in the snow, sledding down the ice-packed hills, and attending "Big Ring," the square dance that no one dared called "dancing" are but a few of the pleasant memories. "For many, bringing in and preserving a God-given harvest was rewarding. Forming class and student governments, contributing to and working on student publications were also pleasurable and a good learning experience," he said. And with a twinkle in his eye, he also commented that even though no serious romantic involvement happened to him, there were opportunities for a few flirtations, always under the careful scrutiny of the faculty.

In assessing those teachers and staff who had been his mentors during those student years, he paid tribute to Dr. and Mrs. Ritchie, founders of the school. "They worked tirelessly for better educational systems in the local public schools as well as Rabun Gap. Dedication, tenacity, and tremendous self-sacrifice...," he commented, were their hallmarks. Carpenter compared their involvement with students as a type of tough love that demanded the best of each student in return for their own total devotion. The few, who were unwilling to work or who did not abide by the rules, were asked to leave.

Dr. Coit, who came to Rabun Gap when it merged with Nacoochee Institute, "was a team player, less visible, but effective in his own right." And Mrs. Coit, he remembered as "reserved and aristocratic, who by example and insistence made you do things properly and right."

As for Dean Fry, whom Carpenter had as a teacher in both high school and college, he described as "a true gentleman, with personality and demeanor to match; a friend who led rather than coerced and pushed."

Between Carpenter's high school years and junior college years, the Ritchies and the Coits retired, with Dr. George Bellingrath replacing them. Although he did not know him well, Carpenter described him as more "Ivy League" with a desire to modernize the school and make it better known.

No biography of those junior college years seems to be complete without the mention of Jack Acree, whom Carpenter painted as "a sports enthusiast, good teacher and coach. He didn't shy away from working you hard scholastically and physically. He was demanding but absolutely impartial and fair A solid rock and friend."

Three teachers, Misses Clayton, Lennon, and Jones, he described as "truly saints, who by teaching Bible and other subjects as nearly as the Lord would have done," greatly influenced those on campus.

Mr. Walker, shop and manual arts; Mr. Berry Floyd, education; Mr. Shotts, chemistry and physics; were all memorable teachers, each with special gifts.

It was Mr. Nicholson, known as Mr. Nick, who occupied a very special place in Carpenter's memories. "Many considered him abrasive," he confessed, "but to me, he was the most profound and logical thinker I have ever known.

"The total thrust of his teaching was to make students think their way through a problem and be tough enough to survive and even prosper, no matter the circumstances."

For many, the junior college years were spent under the clouds of war, and as a cavalryman in World War I, Nicholson was cognizant of this threat to his students. "When Mr. Nick talked to us, trying to prepare us for the imminent conflict, we were aware of his patriotism and love of country. After the attack on Pearl Harbor, Mr. Nick gathered a number of us in his office to hear President Roosevelt's message and declaration of war. I shall never forget Mr. Nicholson's words: 'Your lives will never again be the same.'"

Fired with equal patriotism to serve their country, many Rabun Gap students sought to volunteer for military service. Waiting to be accepted for naval aviation training, Carpenter and a few others, including his good friends, Jim and Henry Dillard, made a trip to Atlanta during the last quarter of the 1942 school year. Unable to pass the vision test, Carpenter was accepted as Seaman, first class, and assigned to Naval Air Station, Atlanta on June 21, 1942, after he had graduated from Rabun Gap in May, with a Georgia provisional teacher's certificate.

"Naval Air Station was probably the best duty one could have in the war-torn years, but it left two of my deepest desires unsatisfied," he remembered. "Since I had two brothers and many friends in combat, I felt I should be actively engaging the enemy, too. And since my other desire was to be a commissioned officer, this assignment afforded me no chance."

Carpenter's excellent enlisted service and his two years in college qualified him for Midshipman School. He was accepted for officer's training and ordered to the University of Notre Dame. He received his commission as Ensign on January 20, 1944.

His tour of duty at Naval Air Station, Atlanta, had also brought an unexpected reward. It was there that he had met his future wife, Geneva Miller who, by his own words, "became and still is the dearest and most significant person in my life."

With six days leave, after graduation from Midshipman School, he and Geneva were married and spent their brief honeymoon at the Biltmore Hotel in Atlanta.

Then came amphibious training at Little Creek, Virginia, and advanced training at Fort Pierce, Florida. In April, Ensign Carpenter, assigned to LST 549, sailed through the Panama Canal to Bora Bora, and then to New Guinea, where he participated in the landing of troops and equipment at Cape Sansapore, New Guinea on the Vogelkop Peninsula.

After that operation, he was reassigned to LST 467, on which he remained until the Japanese surrender in 1945. During that time, the LST made landings on Leyte, Luzon, Cebu, Palawan, and other Philippine islands, and later in what was then called Dutch East Indies. "The excitement came from Japanese air attacks, shellings while we were beached, submarine attacks, kamikaze attacks and surface engagements on the invasion fleets," Carpenter recalled, "with the most frightening episode in the Battle of Leyte Gulf when we were surprised by a major Japanese fleet." Far outnumbered, with the LSTs as sitting ducks, the Americans on the few escort carriers and destroyers fought valiantly and heroically, and to this day, Carpenter says that he owes his life to that "historic charge of the finest of the U.S. Navy."

At the end of the war, Lt. (jg.) Marlar L. Carpenter, decorated with American Theatre and Asiatic-Pacific medals with two battle stars, plus the Philippine Theatre with three battle stars, and the Navy Unit Commendation medal, had the opportunity to stay in the navy, but chose instead to come home. However, he remained in the Naval Reserve for the next twelve years, with an advancement in rank to Lieutenant.

Faced with choosing a career, Carpenter found that his priorities had changed during the war. Upon the advice of a neighborhood druggist, he decided that he would like to go into pharmacy. But due to such a large number of applicants, he had to wait until the second quarter of 1946 to be admitted to the Southern College of Pharmacy in Atlanta.

Those next years were busy ones—going to college, starting a family, working part-time, and building a house with much of the work done himself, by using the expertise that he had learned earlier in the manual arts shop at Rabun Gap.

As a registered pharmacist, Carpenter worked in Decatur for several years. Then in June of 1951, Carpenter made the move to Chatsworth with his wife and four-year-old son, Terry Kent. Thus began the twelve-year saga as the owner of his own drug store that was open seven days a week. "Early on, I learned that laughter is the best medicine," he said, "so I always strove to be courteous, pleasant, and even humorous when appropriate, in order to make my patients feel better.

"Rarely did anyone fail to get needed medications if he did not have the money to pay, or even if he owed an old account. This was definitely not a sound business practice, but I have never regretted it. Those who came to buy medicines to self-medicate themselves or others were always questioned about the severity of symptoms and were counseled as to the wisdom of doing so. Especially where infants, children, and the elderly were involved, I chose not to sell remedies but to advise them to consult a physician. Never did I refuse to return after hours, and never did I charge additionally for this service."

From building his own professional building and several others, where he did part of the work himself, Carpenter prospered as a developer and business owner. Later, after his own house was built, he constructed another as an incentive to attract a practicing physician to the area.

Family-oriented with two sons, Terry Kent and Marc Lawson, Carpenter decided to sell his pharmacy and work as a pharmacist only three days a week, so that he might devote more time to family, church, and community.

He served on the Murray County Board of Education, and has been active as deacon, Sunday School teacher, chairman of the pulpit committee, and for thirty years on the building and grounds committee of First Baptist Church in Chatsworth.

He is justifiably proud of his two sons, both graduates of Georgia Institute of Technology and academically gifted in high school as Star students, valedictorian, and National Merit Scholarship winner.

"I have been well blessed by my immediate family." In a tribute to his wife, Carpenter said, "For more than fifty-three years, Geneva has been my wife, my helpmate, and my friend in the highest sense of those terms." And his pride also extends to his only grandchild, Thomas Kell Carpenter. "Truly I could not have asked for more than I have received from each of my family members."

The ties to Rabun Gap-Nacoochee School for the past sixty years have remained firm. As a past-president of the Junior College Alumni Association and the "Hooverites," those intrepid survivors of the Great Depression, as well as chairman of the junior college's book project, Marlar Carpenter, retired pharmacist, developer, and sometimes poet, said, "There is no doubt in my mind about the stellar quality of that great institution."

In a student poem written shortly before graduation, Carpenter pledged that his classmates and school would never be forgotten. "The picture cannot fade as time descends / For it's painted on my heart."

DINING HALL

Chapter Eleven

SUDIE FRANCES (SUE) COLEMAN CHANDLER
TEACHER AND INTERNAL REVENUE SERVICE TRAINER

ue Coleman Chandler, a graduate of the junior college class of 1939 at Rabun Gap-Nacoochee School, has vivid images of that significant time in her life when she was a student.

As if it were yesterday, Sue can still visualize the bench under the tall white pine tree near the dining hall, where Dr. Andrew Ritchie and some of his students waited each day for the noonday meal.

"We called Dr. Ritchie by his nickname, 'Uncle Fed,'" she reminisced. Yet, no one seemed to know how he had acquired the sobriquet, although it was suggested that since he saw to it that his students were well fed, the name naturally followed.

"Although we were a work school, I never saw 'Uncle Fed' in the everyday uniform of overalls. He always wore suit trousers and a shirt, and he looked particularly nice when he went out of town to solicit funds for the school from his rich friends, whom he had known at Harvard. A company in Atlanta made sure of that.

"I also remember that every morning, especially in the summer, when he was on campus, he would get up after breakfast, ring the bell, and walk to the center of the dining hall. We knew that he was either going to lecture us about something, or report on his travels.

"But one morning, that second year, we turned the tables on him. A good many of us were there for the summer, earning our tuition for the following quarter. It was his seventieth birthday, and somebody decided that each one of us would get up and say something—wishing him a happy birthday. One of the male students stood up and said, 'Uncle Fed, I hope you live to see *me* seventy!'

"Mrs. Ritchie was in charge when Dr. Ritchie was away. She was a true partner, a co-president. And she knew everything that went on, on campus. She always had a favorite expression when guiding the women students against vanity and sundry sins. 'Now, girls, you don't want to become Jezebels.'

"The Ritchies lived in a little white clapboard cottage directly across the road from the dining hall.

"Dr. Ritchie retired in 1939, the year I graduated, and Dr. Bellingrath became president that fall."

The Coleman family of Emmanuel County, Georgia was a close-knit one, with a tradition of helping each other. Growing up on a farm, in an era when cash was almost non-existent, Sue's sister Vesta had been hired as a summer assistant to the local Home Demonstration agent. From the money she made, she enabled an older sister, Bertha, to attend a summer school where she could get a teacher's license. Bertha taught school for a year, and she in turn sent Vesta to Rabun Gap-Nacoochee School with the money she managed to save that year. Later, Vesta, who graduated in the junior college class of 1936, was eager for her younger sister, Sue, to have the same experience. And down the line, Sue helped her younger brother Brinson. Out of the ten children, three attended Rabun Gap-Nacoochee School.

Born on November 24, 1917 to Vesta Florence Allen Coleman

VESTA COLEMAN (1935-36)

and Emmette Caleb Coleman, Sr., Sue was nineteen when she went to Rabun Gap. "I had been out of high school for three years,"she said, "so I was older than most of the other students. Since jobs were scarce at that time, I had stayed on the farm, helping out my mother."

Then, with Vesta's financial help, Sue left her home near Swainsboro and boarded a night train in Midville, a small town in an adjoining county.

Earlier she had packed her trunk with the requisite school uniforms, rayon stockings and walking shoes, and had mailed a letter to the dean of students, to let him know the date and time of her arrival. But unknown to Sue, the dean had resigned and left the school, and when her letter arrived, it had been thought to be a personal one and had been forwarded, unopened, to him at his new address.

"I left Midville at ten o'clock, rode all night, and got into Atlanta about six or seven o'clock the next morning. I didn't have any money to buy anything on the train, so my family had packed a lunch for me. I ate some of it that night and saved some for the next day.

"I had never been out of Emmanuel County before; had never

ridden on a train. And here I had to change terminals in Atlanta—from the Central of Georgia to the Southern Railway—a frightening experience. But my sister had written down what I was supposed to do."

Sue found the right train, boarded it with her suitcase, and traveled on the Southern as far north as Cornelia.

"Now, when you get to Cornelia," her sister had said, "you get off the train and walk through the town until you see a great big red apple hanging in the air. That's the Tallulah Falls train station."

Remembering that hazardous part of the trip, Sue described the train as a cinder box, with smoke and cinders coming back through the open windows. As it creaked, wobbled, and swayed on the tall cornstalk bridge above the rushing Tallulah Falls Gorge, Sue could understand why it was more aptly called "Total Failure" by its passengers. She felt that any moment, the train would plunge into the gorge below. "Dear Lord," she prayed, "if you'll get me out of this mess, I'll never ride it again."

She successfully crossed the gorge, and the conductor soon called out, "Rabun Gap!" When the train came to a stop, he helped her down the steps with her suitcase. Sue breathed a sigh of relief. At last, she was at her destination.

Rabun Gap did not have a bona fide train depot—merely a shed that served to shelter waiting passengers from the rain. It was in the middle of a pasture, with overgrown weeds and grass. And of course, with no one knowing of her arrival, there was not a soul in sight to meet Sue. All she saw were her trunk farther down the line and a group of buildings on a hill in the distance.

"I picked up my suitcase and started toward one of the buildings that I thought might be the girls' dormitory. At that time, there were only two dorms on campus—one for girls and one for boys.

"It was noon on a hot June day. When I reached the dorm, I rang the doorbell. Nobody came to the door, even though I rang the bell a number of times. So I picked up my suitcase and trudged over to what I mistakenly thought was the boys' dormitory.

"It was cool inside the building, but still there was no one in sight. I happened to see a closed door with a nameplate on it, so I walked over and knocked. After a few minutes, a man, who turned out to be Mr. Nicholson, the science teacher, came to the door. I told him who I was and he let me talk for a little bit. Then, without saying a word, he went back inside, closing the door behind him.

"A few minutes later, he opened the door again. He told me that everyone was at dinner—the noonday meal—in the dining hall. But that someone was coming in a school pickup truck to take me to the dining room. Then, they would take care of my trunk, which was still down in the pasture.

"At the dining hall, I met Mrs. Walker, the matron of the girls' dorm. And later, she told me that since I had ridden all night on the train that, if I wanted to, I could sleep in the afternoon. I did, and around six o'clock, the girl who was to be my roommate brought my supper to me.

"That was the end of my first day as a junior college student," Sue recalled.

"Students could accumulate credit for tuition by working either four, eight, or twelve weeks in the summer. Since I had so little money, I worked the entire twelve weeks, the maximum time allowed. The twelve weeks work and the one hundred dollars in cash paid my tuition for the entire nine months, together with the regularly assigned work during the school year.

"My first work assignment was to string beans for the noonday meal in the dining hall. The group of girls sat under the big white pine tree. I had never seen so many green beans in one place. Many months later, there were even more when I was assigned to the cannery crew. That was in the summer of 1938.

"The cannery was my favorite work assignment. Each morning,

we rode in the back of the pickup truck to the community cannery in Dillard. Although we worked long hours, sometimes even up to nine o'clock at night, waiting for the last batch of canned vegetables or fruit to come out of the large pressure cooker, it was fun.

"Mrs. Sophie Roberts, a large woman of German descent, was the most wonderful supervisor. She was so talented and could entertain us with stories of her years before she came to America. And she was very caring. When the sometimes not-too-generous dietician was looking elsewhere, she would sneak out some biscuits and sausage or bacon from the leftovers from breakfast at the school dining hall. And about ten o'clock at the cannery, she would give a secret signal to us to come to the back room, one at a time. There she would give us our midmorning snack. My, how we loved our Mrs. Roberts!"

Other assignments on campus were divided between the boys and girls. While the boys were assigned to do the field work, the cutting of timber for firewood, the dairying, and the slaughter of animals for meat, the girls were assigned to cleaning the dorms, cooking, waitressing, working in the garden, and doing the laundry.

"By the second year, I did a lot of the cooking," Sue related. "Four girls were usually assigned to cook dinner and supper – staple things you'd expect country people to have – almost all of it grown on the farm. We used wood stoves, with six big eyes and two ovens. We made biscuits for breakfast, corn bread for dinner, and whole wheat rolls for supper, with white rolls on Sundays. The wheat flour was grown and milled on the farm, but the white flour had to be bought, so white rolls were a treat.

"Everything was closely watched, so that no food would be wasted. Butter was meted out, so much for each table. We had a milk separator. At that time, the boys would milk by hand and bring the milk into what we called 'the milk house.' The cream and part of the whole milk were sold to the CCC camp in North Carolina – in

Otto, a few miles away. I worked in the milk house in the afternoons and evenings sometimes, when I was assigned to wait on tables, and we served skim milk, or 'blue john' as it was called, to those who wanted it.

"Waitresses had to go early, set up the tables, and put food on the table. There were ten people to a table — with an adult supervisor. After each meal, we washed the dishes — tubs two feet deep, both hot and cold water. Another team would dry the dishes, and then we would reset the tables for the next meal. The breakfast crew lived at the dining hall.

"During the school year, we went to class on a standard schedule. The waitresses did their duty — nothing else — then studied during study hall and at night. We had two days a week to work, and went to class four days."

Sue, who at first thought that she would major in home economics, later changed her mind. Dr. Ritchie had started the junior college with the idea of training much needed teachers for the rural areas.

"By the time I got there," Sue said, "the teaching program was pretty well set up. Mr. Berry Floyd had been instrumental in getting the program started. So I got into teacher training, with educational psychology and practice teaching over in the Dillard Community School, which went through the ninth grade."

Sue was an outstanding student — chosen as monitor for the girls' dorm, and to represent the home economics department at a day's conference in Commerce, Georgia.

At that time, the Chandler twins — Richard (Rip) and Rogers (Rog) — were also making their mark on campus as pitcher and catcher of the baseball team. Sue had attracted Rog's eye, and they began to pair up for school activities, such as the Big Ring, or square dances on Saturday nights; the trips on the school bus to Highlands, N. C., Wayah Bald, and picnics to Warwoman Dell, where they toasted marshmallows over an open fire — all of the activities chaperoned by teachers.

Sue was not only pretty, but athletic, as well, in softball and tennis — winning, with her roommate, the doubles tournament her first year on campus.

On the day of the home economics conference, Sue's instructor took her to the bus at the highway at seven A.M. and made plans to pick her up again at seven P.M. when the bus returned.

On that cold and windy evening in March, when the sun had gone down, Rog decided that he would slip out of the boys' dorm, meet the bus, and walk with Sue back to her dorm at the top of the hill. Only his twin brother, Rip, knew of his intention.

He had settled himself out of the chilling wind, behind some shrubbery that flanked the marker at the entrance to the school. Looking for the headlights of the bus down the deserted highway, he saw instead the headlights of a car, approaching from the campus hilltop. It was Mrs. Broach, coming to meet her student. Rog, hoping that the car headlights would not catch him in their glare, crouched low and waited until the vehicle stopped and the headlights were turned off. Then, as quietly as possible, he escaped from his hiding place and slipped back up the hill and into the dorm, his rendezvous with his sweetheart gone awry.

It was only years later, after the two were married, that Rog confessed to Sue the chance he had taken that night.

The day after Sue graduated, and with Rog remaining for another year at school, Sue went to Waynesville, North Carolina to a summer job that Mrs. Roberts, her supervisor, had arranged, as a waitress in a resort hotel. She went back again the next summer, and in 1941, she and Rogers Chandler were married.

They moved to Gainesville, out in the community where Rog was born. And through her father-in-law, who was a school trustee, she was able to get a job, teaching the primary grades for four years, while her husband was away at war.

Rog's twin brother, Richard (Rip) had been selected for the draft first, and then Rog. After basic training, their mother had written the War Department, requesting that the twins be put together. The request was granted, and the twins went through World War II together. During the Battle of the Bulge in 1944, Rog was slightly wounded by a buzz bomb, but the two survived and came home together after the war.

Prior to the war, Rog had worked at the Army Depot at Fort Gillem in College Park. He returned to work there in 1946, while Sue had a position in the County Public Welfare Department. When he became disabled in 1959, the couple moved from McDonough to Doraville.

Sue became the breadwinner. When the Internal Revenue Department opened up a service center in Chamblee, Sue applied for work there. She was hired in 1962 and worked until her retirement in 1981, first as a tax examiner, and then as a writer of training materials.

"We would go to the national office and various service centers to develop training material for the different service centers—in the processing division. It was challenging, and I enjoyed the work very much."

Aware of the bad press that the Internal Revenue Service has gotten in past years, Sue said, "A lot of people blame the IRS for the ills of the tax system, but they forget that the members of Congress—the House and Senate—are the ones who make the laws. IRS simply enforces them."

When Rog recovered, he worked with General Services Administration in Atlanta. He retired in 1979, and passed away in 1984.

But Sue and Rog had three enjoyable years of retirement together. Rogers maintained a large garden on their property, and

Sue canned many of the vegetables, as she had done so many years before at Rabun Gap. "We were homebodies," she confessed. "We didn't do much traveling, but the best part of traveling was coming into our own driveway again."

They were active in their church and community, and enjoyed their two children, Constance Susan and William Rogers Chandler, Jr. Earlier, a tragedy at a school crossing had taken the life of a third child, their twelve-year-old, Frances Gaynell.

Now, Sue is a dynamo, working with her church, teaching English to immigrants, and serving as secretary of the revitalized Junior College Alumni Association.

The group had been organized from the time of the first graduating class, but through the years, it had floundered.

"In 1982, when Miss Alice Miller, the missionary, came to speak at our meeting in Atlanta," Sue recalled, "someone brought a message from the school: 'Reorganize and get going again.' We did." She was instrumental, with Geneva Mayfield, Harding Cain, James Haynes, and others, in establishing the junior college alumni's scholarship fund, to help outstanding high school seniors at Rabun Gap to further their education.

In looking back over the years, Sue said, "The training that we had at Rabun Gap-Nacoochee School has followed me my entire life. First of all, we were there for a purpose. We wanted to better ourselves. And I think those principles and values that we had instilled in us—we brought a lot of it from our homes, I know—But the values were reinforced, encouraged, developed.

"Everything that has come about in my life is based, first of all, on my Christian home, and the training I received at the school." And in speaking of the closeness of the elite group that shared the years from 1934 to 1945, Sue Coleman Chandler, class of 1939, said, "Sometimes, in our Junior College Alumni Association, we tend to forget that we were not all there at the same time."

Chapter Twelve

HUGH FRANKLIN DAVIS
FROZEN FOODS ENTREPRENEUR AND PHILANTHROPIST

'**ve** found out that you can't out give the Lord. If you're kind to people, it will splash back on you."

This is the credo of faith that Hugh Franklin Davis has lived by all his life. His infectious exuberance and joy, combined with his sense of humor and picturesque speech, have served him well, in all circumstances.

On a quiet, tree-lined street in Rome, Georgia, where his substantial brick house is fronted by a rolling, well-manicured lawn, with the Coosa River flowing nearby, Davis, a 1939 graduate of the junior college department of Rabun Gap-Nacoochee School, began to recall the epiphanies in his life.

Yet, relaxing in the sunroom on that July morning, Davis was also interested in talking about a recent celebration of his wife Helen's seventy-fifth birthday. Surrounded by friends and family, Helen had received seventy-five presents, the number planned by her children and grandchildren.

"We've got some very special kids," Davis said. "They all came for Helen's birthday, with the grandkids. One of my golfing buddies had written a poem in her honor, and while we were all on the boat, he read it, and we had a lot of laughs."

Clearly proud of all his accomplished and successful children and grandchildren, Davis said, "When our granddaughter from Chapel Hill, North Carolina left—she's six feet, one, and a raving beauty—she pinned a two-page note to Helen's pillow, telling her what her grandmother had meant to her, and how much she appreciated what we'd done for her, education-wise. We just said that was one of the best things that had happened within the last two days."

Savoring the family experience that had meant so much, Hugh then returned to the biography of his own childhood.

Born on August 15, 1920, to Benjamin Franklin Davis and Alice Payne Davis at Floyd Springs, Georgia, Hugh started to school when he was five, along with his six-year-old sister.

"Mother was a schoolteacher before marrying Dad," he said. "And I was the only boy, with two sisters—Jeanette and Avaleen.

"Dad had sixty acres and drove a school bus sometimes—he'd built our own school bus. He didn't have more than a third-grade education, and never made a thousand dollars a single year in his entire life. But in a lot of ways, he was like Dr. Ritchie at Rabun Gap. Keeping your word, being on time, paying what you owed, and doing a good job—these were strong with him. If you promised him something and you didn't come through, he couldn't understand why you were like that.

"My mother taught me how to debate, and she would take time with my two sisters and me. When I graduated from grammar school as valedictorian, my dad gave me a quarter."

That impressed Hugh. "What would you do if I was number one in high school?" he asked immediately.

"Well, I'd give you another quarter."

Hugh looked at his dad and said, "Start saving the money." Four years later, when Hugh was fifteen, he received the second quarter.

He was first honor graduate, with his sister as salutatorian.

After high school, during a revival that summer, "I accepted Christ as my Lord and Savior," he said, a decision that influenced the rest of his life.

With high school behind him, Hugh began to dream of going to college. The logical choice was Berry College, located in Rome a few miles away from Armuchee, where the family lived. But by the time he investigated that possibility, the freshman class had already filled. Tuition to go to any other school seemed out of the question.

Then, the family remembered that a neighbor had gone to Rabun Gap-Nacoochee Junior College. So Hugh applied and was accepted.

Davis was five feet, four inches tall and weighed one hundred and four pounds at the time, and he soon acquired the nick-name "Pee-Wee" from his classmates. "That first week around the dining hall table at Rabun Gap," he recalled, "they put two or three Sears, Roebuck catalogues in the chair seat, to get me up there with everyone else. Because of my size, people sort of adopted me, or picked at me. But I enjoyed the attention, and it was a good experience."

That first year, he gained forty-five pounds and grew to six feet. The growth spurt, natural to one so young, was helped along by the advice of a classmate, when Hugh became interested in one of the student waitresses in the dining hall.

"Myra Nell was short, so I could relate to her," Davis said. "But she was already dating a boy who was six feet, three inches. When I confided that I wished she were interested in me, my classmate said, "Well, you know how to get things started your way, don't you?"

Hugh listened as the plan was revealed. "Get her to keep bringing you something," his friend advised. "Ask her if you might have another roll, or another glass of milk. Keep her busy, without overdoing it."

Hugh took the advice. He kept eating and kept asking for more. Within three months, he had not only gained a date with Myra Nell, but also quite a bit of weight from eating all the extra food.

"But the school was really strict when it came to dating," Davis lamented. "Not much opportunity for kissing or holding hands. When we went to a movie, we'd have adults with us to chaperone. It was not like a modern-day college, I assure you."

Speaking of the types of work he did to help pay his tuition, he said, "Work was natural for me. My first year, we did all kinds of odd jobs. We had a school dairy, so we cleaned out the stalls. We also raised corn and other crops. Sometimes, we'd help the farm families gather their crops."

Perhaps the chore that Davis remembered best was going to the woods to cut timber to be used in heating the buildings. Amid the tremendous amount of work that involved, it was also an opportunity to initiate the novices by the more seasoned students.

"We were back about three miles in the woods behind the school, and the group decided that somebody ought to walk back and get some sky hooks to help bring out the timber," Davis recalled. "Since I was one of the smaller ones, they selected me.

"Now, I had heard rumors about this, and suspected it was a little like snipe hunting, where one person gets left holding the bag. But I walked the three miles back to the school and stopped by the dining hall where Alice Miller was in charge.

"They baked these biscuits, or some called them rolls, from wheat and rye flour, and they were just as good at eleven o'clock as they were at seven in the morning. I talked someone into buttering me two rolls. Then, I went to my room and took a good, long nap. After I ate lunch, I finally went back to the woods.

"Look,' I said, 'I couldn't find any sky hooks anywhere.' I told them I'd gone to Mr. Walker. He didn't know where they were. Then he sent me to another place... While I was telling them all the places I'd gone, they were falling out, laughing. I never told them to this day what I'd really done.

"On Sundays, we marched in an almost military formation toward the Dillard House, to the Presbyterian Church for services. Almost every Sunday afternoon, our houseparent, Mrs. Nick (Nicholson), who was one of the kindest, sweetest Christians I've ever known, would have vespers or Bible studies, or she'd have a singing group come in. And Mr. Nick really knew what was going on in the dorm. I don't know how he did it, but he could pinpoint exactly where the noise was coming from. He'd caution us by saying, 'You need to cut down on your activity in there.'

"Then, we'd have chapel during the week. I remember one incident especially. We had a man in our class—Denver Truelove. He was killed later, after the World War II Tokyo raid with General Doolittle. Well, Denver had beautiful hair, and he always spent a little extra time with it. But it was known among the rest of us that you didn't mess with Denver's hair.

"That day in chapel, we had a guest speaker—a red-headed man with a ruddy face. He'd come off the platform at times, walk around, and tousle someone's hair. Well, Denver was sitting on the front row, and the excitement mounted as to whether the man would get to Denver. Because of that, nobody heard a word that the man was saying. But the crisis passed. The speaker finished without ruining Denver's hair.

"My two years at Rabun Gap were special, as we were taught to work two days a week, go to school for four days, with Sundays for rest and worship. It was like a large family to me. Do your share; help each other; enjoy each day; be thankful for the food and the chance to learn."

Davis, interested in wrestling and boxing, remembered going to the Fry farm house to listen to championship bouts broadcast on the radio. But he admitted that his own foray several years later into the boxing ring did not turn out well.

Davis graduated in the class of 1939, with teacher certification, but he was deemed too young by the superintendent to teach in the rough and tough schools of the nearby rural areas.

Instead, he found work in a sawmill and did other odd jobs for a year. Then, his teaching opportunity came—a trial position for three months in a school where the students had "run off" the former two teachers.

"At the school, we had an auditorium— a large room built on the side of a hill, with the two classrooms underneath one end of it. I remember one of those first days when I overheard two high school boys talking. 'Fresh meat, boys! Fresh meat.' So I was wary that something might happen.

"I had to walk up a few outside steps to get into the classroom. When I heard some talking behind me, I glanced out of the corner of my eye and saw a high school boy with a rope in his hands, and about twenty students following him. From that, I knew that he would probably throw that rope and try to jerk my feet out from under me when I walked up the steps.

"Whether it was God-given or just intuition, when he made his move, I reached back and got his ear and twisted it. It really hurt him, and while he pleaded for me to let go, I twisted it a little bit more. Then I threatened, "I'll take it off. You see, I like this job, and I'm not going to give it up. And I'll do whatever it takes to stay here.'

"I never had a bit of trouble from him from then on. But that was the time when a teacher had authority, a time when you could discipline a child without being sued."

Davis survived discipline problems, fathers threatening to beat him up, and assorted other threats. But he taught only one year. He pulled up stakes, going to Nashville with another man by the same name—Hugh Davis—to work in the aircraft industry. A short stay in Baltimore with Martin Aircraft preceded his going to California in 1941, where the two were hired by Lockheed Aircraft, building wings for airplanes. After Lockheed, the two Davises parted company, with Hugh going into military service.

"I was placed under a navy training program at Bakersfield, California and was being trained to fly a piper cub," he said. "Solo flying was a great thrill that I'll never forget."

Then he asked to be trained back East. During the six months of waiting, the other Hugh Davis and his girl friend, Vera Nell, arranged a blind date for Hugh — with Helen Dougherty.

"Man, was she pretty!" Hugh exclaimed. "Then, during my training, Helen and I talked about life together, and on April 29, 1944, we were married at New Bern, North Carolina."

Davis was commissioned as a U.S. Marine pilot, trained by the navy. "Flying was just about number one in my life," he admitted. "Being a pilot was far more exciting than being an infantryman. But I've always said that to be a fighter pilot, one oar's not in the water, or your elevator doesn't go to the top floor.

"Once I left the States and the West Coast, I was stationed on an island where I stayed for three months. During that time, I did patrol work, and made ready for the invasion of Okinawa. Ten days after the invasion, the Marines had secured the airfield, and we went in. Anytime enemy planes were in the vicinity, we were up in the skies. It didn't take but a few weeks before the Japanese Air Force was not a problem."

In talking about his experiences in the air, Davis made light of the close calls and narrow escapes. But the pilots were equally at risk on the ground. "They never did capture all the Japanese who were holed up in the caves," he said. "Word would come down that some had slipped into camp and slit some of the pilots' throats, so we were careful. Occasionally, while an outdoor movie was being shown, the patrols would find a few at the rear. watching the movie."

One night in late 1945, before Hugh was scheduled to go to Japan to get ready for that invasion, he was worried about his wife. He had not heard from her in nearly two weeks. In the last letter he'd received, she had written that she was on her way to the hospital to have their baby.

"The day before, they sent up twenty-four planes," Davis said. "By morning, only eight of us came back. That night, as we talked about our group leaving the next day, I did not know that our orders were being cancelled by the Generals of the U.S. Army, Navy, and Marines, since our planes were not built for such a long flight. That next day, letters arrived, announcing that Stephen Hugh Davis and mother were doing well.

"Earlier, in August, when the atomic bomb was dropped on the two cities in Japan, some people talked about the devastation. But that saved over one hundred thousand American lives.

"I was in the air force for four years, from 1942 to 1946. I did everything that I was supposed to do. I had duties; I had patrol. And later, we had to pick up prisoners of war on the various islands. Stationed on Okinawa, I stayed in the service until February 1946. During that entire time, as a born-again Christian, I knew I was coming home some day."

Davis returned home to his wife and his son, Steve, and began to look for a civilian job. Through family connections, he was hired to head the office of a new car dealer. Two years later, when going to Atlanta to sell Mack trucks, he rode with Helen's uncle and brother, who had decided to get out of the fish and poultry business.

On the way back home, Davis struck a deal with his wife's uncle to take over the business—leasing the equipment and buying the produce. During his military service, Hugh had sent his money home and Helen had saved it. So after buying their first house for $1,950, he was able to purchase the business for $4,500 cash and his automobile.

"I drove one of the delivery trucks for the family to go to church and get around," Davis said. But it was during that time, that Hugh's faith was tested time and again.

The grocer and the bread man kept inviting the Davises to Calvary Baptist Church. It wasn't until that second year, that Davis truly became a dedicated member. He began tithing; his faith increased.

Generous to his employees, Davis also gave himself a bonus that particular Christmas. "I was going to use the money to buy a new overcoat that I needed," he said. "It was an unwritten law at one time that a man had to have an overcoat down to his ankles.

"I didn't know it, but all the employees had decided to get me a present, too. When they called Helen, she told them that I had said something about needing a new overcoat. And they bought me a nicer one than I'd planned to buy.

"That night, while I was lying in bed, I said, 'Now Lord, you gave me this overcoat and I've still got these five twenty dollar bills, my bonus, in my pocket. I'm going to give you these five bills. Nobody knows it except you and me.'

"Three or four days later, after I'd eaten lunch at home, I felt like calling one of the pastors that I'd met at the Peachstate Bible Camp, where we took boys and girls in the summer. We decided to meet for a cup of coffee, so I went by and picked him up.

"On the way to a drive-in, he had his hand in his pocket and I could tell that he was counting up his change. I didn't want anything, so he just ordered a cup of coffee."

While sitting in the car, Hugh reached into his pocket and pulled out one of the twenty-dollar bills. "God said to give you this.

"The tears started out of his eyes," Davis recalled. "He reached over and touched my shoulder and said, 'Hugh, at ten-thirty this morning, a couple came by the church. They needed some food and gas money to get to Chattanooga. In my pocket I had this one ten-dollar bill, but it was supposed to go to something else. Yet, the Lord seemed to be telling me to help that couple. So I did.'

"Gratefully, he looked down at the money in his hand and said, 'You know, you really didn't have anything to do with this, Hugh. And I didn't have anything to do with it,'"

Four more times, Hugh found a need. "I don't understand it, but sometimes you do a simple little something, and people tell you how much it means to them. I guess that's what Christmas is about."

The more Davis gave, the more successful in his business he became. From an auto office manager, to the owner of Rome Fish and Oyster, Rome Chickery, Rome Frozen Foods, to Sysco Rome, Hugh always dealt with his customers in an honest, straight-forward way. When he sold out to Sysco Corporation, it was not because of the size of his business, according to Davis. The corporation wanted Hugh, as well, paying him nearly a half million dollars in stock. Davis wanted cash to help his children, but the company would only pay in stock, which he could not sell for two years. "That became a business boom. Thanks again, Lord!

"Through the years, it just kept growing. So all my children have done well. It's knitted us together."

Two doctors, a CEO of a company, a shop owner, a computer programmer, and a teacher—these are the occupations of the six Davis children—Steve, Kenneth, Bob, Karen, Robin, and Susan.

Davis has not only formed the Hugh and Helen Davis Foundation, but has endowed the Hugh Davis Center for Ministry Education at Shorter College.

He has helped to build churches and schools in South America, Africa, Belgium, and in the state of Alaska. Traveling the Ukraine, China, India, the Philippines, and other countries, he is still busy ministering, teaching, and sharing.

He has served or continues to serve as a bank director and

trustee for two colleges – Shorter and Truett McConnell – and also as trustee for two youth camps, and for the mission, Titus International.

Wearing a pacemaker has not slowed him down. Davis seems to be busier than ever. For him, each day is exciting; each day is an opportunity to serve. He truly lives by his credo: "If you're kind to people, it will splash back on you."

WAITING FOR THE COWS TO COME HOME

Chapter Thirteen

FRANCES FRY AND JAMES F. DEAL
UNIVERSITY EDUCATOR, ADMINISTRATOR, WRITER

ith a forty-year career in the dairy industry, including the Academic Head of the Agriculture Department at Berry College, James F. Deal, with his wife, Frances Fry, has led a many-faceted life in various sections of the South. Yet, this couple's love for the valley of their early years has drawn them back in retirement, where they now live in an earlier family home.

Their childhoods could not have been more dissimilar—one nurtured by a mother and father in one community; the other the son of a young widow with eight children, whose family was divided early in life, with frequent sojourns in church boarding schools and with relatives.

Frances Fry was six years old when her father, Henry Lee Fry, became associated with Rabun Gap-Nacoochee School—first as agriculture teacher in the high school and administrator of the Farm Family program, and then later Dean and Vice President of the school. According to Wes Williams, another former junior college student, he had also been a star pitcher for the University of

Georgia. And he would often pitch, coach, or umpire for the Rabun Gap community baseball team. Dean Fry remained at the school for twenty-eight years, until 1959. It was on the Rabun Gap campus where Frances grew up.

"I was privileged to be a part of the unique years of the school, those of the farm family and the junior college. Those programs gave many a chance to get a quality education and to better themselves. I feel that my father was a big part of this process.

"He loved his work," she recalled, "and he loved working with the farm families—to help them get a start, whether it was dairying or poultry, or whatever.

"My parents and Dr. and Mrs. Ritchie soon became close friends. We always felt that they were there for us, and we respected and loved them.

"I remember Dr. Ritchie appearing at our door at 5:30 or 6 o'clock in the morning. If he had something on his mind and he wanted to talk it over with Daddy, he'd come to the house, even though Daddy would have been at the office in another thirty minutes. Often, Dr. Ritchie would have a cup of coffee with us, or sometimes, breakfast.

"My mother Martha, whom everybody on campus called 'Ma Fry,' was right in the middle of everything, helping any way she could. She belonged to the clubs that some of the farm women belonged to. And even the doctor called on her to help, especially in childbirth.

"I remember that when Mrs. Hopper died in childbirth, we kept the baby for six weeks in our home. There were a number of children—the oldest was ten or twelve, and they didn't think she could take care of a newborn, with all the others. I must have been about fourteen at the time, and when we had to take the baby back to the family, we all cried."

The Fry cottage was evidently a popular gathering place, a

"home away from home" for boarding students and children of both the faculty and farm families. "I remember one time," Frances said, "when a lot of us were out in the yard, playing ball. A woman came by and asked if my mother were running an orphanage."

By the time Jimmy Deal arrived as a high school student at Rabun Gap, he had spent more than his share of years in a home away from home. "I had had such a strange life up to that point," he confessed, "that I wasn't homesick, as so many other students were. I'd gotten over that when I was eight years old, when I was sent to Crossnore. Dr. Sloop, head of the school, seeing how homesick I was, called me in and referred me to the chaplain. We sat down and talked for a long time. The chaplain probably helped me more than anyone else. But once I got over the homesickness, then, wherever I was..." Deal smiled and continued, "I was kinda like St. Paul. I learned that in whatever state I am, therein to be content."

He was only eighteen months old when his father died, and his mother moved the family back to Hamilton, North Carolina, where her mother and stepfather lived. He remained in Hamilton until he was sent to Crossnore.

From Crossnore back to Hamilton for two years, then to California to live with an older brother who had been in the navy, Jimmy spent his childhood, until he followed in a sister's footsteps and entered the high school at Rabun Gap-Nacoochee in 1938.

"In the three years I was at Rabun Gap," he said, "nobody in my family had any money to help me, so it was a matter of what Dr. Ritchie was so pleased to be able to do — simply to support kids that needed an opportunity to get an education.

"It's a strange thing. We did whatever needed to be done in those days. We didn't resist.

"The first job I had at the school was cleaning out the septic tank — by hand. I thought nothing of it since a bunch of other kids were doing the same thing. But we had another new boy on the crew. About fifteen minutes into the work, he threw down his shovel, went back to the dorm, packed his clothes, and went down to the highway. We never saw him again."

By the time Deal graduated from high school in 1940, he was sixteen years old. With few jobs open for one so young, he decided to join the navy as his two older brothers had done. But when he arrived at the recruitment center in New Bern, North Carolina, he realized he was not "a good enough liar" to pass for seventeen. So, instead of volunteering for the navy, he joined the Civilian Conservation Corps—the CCC—a program to give work to young men who would otherwise be out on the street.

For that year, he worked in such activities as soil conservation and timber stand improvement. Then, since he had learned to type, he became the clerk and chauffeur for the district inspector. After the year was over, he returned to Rabun Gap to attend the junior college. By that time, Ritchie had retired, and Dr. George Bellingrath was president.

Deal, a seasoned raconteur, with a wry sense of humor, is famous for the many stories involving his own junior college classmates and some of the teachers, including Mr. Nick, the agricultural teacher.

"Mr. Nick was fantastic. Anybody who got through school without getting to know him really missed something. He always had a loaded question when he walked into class. One day, when we'd been studying marketing in agriculture, he looked at a red-headed fellow named Ross Cathey, who lives near Helen, Georgia. He said, 'Cathey, what's the price of corn in White County these days?' Without batting an eye, Ross said, 'Two dollars a quart.' Mr. Nick started laughing. It made the day for all of us."

And in speaking of spirits, Deal recounted the time that he and his roommate, Goodwin Nix, managed to get some grapes. "We pressed the grapes and put the juice in a bottle—hoping to make some wine. Mr. Nick found out about it. He brought the bottle in and said in effect, 'You bunch of dummies, this isn't how to make wine.' And he proceeded to tell us how. But we never did get to make any."

While Deal and his friends were busy with such antics in their spare time, Frances was enjoying the bike rides with her friends to Rabun Lake Beach. "When it was time to return," she said, "we would flag down the train. Our bikes would be loaded in the freight car and when we wanted off, we'd pull the cord. They were very lenient about letting students ride the train."

This was the Tallulah Falls train line that connected Cornelia to Franklin, North Carolina, a distance of a little over sixty miles. During particularly hazardous times, according to John Knox Coit, Jr., the conductor of the spur that was quite often referred to as "Total Failure," would announce at the start of the trip, "This train is for Demorest, Clarkesville, Turnerville, Hollywood, Tallulah Falls, and Prepare to meet thy God!"

Other reminiscences of that era for Deal were the time he and a friend, who is an outstanding educator today, were working in the milking parlor. His friend had on a stiff new pair of overalls, with the pocket sticking out. Tempted by this sight, Deal proceeded to squirt warm milk into the pocket, filling it up before it began to seep. A chase ensued; a bucket of milk was thrown in self-defense. Yet, the two are friends today. But Deal vows that the reason his former classmate is so good looking is the milk bath he had all those years ago.

Deal was in the junior college for one year. With the outbreak of World War II, he went into the navy, where he remained for forty-four months. In the meantime, Frances had finished the two-year program and enrolled at Georgia State College for Women in Milledgeville, where she received her degree in dietetics. Her first job was as dietician at the renowned Davison's Tearoom in Atlanta and later taught kindergarten. In 1944, she and Jimmy were married.

Basic training, Yeoman school, a Naval Academy Prep School appointment, which he decided he did not want, finally led Deal into amphibious training. Assigned to the staff of the Amphibious Training Command for the Pacific Fleet, he remained on Admiral Royal's staff for the remainder of the war. "I never heard a shot fired in anger anywhere," he remarked.

When the war was over, he was sent to Jacksonville, Florida to work as a yeoman, processing the discharges. When the time came for him to go back to school—at the University of Georgia—he merely wrote his own orders for discharge.

Going to school year round, Deal graduated at the end of the winter quarter in 1948, with a degree in Dairy Husbandry, now known as Dairy Science. His first job was at the oldest orphanage in the United States—Bethesda Home in Savannah, Georgia. And although he loved his work there, a call from the Head of the Dairy Department at the University of Georgia took him back to Athens to do graduate work and manage the university farm.

"During my graduate status, I had an interesting student—one of the Mayfield brothers who owned Mayfield Dairy. He had come, not to pursue a degree, but to take some specialty courses. Later, when their farm manager was being replaced because of health problems, they asked the department head to recommend someone. The letter was passed to me, and I decided to recommend myself." He left the academic world and became farm manager for Mayfield for eight years.

Another eight years with the American Jersey Cattle Club finally brought him into the academic world again—at Berry College in Rome, Georgia, where in 1969 he became Head of the Agriculture Department, as well as Director of Agriculture and Forest Resources, with a responsibility for 30,000 acres. He was also instrumental in securing a one-million-dollar gift to develop the

Agricultural Research Center.

"Retiring from Berry at the end of 1982, we came back to Dillard."

Deal's plans to do agriculture consulting were cut short when he went to his alma mater to meet its new president, Bruce Dodd, for whom he developed a great respect. "He talked me into going to work as Director of Advancement for Rabun Gap-Nacoochee School, so I did the fund raising and PR for five years before I re-retired.

"I did a fair amount of traveling doing fund raising and writing proposals and grants.... That group from Dr. Ritchie's time—the Rockefellers and so on—had pretty much gotten out of the picture. We still had the Woodruffs in Atlanta, the Hodgsons in Athens, and the women's groups, the Guilds, in Atlanta. But the support of the church had fallen off considerably." So trips with President Dodd to various churches in the Synod began, many times taking along the Gap Singers, an asset in the major presentation of the school.

"Another problem I had was selling the school on the basis of what it had been, as opposed to what it was, and what it could be. Those were three different avenues entirely."

Deal did not hide his strong feelings as to the reason for this. "The school had developed a reputation among a lot of people as being a home for undesirable troublemakers. Some people still think that.

"You see, we'd gone through a period where there was never such a thing as a 'bad kid—only a bad environment.'"

Deal attributed this situation that had to be dealt with, head on, to the disproportionate numbers of ministers on the board. "Out of thirty-five members, a large percentage were preachers. Some of them were naive, at best. They would call the school and say, 'We've got such a wonderful little fellow here, but if we don't get him into a better environment, he's going to jail'."

Deal praised Director of Admissions, Marion Rector, whom he worked with closely. "Marion, as an old school admissions man, had an insight into these kids that no one else had. He had the ability to take a youngster and, by the time he got through with his interview and testing and the interview with parents, he didn't make too many mistakes on the kids he brought in. If the student needed to be given a lot of psychological counseling or was into drugs, and Marion was able to find that out, he would tell the parents: 'We're not equipped to handle your child. We don't have the counseling staff. But here's a school that is equipped.' He would recommend three or four schools, and the parents of those youngsters were so pleased with the results and what Marion had done for them, that they would talk about Rabun Gap to their neighbors and friends. We got a lot of referrals that way."

When Deal retired from his position at the school, he still had goals and interests to pursue. Retirement "gave me the opportunity to do what I had wanted to do for a long time—and that was writing. I had written for dairy magazines before I retired, so I did stories from Texas to Florida to New York."

He has reason to be proud of his work, which resulted in published articles in six national magazines, several regional and state publications and local newspapers, with twelve featured picture covers.

Frances and Jimmy also have reason to be proud of their children—Stephen, Vicki, and Meagan—and their grandchildren. "One of the interesting things about our family," Deal said, "is that all three are in education, either our own or their spouses." Two of their grandchildren are grown, one still in college, and then there are the granddaughters, aged ten and fourteen, who have plenty of time to decide on careers.

Frances and Jimmy are both active in the Dillard community and in the Methodist Church, while Deal is on the city council, the police commissioner, and involved with Appalachian Regional Community Resources.

In recounting the blessings of his days as a student, Deal is still grateful for the good friends he made there, the life-long fellowship that resulted, and that early chance to earn his own educational expenses. But "best of all, like so many other Gappers," he said, "I found my future wife there."

With typical Deal humor, he winked at his wife Frances and teased, "We've had forty-five wonderful years together, and forty-five out of fifty-three ain't bad!"

FARM SCENE

Chapter Fourteen

DR. EMMETT URCEY DILLARD
UNIVERSITY ASSOCIATE PROFESSOR, LIVESTOCK RESEARCH SCIENTIST

r. Emmett Urcey Dillard boarded a DC-3 in Lima, Peru, and began to fly to one of the research stations deep in the Peruvian jungle. The weather worsened with each mile as the plane headed for the small airport, with its less than adequate landing strip adjacent to a grove of tall trees.

Dillard and his research team had taken this trip regularly, but on that particular day, they all felt a slight trepidation. Finally the landing strip became visible out of the mist, and the pilot began his steep descent.

The plane landed without incident on the rough runway, or so Dillard assumed, until he looked back and saw the wings of the plane decorated with twigs and leaves. Coming in for the landing, they had skimmed the tops of the trees.

The long journey from the Southern Appalachian Highlands to the isolated Andes Mountains of Peru encompasses the life story of Associate Professor Emeritus, Emmett Urcey Dillard, Ph.D.

Urcey's roots were in the Highlands. Born on August 12, 1917 to V.N. "Polie" Dillard and Minnie Cope Dillard, on a farm near

Sylva, North Carolina, he was fifteen years old when his family moved to the Rabun Gap-Nacoochee School campus in north Georgia, as part of the Farm Family program.

As to how the farm families were selected, Urcey said, "I know my mother had a sister living there before we went. And I remember that the previous fall, Dr. and Mrs. Ritchie visited our family in North Carolina. We were living on a small farm at the time. I think preference was given generally to people who had reasonably large families. I had five brothers and a sister who also attended the school, as day students.

"The design of the program was 'education for the total family.' The men had to go to classes on agriculture, while the ladies were required to go to classes on home economics and other homemaking programs. They met once or twice a month, on the average.

"All of the farm houses were designed alike," he added, "but some were newer than others. The house we moved into had been occupied by one other family. We were also assigned a certain amount of land that we farmed as tenants. Since students in the farm families had their own chores to do, they rarely worked in other areas. But a lot of the men—heads of the farm families—supervised the work crews, made up of the students who lived in the dorm. Sometimes, I would do extra work at the school and would be paid a little for that work.

"Our next door neighbors were the Bennetts from Hayward County, North Carolina. They had lived in a part of what is now known as the Great Smoky Mountain National Park. When the park was started, all farm property in that area was purchased, and the families were moved out by the park service. The Bennett family, which included a daughter Della, came to Rabun Gap and stayed the normal length of time in the farm program. Then they bought a farm up in Wolf Fork Valley, several miles from the school."

The farm families were a close-knit community. After the essential chores were done on weekends, they did quite a bit of visiting on Saturday nights and Sunday afternoons, between church services, which they attended both in the morning and in the evening. Dillard remembers that at least once or twice a month, the teenagers would have a party at one of the farm homes.

During the week, with going to classes, studying, and helping to run their own farm property, Urcey did not have much time for outside activities. Although he played some sports for recreation, his favorite pastime was swimming in Betty's Creek, which ran through part of the land they farmed.

While Urcey was a senior in high school, the junior college department was established and, upon graduation, he entered the second class. "Had it not been founded at that time, I don't know where I would have gone. There was a strong likelihood that I would not have gone to college at all."

Dillard's mother had been a schoolteacher before her marriage, and he had three paternal uncles who were also teachers. So education was quite important in the family.

Berea College in Kentucky, with its four-year-program, had also been designed to give students from Appalachia an opportunity to work their way through school. So Urcey was able to finish his undergraduate education there, graduating in 1940 with a B.S. degree in Agriculture.

"I had been interested in animals as a part of agriculture for a long time. In fact, when I was at Berea, I did some livestock judging, although I was not a member of the school's livestock judging team.

"Primarily in judging livestock, you judge them pretty much on appearance—how much muscling they have for meat production and something about the conformation of the body. It's a little like a beauty pageant for animals." Beauty on the hoof.

When Dillard finished at Berea, he made a trip to the farm in Wolf Fork Valley, where the Bennetts had moved. On February 4, 1940, he married their daughter, Della Edna, who had been his next door neighbor at Rabun Gap.

"After Berea, I went to the University of Georgia for a spring term of regular school and then for one summer term. While I was there, an employment opportunity came along, and I started working with the Farmer's Home Administration, which at that time was known as Farm Security Administration.

"We made loans to low-income farmers who didn't have, and couldn't get money at a reasonable rate from the banks. We not only provided loans to buy equipment, fertilizer, seeds, and so on, but also had a small program to help farmers buy land. Mainly though, we advised them and helped them set up their farming operations so that they, hopefully, could get out of debt and repay the loan."

He was assistant county supervisor in Forsyth County for three years, from 1940-43, in a five-agent office. Then, he moved to the northern part of Georgia, to Habersham County, where he was county supervisor, with total responsibility for all the programs.

In April 1944, he went into military service, the U.S. Naval Reserve. Stationed aboard the U.S.S. *Duxberry Bay*, he served in the Pacific Theatre of Operations. By November 1945, Dillard was discharged as Radarman, second class.

Unscathed by the war, he returned home to Della and their three children, David, Sandra, and Gerald. Clifton, the youngest, was born in 1951.

Wanting to continue his education, and having initially done some graduate work at the University of Georgia, Urcey applied there. But at that time, the school did not have an approved master's degree program in animal science, the area in which he was interested. Although assured that the certification would be in place by the time he was ready to receive his degree, Urcey decided not to take the chance. Instead, he applied at both Iowa State and North Carolina State.

"I was accepted by both," he said. "But with a wife and children, I wanted to be closer to home than Iowa. So we went to North Carolina State in the spring of 1946."

He was offered an assistantship starting that next year, and during the summer, he also worked part-time at the livestock farm there, doing research and helping with the breeding research program.

In 1947, Dillard received the Phi Kappa Phi Graduate Scholarship Award, and in 1948, his M.S. degree in Animal Industry.

"My research project for my master's degree was working with different breeds of beef cattle, to see how they responded to treatment in range grazing in forested land that had an undergrowth of switch cane, or reeds. This plant used to grow all the way from Ohio to Florida, but now is pretty much limited to the Southeast. From this work it was determined that, if properly managed, switch cane was a valuable nutrition source for mature cattle and that cattle production could be compatible with timber production in the pond pine areas of eastern North Carolina."

During the ensuing years, Dillard became Assistant Professor and then Associate Professor at North Carolina State, where he continued his research. For the first four years, he was a full-time research employee, but also served as a laboratory instructor part-time. For the rest of his tenure, besides his research, he co-taught courses, or was responsible for teaching at least one course each semester.

In much of his research with beef, sheep, and swine, the data provided the involved graduate students with material for several master's theses and Ph.D. dissertations. Information from these projects was also published in scientific journals and oftentimes became the basis for articles written for the general press.

Explaining his various research projects with beef cattle, Urcey said, "We were looking for cattle that would be heat tolerant, because in the eastern part of North Carolina, the weather is very hot and humid in the summer, and the Hereford, Angus, and Shorthorn, the principal U.S. breeds of beef cattle, suffer from the heat and high humidity.

"At that time, many people were looking at Brahman cattle. We were doing some crossbreeding work with those.

"We crossed the Brahman with Hereford, primarily. Then, because we got them through the King ranch in Texas, we also used another breed, the Afrikander, imported from Africa. They resembled to some degree the Brahman, but they didn't have the big hump on their shoulders. We used some Afrikander crossbred cattle in those evaluations, but discontinued them because of their temperament. But we did continue with the Brahman for several years."

Dillard named other crossbreeds he worked with, to find a superior animal suited to the North Carolina environment.

"We were interested primarily in comparing the Hereford, which was the main breed being used in North Carolina, with other breed groups. Semen was imported from a breed of cattle in Colombia, South America, called Romo-Sinuana. Romo simply means 'without horns,' and bald. The cattle were developed in the Sinu Valley in Colombia. Thus the name. They had heat tolerance, which we were looking for, plus they were a much more docile animal than the Brahman or Afrikander."

Prior to that, in 1953, Dillard had acquired his Ph.D. degree in Animal Husbandry at the University of Missouri.

Also in 1953 through the Department of Agriculture and the Agency for International Development (AID) in Washington, D.C.—Peru and North Carolina State signed a contract to work together. AID would furnish the money, the university the technical assistance, and Peru would provide the opportunities for research and some teaching, as an effort was made to improve agricultural production of selected crops and livestock of Peru.

"When the research project in Peru first started," Dr. Dillard said, "there were six of us who went there from North Carolina. I worked with the livestock, while others worked on forage plants, wheat, and small grains."

The Dillards sold their house, shipped all their furniture, and moved to Lima, the Peruvian capital city on the coast, where most of the other families on the team also located.

"In a way, the men had it easier than the wives," he said, "because we were working most of the time in agricultural situations, whereas the wives had to learn to communicate and get along by themselves with the day-to-day operations of the home.

"Typical in most underdeveloped countries, many people have servants, even though they, themselves, don't make a lot of money. We had one regular maid, who went to the market everyday to do the grocery shopping and was responsible for most of the housework. Once a week, two other people came by, one to clean and wax the wooden parquet floors and tile, and the other—a gardener—to tend the small yard. Since there is almost no rain on the coast, everything was under irrigation.

"Some of the other families, who had small children, also had a maid to take care of them, but our four were all of school age. They were enrolled in a school where English was spoken half the day, and Spanish the other half.

"When we first went to Peru, there was not much fresh food to buy except at the daily market. Meat was a little difficult to come by, but being a port city, Lima had a good supply of fresh fish. The city also had several nice dairies, although you took a chance, drinking the milk from some of them. So we also bought powdered milk. And as for the water, we had been told to boil and filter it. We did.

"Della, my wife, should have kept a diary of all the things that happened. Her letters, written back home to family and friends, kept them entertained.

"There was always a problem with the doors and locks in the house we rented. Of ancient vintage, the slide locks and the pins that pushed the lock forward were unreliable.

"One time, we were having about twenty people for dinner, and the lock on the door from the kitchen to the dining room stuck and broke. So the maid, to serve each dish, had to walk all the way around to the hall, come back in through the living room, and then into the dining room.

"And I think that same week, one of our boys, Jerry, who was about twelve at the time, got stuck in the bathroom. All the doors and windows had bars on them because of theft. But one of his friends, a neighbor, who was about the same age, was determined to help him. He climbed through the small window, but it was such a tight squeeze for him, that his pants came off in the window. Neither one of the boys could get the door open. So then, one of the workers nearby said that he would go in. Both boys shouted, 'Well, when you come through the window and your pants come off, we're getting out of here!' But the worker got in and rescued both boys."

From November 1957 to December 1960, Dillard served as Livestock Advisor in Peru through the AID contract, Acting Chief of the North Carolina Mission to Peru from July to December of 1959, and then returned as National Beef Cattle Production Specialist from December 1966 to January 1969.

"There were three research stations I worked with that were located in the Andes," he explained.

"Perhaps the biggest problem was mountain or altitude sickness.

The research stations were located about twelve to thirteen thousand feet above sea level, and until you get acclimated to the thin air, it can be bothersome. I had headaches sometimes. The Indians (about seventy-five percent of Peru's rural population) were quite used to the altitude.

"We had one farm that I worked with where there were alpacas. They're in the llama family, but whereas the llama is used more as a beast of burden, the alpaca is raised more for its fleece and for its meat."

The government of Peru changed hands several times while he was there, the coups occurring usually without gunfire. One time Urcey was in the jungle, and when he arrived at the outpost airport, it was surrounded by soldiers. After an extra day, he was allowed to return to Lima.

For the first three-year tour of duty, Dillard averaged being out of town one hundred and five days a year. He had more than his share of rough plane rides, braving rain squalls along the Huallaga River, traveling on some almost impassable roads, and learning to be productive in another culture.

When Urcey and his family returned to Raleigh and North Carolina State, he took a six-month leave of absence to brush up on the changes that had occurred in research while he was away. They purchased another house, another car, and returned to life as usual. But he confessed that it was a little difficult to settle down again, after being in a totally different culture.

On his second tour of duty as National Beef Cattle Production Specialist in Peru, from 1966-69, Dillard derived great satisfaction in successfully working on a project that he considered rather outside his area of expertise.

"In Peru, the guinea pig is the poor man's meat animal. The Peruvians and other Latinos are very neighborly and generous with what they have in providing for their guests. They did as we used to do years ago on the farm. If company came for dinner, we'd go out and select the best chicken in the yard and fix it for dinner.

"But with Peruvians, instead of a flock of chickens running around the yard, many families had guinea pigs running around the house and eating the scraps and a little extra food. And when company came, they would put the best meat on the table—which left the less desirable animals for their breeding stock.

"When we started working with this project, we set up a breeding group for the purpose of improving the meat production of this animal species. We were running five hundred animals maximum, with a selection from two different areas in Peru. It took almost a year before we had one of the male animals reaching a kilo (2.2 lbs.) at three months of age, which is pretty much grown by then. We started selecting these large animals, and by the time I returned to North Carolina, we had produced over thirty males that had reached that weight—what we would call 'slaughter weight' in our swine or cattle here. We usually got up to three litters a year, so it was a fairly rapid turnover. I think in the time that we were serving there, we did something like twelve generations of selection.

"I know they've kept the program going through the years, but I haven't kept up with the actual statistics as to how effective it's been in improving the welfare of the general population of the country."

Dillard also helped to train Peace Corps workers at North Carolina State before they went overseas. When he was in Peru, quite a few volunteers were in various parts of that country.

"We would go and hold a school—those of us who were technical people there. I remember one time we were holding a Peace Corps school in Huancayo, which is at the top of the Andes, not too far from where the guerrilla area was. We were about halfway through the course when we had to call it off, because there was a threat that the guerrillas might do something. They allegedly wanted to get rid of the Peace Corps.

"Now, you have to understand that maybe seventy-five percent of the people are very, very poor. Anything that will promise them some food and clothing—they'll go for. It's hard to combat the Communist influence in some areas, because the country still has so many poor people."

Returning to North Carolina State, Urcey started a new selection project with beef cattle, doing an evaluation of possible genotype by environment interactions within the Hereford breed of cattle—genotype meaning: sharing a specified type of genetic makeup.

"We probably had one of the earliest projects of genotype by environment interactions in cattle. Genetic material was brought from Montana and other places in the United States. We had one research station in North Carolina near the coast; another up above Asheville, where the elevation is three thousand feet, with a lot of snow and ice in winter. We split the progeny of a particular sire, took a part to each location, and measured their performance to see if they did better in one location than the other.

"Another project I was responsible for had to do with the selection in swine, using both a control population and a selected population to evaluate performance traits—also one of the first studies in which both were used in large animals.

"North Carolina is not so prominent today in raising beef cattle. However, we have become the second largest producer of swine in the United States. Only Iowa beats us. But North Carolina has more large commercial operations, where producing swine has become an industry, rather than a farming operation."

Through the years, Dr. Dillard has been honored by his peers for his achievements. He is a member of the American Society of Animal Science, and the honor societies—Alpha Zeta, Phi Kappa Phi, Sigma Xi, and Gamma Sigma Delta. He is listed in *American Men of Science* and *Who's Who in the South and Southwest*. In 1975, he received the Educator's Award from the North Carolina Beef Cattle Improvement Program and in 1980, was inducted into its Hall of Fame by the Animal Science Club at North Carolina State University. In 1986, Rabun Gap-Nacoochee School recognized him with the Outstanding Alumnus Award.

Now retired, Dr. Dillard still keeps up with trends in research, as well as what is going on in Peru. "But you soon find out that, being retired, you never have as much time as you thought you'd have," he confessed. "I've been active in the church for years (he's an ordained deacon, as well as church historian). And while I was still working, I was on a bowling team for twenty years. I won't say that I'm a stamp collector. I'm an accumulator. I've also become interested in family genealogy and have written a book on the Dillard family. This I have already revised and updated several times."

In his genealogy research, he discovered that the John Dillard, who originally settled in the Rabun Gap and Dillard area, was the ward of his paternal ancestor from Virginia – a link to the valley in Rabun County.

As to his philosophy acquired through the years, Urcey said, "I'm a firm believer in the fact that I'm a different person from what I was yesterday, and I'll be a different person tomorrow from what I am today. Because we're building every day on what our background is. Just how much the five or six years spent at Rabun Gap put into my total being, I couldn't say. But obviously, it was quite important.

"I think the teachers there instilled in many of us the desire to be teachers. The two who were the most influential were Mr. Nicholson, my philosophy mentor, and Mr. Shotts, my chemistry teacher.

"In working with my own students, I attempted to instill in them a desire to learn and to be inquisitive about the world in general and animals—including man, in particular."

He also feels that young people should be exposed to foreign languages much earlier in their education, to be able to communicate effectively in a global community.

"I have been very fortunate in having a wife who has been very supportive of me throughout our lives together, and we are the proud parents of three sons and a daughter, who have been reasonably successful," he added.

When asked in looking back on his life, if he would have done anything differently, he said, "Not in terms of my education. I think I've done a lot of good research, but I don't like to write. So my publication material is not that extensive. Perhaps I should have written a little more."

He laughed and said, "That question reminds me of my brother who did an interview with our father when he was in his eighties.

"In answering a similar question, Dad said, 'Well, I might "lay by" the corn a little earlier.'"

All in all, Dr. Emmett Urcey Dillard seems equally content with his own life.

STUDENT WORK CREW

Chapter Fifteen

DR. ALBERT H.H. DORSEY

CHIEF OF CURRICULUM SECTION, SOUTH CAROLINA STATE DEPARTMENT OF EDUCATION

Dr. Albert H.H. Dorsey, one of the outstanding educators in America, was the first in his family to pursue an education beyond the high school level.

Born on May 22, 1918 to the former Mary Rosalene Crumley and Augustus Lee Dorsey, the sheriff of White County, Georgia, he often jokes about the place of his birth.

"At that time, the sheriff's family lived on the first floor of the jail," Dorsey confided. "Since I was delivered at home, I suppose I'm a jailbird by birth."

After graduation from Cleveland High School in 1935, Dorsey's only chance of higher education hinged on his being accepted in the junior college department of Rabun Gap-Nacoochee School. "I had no money, and it was only by the grace of God and friends like Mr. E.J. Huff that made it possible.

"Mr. Huff, the county agent for White County, had known the Nicholsons while enrolled in North Georgia College at Dahlonega," he said. "He drove me to the Gap and pled my case." Dorsey still remembers the happiness he felt at being accepted, with the opportunity "to live and learn with a wonderful bunch" of people.

He did not mind the hard work to earn his tuition, for the chores were done alongside others. The feeling of love and respect and the introduction of a sound program of worship far outweighed the minor mishaps of a few mule kicks and a few hay wagon turnovers. "On the two work days each week, we were assigned various types of work, from cutting wood for fuel, to campus beautification, to working in the dairy."

As to the sights, sounds, and smells that he remembered, Dorsey penned: "The sights were as beautiful as today,/The sounds seemed most happy and gay,/The smells, to me, were new mown hay,/The tastes were rye biscuits and sorghum every day."

Active in sports, particularly basketball, he was also involved with the music program, and the "Hooverites," that special club of the Great Depression.

"I remember one basketball game, when a member of the opposite team, weighing over two hundred pounds, and wearing shorts several sizes too small, made a quick bending maneuver to get a free ball off the floor. His shorts split—belt to belt leaving more of him outside than inside. You can imagine the uproar of the crowd and the speed with which he vacated the court."

Besides basketball, Dorsey enjoyed the planned hikes and picnics off campus, and the occasional ride into Clayton to attend the movies.

"Dr. and Mrs. Ritchie were as a father and mother to me. I was often asked to drive for Dr. Ritchie when he had meetings."

The students were well chaperoned when dating, and Dorsey stated, "It was rather hard to do more than hold hands and chatter a few sweet words when two to six eyes were watching to make sure that you didn't go wrong. I finally decided to go off campus to date a beautiful young lady. This happened several times near the end of my first year. But yes, I got caught coming in one night. A kangaroo court is a jar of jelly beans compared to six faculty members reading the riot act."

Dorsey admits learning to love them all– the faculty, that is. "I had their supporting recommendations when I applied to Berea College.

"Berea was a second shot of the same type of work/study/ worship situation as the Gap," he said. "However, the rules were less rigid, and I felt freer." But the preparations for life were similar at both schools. "At both, I learned that I must depend upon myself and select and follow those traits that would allow me to be respected, trusted, and loved by my fellowmen."

In June 1940, Dorsey graduated from Berea with a major in vocational agriculture. That same month, he and Daisy LaVerne Murphy, class of 39 at Berea, were married. And for the next three years he served with the U.S. Department of Agriculture, first making subsistence loans to farmers in Knox, Bell, and Harlan Counties in Kentucky, and becoming a meat inspector for one year in the Neuhoff Packing Company, a subsidiary of Swift, in Nashville, Tennessee.

He resigned in 1943 to volunteer for the U.S. Navy. After completing officers' training in the University of Notre Dame NROTC program, Ensign Dorsey became an amphibious officer on board AKA-70, U.S.S. *Tate*, in the South Pacific. He served as Wave Guide Officer on a number of dangerous beach assaults, from Okinawa, Saipan, Guadalcanal– from the Marshalls, the Marianas, and Solomon Islands. He was also the officer assigned to train and direct the crew operating the number one dual mount 40mm anti-aircraft station on the bow of the *Tate*.

Several years after the war, Dorsey was at a meeting of vocational agriculture teachers in Kentucky, when he heard one of the participants describing his narrow escape during a particular naval battle between Japanese dive bombers and a convoy of American ships. The story sounded familiar. "Were you, by chance, on the *Rixie?*" Dorsey inquired, speaking of the converted hospital ship that had traveled in convoy with the *Tate.* When the surprised man nodded, Dorsey began recalling the events of that day, when the anti-aircraft crew that he had trained brought down the Japanese bomber headed straight for the hospital ship. "...They never faltered. The crew fired constantly until we saw the enemy plane go down about fifty yards short of the *Rixie.*"

Going back to the beginning of the naval battle, Dorsey said, "There were twelve ships in our convoy, circling at sea....One ship was sunk, and three others were hit, including an APC, a personnel ship on our starboard beam, serving as our flag ship. A planning meeting was in session..." He continued to describe the devastation—the wiping out of the flag staff, the captain of the ship, and the entire army field command officers group who were holding a meeting in the wardroom—seventy men in all. The only naval officer left to take command of the crippled, burning ship was a naval lieutenant.

Later, when Dorsey was employed by the S.C. State Department, he had another unusual encounter. "A book salesman entered my office and asked me to review a science book. After a few minutes, I asked if it were possible that we had met before. He turned out to be the navy lieutenant who had to take over command of the crippled ship alongside the *Tate* in the South Pacific."

From 1946-59, Dorsey taught veterans classes under the G.I. Bill. He developed a department of vocational agriculture in Ezell High School in Kentucky and taught classes for high school students, young farmers, and adult farmers.

Then, he entered the graduate program at the University of Virginia in 1959, and by 1962, he had received a master's degree, Specialist in Education, and completed class work for his doctorate.

A new era in education began when he was employed by the

South Carolina State Department of Education. As state supervisor of science, he secured a grant to develop teachers' guides in environmental concepts as part of the science curriculum.

During the time he worked with a select group of thirty-four teachers from various grades to develop and write eight guide books, he moved to the University of South Carolina campus. Four hundred and ten units were written in twenty-one days, and then evaluations, revisions, and editing followed, resulting in the guidebooks being published by a division of Doubleday.

After completion of the project, Dorsey returned to the state department office as Chief of the Curriculum Section, with twenty specialists as staff members. In 1972, he became director of teacher education and state coordinator of teacher centers and teacher corps.

After thirty-two years of public school service, he retired.

During his outstanding career in education, Dr. Albert Dorsey published articles in professional publications, presented papers at prestigious conferences, served on national advisory councils, and participated in professional environmental workshops for other state departments.

Listed in *Who's Who in American Education*, *Personalities of the South*, and *Academy of American Educators*, Dorsey has taken a leadership role in his church and community. When pressed about his various honors, he reluctantly named a few.

"As to honors or awards, I have many, but they are not as important to me as friends. I have letters of commendation from President Harry Truman, Secretary of the Navy James Forrestal, and Chief of Naval Personnel J.L. Holloway, Jr., relative to my being in the service during World War II," he admitted. He has also been honored with certificates of appreciation from the national, state, and local associations of conservation; from the Space Agency for the review of space research "which might lend material to high school curriculum development... and from several colleges and universities for helping them to develop better teaching programs."

Dorsey has also served as Master of his local Masonic Lodge and Deputy Grand master for his district.

Honored by the Rabun Gap-Nacoochee School as an Outstanding Alumnus, he is especially interested in preserving the unique past of the school. Consequently, he is helping to spearhead the museum projects that include the life-sized statues of the school's founders, Dr. and Mrs. Ritchie.

Since retirement, Dorsey has rebuilt a 1963 Jaguar XKE sports coupe; has built a grandfather clock out of prime solid cherry, and has recently begun other hobbies of woodcarving and writing poetry. An ardent mountain and beach traveler, he and his wife celebrated their Golden Wedding Anniversary by touring the "heart of the Canadian Rockies as a gift from our most wonderful children—" Cheryl Ann, Linda LaVerne, and David. He is equally proud of his six grandchildren.

"I have tried to instill in my children, and now my grandchildren, the tenets of integrity, honesty, trust, and respect—and admonished them to rely on themselves and treat others as they expect others to treat them.

In summing up his lifelong interest in education, Dr. Albert H.H. Dorsey said, "Teaching is a mercy, and there is no profession that comes close to the satisfaction one gets in seeing a mind and soul being awakened by his or her efforts."

Chapter Sixteen

JAMES FOSTER GOOLSBY
SCHOOL ADMINISTRATOR, EXECUTIVE DIRECTOR

ike so many couples who attended the junior college of Rabun Gap-Nacoochee School, Foster Goolsby and Frances Taylor became life partners.

"The year after I graduated in 1940, I returned to the campus as often as possible to see Frances, who was a year younger," Foster confessed. Yet, the strict rules of dating were difficult to observe on one particular day. "I proposed to her while we were sitting on the lawn of the girls' dormitory. When she said, Yes, all I could do was to briefly grasp her hand. But I want to tell you, I made up for that later.

"Frances was not a professional educator, but was a tremendous asset to me during my forty-six years in education."

James Foster Goolsby grew up on a farm outside Woodland, Georgia, in the west central area of the state that bordered on the Flint River. This was the region of the Appalachians along the Fall Line or divide, that governed the direction of rivers flowing either into the Gulf or the Atlantic Ocean.

Born February 14, 1922 to Irene Hendricks and Lawrence

Nelson Goolsby, Foster was one of five boys and two girls. Their grandmother also lived with them.

At the time he graduated from high school, he thought he had no chance of a college education. But during the summer, he found out about a school two hundred and twenty-five miles northeast, where he could work for his tuition.

Three weeks later, in July 1938, Foster arrived on campus, taken there by the family minister and his mother and father.

One of the first teachers he encountered as he began his days as a student at Rabun Gap-Nacoochee Junior College was Professor Eugene Nicholson. "I'd never been away from home, but I'd always worked hard. Professor Nick, my agriculture teacher, was landscaping around the main building, and a nice fellow from South Carolina was trying to plow the soil, to try to loosen it before removing it with a dirt pan pulled by a mule. Well, the boy didn't know how to plow. He was really wrestling with it, and it was throwing him around all over the place.

"I said, 'Mr. Nicholson, I can plow.'"

"Well, hell, boy, I wish you'd get at it."

Foster recalled the initial shock of hearing that word come from the lips of one of his professors. "Back then," he explained, "the only two ugly words I'd ever heard were hell and damn, and if you used one or the other, you were sure to go to hell before the sun went down."

For those who now hear much worse words today, the expletives seem quite mild. But this was in the same era of the movie *Gone With the Wind*, with the great discussion as to whether Rhett Butler would be allowed to give his "Frankly, my dear," speech to Scarlett for the world to hear.

Goolsby was at the school for one year before the Ritchies retired. "Uncle Fed was still president, and it was all right with him when we'd say, 'Good morning, Uncle Fed.' It was an honorable title.

"And I remember Mrs. Ritchie so well. A little bitty woman. Whereas Uncle Fed could be as gruff as he needed to be, Mrs. Ritchie would seek opportunities to transmit her interest in each student." This capable, motherly woman knew each student's name. "Both my wife and I felt her interest in us."

Being so far from home, with no money for bus fare, Foster, like many others who lived far away, did not go home during holidays.

"Professor and Mrs. Nick had a farm on the Georgia side of the Chattooga River," he said, "and both Christmases, he employed another student and me to work on his farm for a dollar a day, room and board.

"From sunup to sundown, we worked, clearing off new ground—grubbing or cutting new growth where trees had been cut down. We'd cut firewood, too. I remember he'd get us up at an ungodly hour, and by Saturday night we were marvelling at the fact that the next day would be Sunday. But it didn't make any difference to 'Prof.' He called us at the same time, and we worked until dark."

When questioned about the observance of Christmas Day, Goolsby said, "Mrs. Nick—bless her heart. She and Mrs. Ritchie must have been related, because their personalities and concerns were so similar. For Christmas, she had bought us some little inexpensive gift. But of course, we were thrilled.

"All the students knew that Mr. Nick's greatest asset was Mrs. Nick who, as far as we knew, pretty much ran the school office."

There were other teachers who greatly influenced Goolsby during those two years—who not only taught but lived their faith. Dr. and Mrs. Ritchie, Mr. and Mrs. Berry Floyd, Mr. and Mrs. Walker, and Dean and Mrs. Fry were especially remembered with admiration.

The teacher whom Goolsby attributes as the one who had and continues to have the greatest positive influence of anyone outside his own family, is his former math teacher, dormitory manager, and basketball coach Jack Acree. "His influence is woven throughout any measure of success I have experienced. He has been my personal friend over the decades."

In recalling the intrinsic lessons that were equally important in his student days, Goolsby said, "I learned that the largest part of any major accomplishment is what Uncle Fed called, 'Sweat.' You know, there are so many people of intellect who don't want to put their feet on the floor in the morning.

"Then, Honesty. I learned from my classmates and my professors that if you are able and willing to work, and have honesty, then you almost have it made."

Currently serving as president of the Junior College Alumni Association, Goolsby said, "I never ceased being interested in the school." And in tribute to the examples set by his classmates, he added, "My appreciation of Rabun Gap has grown as I have followed the careers of people like Joe Martin, Bill Stegall, Marlar Carpenter, and Wesley Williams. There's something to this business that, by gosh, if they can do it, I can too."

That 'can do' attitude followed him to his first teaching position—in a two-teacher elementary school in rural Stephens County behind Curhee Mountain. "Back then, in 1940, if you'd walked across a college campus, they'd give you a teacher's certificate," he exaggerated, as he explained the procedure for becoming certified to teach.

"I had seventeen students altogether, in fourth, fifth, sixth, and seventh grades in that one room," he said. At the age of eighteen, he was only three years older than some of his students. "I wasn't much larger than they were, but I was a lot stronger because of my work experience." This strength stood him in good stead, when the inevitable challenge to his authority came.

"Two older boys attacked me, but they didn't scare me. One had a knife. But I just grabbed his arm and squeezed it until the knife dropped. You know, I milked cows at Rabun Gap."

With his adroit handling of the troublemakers, Goolsby was then able to direct his attention to teaching his students.

At one end of the room, "we had a recitation bench," he said. "It was just an old church pew. I'd call one grade out of the four, and they would move from their desks to the bench, where I would teach them. Having only seventeen kids, I could do a lot of individual or small group instruction. Then, when I'd get ready for another grade, that group would retire to work on their assignments."

During that seven-month term in the rural school, Goolsby boarded with a mountain family. "They were tremendous people," he commented. "I stayed out in a bunkhouse in the yard. It was heated with a wood heater. And I drove the school bus from where I boarded and picked up students on the way—both elementary and high school. Another bus came by the elementary school to pick up the high school students. The bus I drove stayed in the school yard."

The following year, with a wedding planned for December 1941, Goolsby began work at LeTourneau Company in Toccoa, the company that manufactured heavy grading equipment. Seven days after Pearl Harbor, he and Frances Taylor were married. But by 1942, he was in the U.S. Army Air Force, stationed at Miami Beach, Florida.

After basic training, Goolsby was sent to Tennessee Tech, to a college training attachment. "They were waiting on the construction of airports and airplanes, and they had to do something with us until they were ready," he explained. "Then, we went to a classification center in Nashville, where we were classified as a pilot, a bombardier, or navigator. We pilots then went to Maxwell Field in Alabama, where they tried to kill us before we got in the war."

B-17 training and combat training followed, and Goolsby was

soon headed for Europe, sailing on the luxury ship, *Ile de France*. But as was the custom in wartime, the ship had been stripped of its luxuries, to serve as a floating dormitory.

"There were fourteen of us in one stateroom," Goolsby lamented. Departing from New York City harbor, the luxury cruiser held to a zig-zag pattern to outrun the German U-boats. Ten days later, the ship safely docked outside the harbor at Glasgow, Scotland, and the men rode to shore in small boats.

After a few practice missions, it was not long before Lt. Goolsby, B-17 pilot, was flying bombing missions into Germany.

Explaining why the Americans were the daytime bombers, while the British became the nighttime bombers, Goolsby said, "It was the Americans' choice. The Flying Fortress was built specifically for high altitude, daylight bombing. The British tried to talk them out of it. 'It won't work,' they said. 'It can't be done. You'll be destroyed.'"

Despite those dire predictions, the U.S. Eighth Air Force was tremendously successful, although casualties were high.

As squadron leader of twelve B-17s, Goolsby found himself flying in strict formation in a steady stream of squadrons that blackened the sky one eventful morning. The primary target was a strategic German airport.

"Pilots don't look at the targets," he said. "They're too busy flying in formation. It's up to the bombardier, who can see far ahead with binoculars and a bombsight. Because of this, the bombardier is aircraft commander on the bombing runs. At all other times, the pilot is commander, even if a general is flying co-pilot.

"My bombardier was able to see that the airport was destroyed, so he determined that we would deviate from the bomber stream and head for the secondary target, which was a marshalling yard, or railroad yard in Oldenburg.

"It wasn't a safe maneuver. But our squadron left the formation.

Every bomb from each airplane exploded on that railroad yard, with the camera in the bomb bay recording the action. When the colonel had the pictures developed, he said, "This is one of the best pieces of bombing I've seen during the entire war."

With modesty, Goolsby admitted that for this dangerous but successful maneuver, he and his bombardier were both awarded the Distinguished Flying Cross.

Describing a typical day, Goolsby said, "If we were to fly a mission the next day, we were notified the night before. Since it took so long for briefing and getting the planes ready, we were usually awakened anywhere from 1:30 to 2:30 A.M. The missions usually lasted for about eight hours. The longest one I flew was ten hours, twenty-five minutes."

On that particular one, with enough fuel to last ten and a half hours, only two planes out of thirty-six landed back at home base. One was flown by Goolsby. The others landed in France and Belgium, then held by friendly troops.

Explaining why he was determined to cross the Channel to reach home base, he said, "I got a letter from my wife every day, and she got one from me every day. I wanted to get back, to get my letter."

Goolsby was in the air force for three years, serving overseas for seven months. "Combat air crews either finished their number of missions or were killed or shot down. Our casualties were approximately fifty percent." By the time the war ended, Goolsby had flown twenty-three combat missions.

Instead of returning to the States on an ocean liner, Lt. Goolsby flew one of the B-17s home, with twenty passengers and all their equipment. Stopping several times to refuel, Goolsby landed on American soil, and soon headed for Toccoa on a thirty-day furlough.

Frances, having remained in Toccoa during wartime, heard the doorbell ring one afternoon. When she opened the door, she found Lt. James Foster Goolsby, war hero and combat pilot, standing there.

"After getting out of the air force, I went back to work at LeTourneau," he said. "By that time, I had enjoyed a measure of success, and I was stimulated. But I learned that while I was in the war, I hadn't learned a single skill that would help me in the steel factory. That prompted me to want to go back to school.

"We continued to live in Toccoa, and I drove over to Piedmont College. I got credit for my college courses at Tennessee Tech and the academic courses at Maxwell Field in navigation and meteorology. So I finished in one calendar year, going the year round."

From Piedmont, Goolsby went immediately to the University of Georgia for a master's degree in school administration. Taking an extra load each term, he was able to complete his master's in one calendar year, also. Later, he completed another year at Florida State.

"My first job was at Edison, Georgia, where I was principal of both elementary and high school." After three years, he was invited to come to DeKalb County by then superintendent Jim Cherry, a former resident of Edison, who had heard of an outstanding young educator in that town.

"Cherry was the greatest paradox I have ever known," Goolsby commented about this exacting man. "He'd make an 'F' in diplomacy, but I'm thankful that I worked for eleven years under his direction."

After principalships at Tucker, Chamblee, and Cross Keys high schools in DeKalb County, Goolsby became principal at Thomasville, where he worked with his colleague, Charlie McDaniel, who had also gone from DeKalb County to become superintendent of schools in Thomasville.

Five years later, the chairman of the board of Valdosta Schools invited Goolsby to apply for the superintendent's position in that city.

"The man who was superintendent planned to retire in a year, so the board wanted his successor to be in place, ready to take over. So I was assistant superintendent for one year, but had the extended contract in my pocket that assured me of the superintendency.

"It was a plum assignment. People patterned their philosophy of education very much like Thomasville, which was a city of refinement, as was Valdosta. I've always been happy to say that there were twice as many academic achievement trophies at Valdosta High as there were athletic trophies, but they didn't get equal press. I was there for ten years.

"Three years prior to that, I told my board that I was going to retire. At the time I was taking math refresher courses on campus at Valdosta State. I was sitting by a lady who knew that I was superintendent of schools. She said, 'Our private school is looking for a headmaster. Do you know anyone you could recommend?' I said, 'Yes, I do.'"

Irwin Academy in Mystic, Georgia was a small school of two hundred students, whereas Valdosta had seven thousand students. Goolsby became headmaster for seven years, until the school closed. Ready to retire, another opportunity suddenly came his way—to become the executive secretary of both the Southeastern Association of Independent Schools, and then the Georgia Independent Schools Association, when the two merged.

Looking forward to his retirement years and more time on the golf course, Goolsby finally retired from the educational arena. He served as a volunteer for the Ben Hill Literacy Program for a year, and then joined the staff of the *Fitzgerald Herald-Leader*, a weekly newspaper, until 1995.

Once again, he was called out of retirement to serve as interim headmaster of Brookwood School in Thomasville for one year, from

1995-96. "My wife and I kept our house in Fitzgerald, but we moved to Thomasville because the school furnished us with very adequate living quarters. I came home on weekends," he said, and with a twinkle in his eye, he added, "And Frances came home when she pleased. She enjoyed Thomasville, since we knew quite a few people from our earlier years there."

The Goolsbys have a daughter Susan, and a son Jimmy, who is an elementary school principal in Valdosta. They also have three grandchildren, of whom they are equally proud.

Since July 1996, Foster admits that he has done whatever he has been called upon to do if he felt capable. And that includes his golf game. In 1997, he shot a 75 on his seventy-fifth birthday.

Active in his church and his community, James Foster Goolsby admits that his fondest memory of Rabun Gap-Nacoochee School was meeting his wife Frances. "I don't mind admitting that it's still an emotional experience every time I go back to the school. Frances has been a great wife, a great mother, and a great grandmother. And it's just made me so proud.

"She's also an amateur decorator and flower arranger. There's not a week that goes by that she's not involved in those two activities. Civic and community, as well as private organizations, call on her constantly. I'm glad, except that things have to be transported." And Foster gets that job.

At the entrance to the Goolsbys' flower garden in Fitzgerald, there's a sign that reads: "Garden Tour, 5¢." But the experiences that James Foster Goolsby remembers in his life of service in education with a loving partner at his side are beyond price.

Chapter Seventeen

LOUISE WILSON HAYNES   JAMES F. HAYNES
VOCATIONAL EDUCATOR, AUTHOR   PARTNER, CONSULTING FIRM

he was the best basketball player we ever had," one of her former teachers at Rabun Gap-Nacoochee Junior College commented, in reminiscing about Louise Wilson Haynes, class of 1939. Later, a fellow student in her class confided that she was also one of the prettiest girls on campus.

Louise's charm and sense of responsibility have not dimmed in the almost sixty years since graduation. And through her successes—her many awards, accolades, a television style show, and a book, Louise has always given credit to the remarkable influence of the work/study school and its teachers.

"We were not just working for our room and board," she insisted. "We were learning how to live. Rabun Gap opened up an uncharted horizon for all of us."

But that journey began with tears, as her mother and father drove her to the school in the Blue Ridge Mountains on a summer day in 1937. Louise had never been to the mountains, had never been away from home before. So with each mile, she felt the impending separation.

"I came from a farm near Covington, Georgia," she said. "We were poor, but so were our neighbors." That was the era when ready cash was not easy to come by. Yet, with a mother and father who reached out in love to the seven children in the family, she did not consider herself underprivileged.

Born on June 30, 1919, Louise Wilson was almost eighteen when she arrived at the school and began her work toward the tuition credit that would supplement the sixty dollars her parents, Joseph Oliver and Beulah Wheeler Wilson, paid for the ensuing year.

Louise went to work immediately, with Alice Miller as her supervisor. "The work was real and very physical, but I enjoyed my work. Those were good days." Besides working in the vegetable garden, she also did laundry "the hard way."

"The school was engaged in an endowment drive, and Dr. Ritchie, the president, was on the road a great deal. Mrs. Ritchie was there and she really knew what was happening. This must have been the best of times and the worst of times.

"Dr. Ritchie was a great communicator, and I can hear him now as he would ring the bell after meals, and bring us a report of his efforts. In him, we had a shining example of faith and works. From his persistence, we gained a great respect for the dignity of labor."

But that dignity was put to the test for Louise in the chicken house, another of her assignments.

"Cleaning the chicken house was absolutely the worst job I ever had," she confessed. "When another girl from Covington was given the same assignment, she packed her suitcase and caught the next bus home."

But Louise persevered and soon she was given better assignments. "The best work assignment I ever had was grading papers for the teachers, Jack Acree and Berry Floyd."

Other pleasant memories included the picnics arranged by Dr. Ritchie, the Big Ring or square dance on a Saturday night, and the unforgettable aroma of fresh yeast rolls.

Louise Wilson graduated in 1939 with a two-year teaching certificate and went back to Covington to teach. During that time, she also took extra vocational classes, which qualified her for a four-year certificate.

In December of 1940, she married Raybun F. Stone and moved to Macon, Georgia. But she kept up her teaching and her vocational training through the years, with pattern drafting and design courses at Wesleyan College, men's tailoring with a master tailor at the Macon vocational school, and women's tailoring at Rich's, an Atlanta department store. She also took courses at the University of Georgia, and later at Florida State University, University of South Florida, and Colorado State.

During World War II, Louise helped to train workers for a defense plant, in vocational power machine operation and clothing construction. Later, she worked for the Singer Sewing Machine Company and taught vocational home economics at Dudley M. Hughes Vocational School in Macon.

"In adult home economics," she said, "I was the first to teach men's tailoring at the vocational school. What an experience! As I taught teachers, the course spread all over Georgia. Then, when I moved to Florida, I was also the first to teach men's tailoring in Florida.

"In the early '50s, television was new to us. I did style shows for our department, with McCalls and Vogue Pattern Company. The children were very excited, seeing their mother on TV."

By 1964, Louise, with her two children, son Raybun, Jr. and daughter Freida, moved to Florida, where Louise became even more outstanding in her field.

During the next fourteen years, she served as a consultant for the Florida State Department of Education, conducting teacher workshops for secondary and adult home economics teachers over the state, and contributing the unit on "Tailoring" for the Florida curriculum resource guidebook.

She helped plan the new vocational school in St. Petersburg, and in 1974, Louise was voted the outstanding Home Economics Vocational Teacher of the Year. She was again honored in 1975 for her contributions in Pinellas County.

During her summers at Colorado State, where she was working on an advanced degree, her advisor had suggested that she write a book on men's tailoring, since no book had ever been published on the subject, prior to that time. In 1973, the book, *Men's Tailoring*, by Louise W. Stone (Haynes) was published and later revised in 1974 and 1976.

When questioned about her successful career in adult vocational education, Louise said, "Effective learning takes place as a result of effective teaching. I have found that the key to good relationships in the classroom is understanding and communication. In adult education we do not have a captive audience. Students attend of their own free will. We must try to understand their needs, give them the tools and the skills, and create an atmosphere that will hold their interest."

Louise's own interest in her alma mater brought her back at times to the reunions of her junior college classmates. It was at one of these reunions that she became reacquainted with James F. Haynes, who had also graduated from the school in 1939.

Shortly thereafter, in November of 1977, the two were married, and a new chapter in Louise Wilson Stone's life began, as the wife of James F. Haynes.

James F. Haynes was born on July 7, 1919 at Clermont, Georgia, and after skipping two grades, he graduated from the local high school in 1935. In 1936, he took a business education course, learning to type and take dictation.

By the time he enrolled at Rabun Gap-Nacoochee Junior College in the summer of 1937, his secretarial skills were much sought after by both Mrs. Ritchie and Mrs. Nick (Nicholson) who worked in the office of the school. But Dr. Ritchie put a stop to that plan. "No man should be behind a typewriter," he said. "He should learn to plow." So off to the fields James went.

Years later, his business partner, Guy B. Arthur, wrote of that day in 1939 when he met James Haynes and interviewed him for his first job.

"As plant manager for R.G. LeTourneau Company in Toccoa, Georgia, I asked the personnel manager to hire a male secretary. I needed a young man who could go out into the shop, and even into the men's room, if need be. I was told that they never had such an applicant. So I said, 'Do the best you can.'

"A young man came into my office and introduced himself as Jimmy Haynes." After the preliminary questions, James was given a memorandum and asked to make a copy of it on the typewriter in the next room. A few minutes later, he came back with a perfectly typed memorandum.

Impressed, Arthur then asked, "Can you take dictation?"

"Yes, sir," was the reply.

"I handed him a steno pad," Arthur said, "and started dictating a letter. Shortly after, he came back into the office with a perfectly typed letter, a copy, and an envelope."

A week later, after references were checked and the personnel manager had explained his benefits, Haynes began work for the company in an office next to the plant manager's.

"Every month he became more invaluable. We could discuss a matter and he would take care of it."

In the early days of World War II, when the company was under orders from the Ordinance Department, one of Haynes' jobs was to go to Atlanta for approval of any changes the company wanted to make in wages, salaries, or benefits.

His tenacity became well-known in the Atlanta office. He might wait all day to see someone, even though he'd been told everyone was too busy. He never went back to Toccoa without the needed approval.

For four years, from 1940 to 1944, Haynes worked at LeTourneau Company. Then, he entered the Armed Services, where he was assigned to the Army Postal Service on Governor's Island.

By 1945, after he'd received his honorable discharge, Haynes enrolled at the University of Georgia, receiving a degree in Business Administration in 1947.

Taking up the story, Arthur said, "We met to talk about our future. I told him that I was tired of living in New York and wanted to move back to Toccoa. And that I was thinking of starting a consulting business."

The two worked out a partnership deal to carry on research in the field of personnel opinion studies. When told that the new company probably would not make any money for the first two to three years, Haynes replied, "That's no problem. I've saved all the money I made in service."

Guy B. Arthur and Associates was formed with Haynes as treasurer. He would manage the office and also conduct the surveys. Haynes rented an upstairs office, and for twenty-five years, he and his employees walked up those same stairs.

He was well-known to have an overflowing desk at all times, yet able to find any needed information within minutes.

Responsible for clients in forty-three states, Haynes, with the help of associates from each area of the United States, actively participated in the planning, interviewing, reporting, and follow-up phases of personnel opinion studies. Also experienced in the installation of job evaluation programs and other activities in the industrial field, he published a number of articles during his career.

In paying tribute to his partner, Guy Arthur said, "Jim was a wonderful friend, a dedicated Christian, active in his church, and someone who talked little, but when he did, it paid to listen."

Louise recalled their years together as good years. "After moving to Toccoa, I did part-time teaching and worked with James, bringing some of my vocational experience into his managing and consulting firm. I also traveled all over the country with him."

The two were active in the United Methodist Church in Toccoa, where James was a certified lay speaker, Sunday School teacher, and chairman of the Administrative Board. Louise was equally active.

Through the years, the couple never forgot the school in the north Georgia mountains where they had been given their first opportunity of higher education.

James Haynes served as president of the Rabun Gap-Nacoochee School Alumni, and a member of the Board of Trustees. Both James and Louise also became presidents of that very special group, the Junior College Alumni.

Upon retirement in 1986, after the consulting business was sold to a California company, the couple moved to Florida, where James Haynes died on February 3, 1989.

Proud of her children, Freida Stone Burris, a teacher in Orlando, and Raybun F. Stone, Jr., an attorney in Ocala, and her five grandchildren, Louise Wilson Stone Haynes has continued her tradition of leadership in her church, community, and professional organizations.

At a meeting of the junior college alumni group that also included her two younger sisters, Lynda Hasty, class of 1942, and Ruth King, class of 1945, then-president Louise Haynes looked out at her peers. "In this group, I see people who have risen to positions of great responsibility in education, religion, business, medicine, and other areas. I'm sure getting to the top wasn't easy. But we all share one thing in common.

James would have said that it's the 'Spirit of Rabun Gap.'"

THE WILSON SISTERS
LOUISE WILSON CLASS OF '39, LYNDA WILSON CLASS OF '42, RUTH WILSON CLASS OF '45

Chapter Eighteen

DR. WILLIAM RANSOM LEDFORD
UNIVERSITY PROFESSOR OF ROMANCE LANGUAGES

n 1970, after completing his doctorate in romance languages from the University of North Carolina, Dr. William R. Ledford was given a semester sabbatical from his teaching at Meredith College to do additional research in the libraries of Spain.

One afternoon, while sitting in a sun-drenched park in Seville, he watched Spanish workers proudly tending to the park, with an all-too-familiar odor of barn fertilizer pervading the air. Instantly, he remembered his earlier days as a junior college student at Rabun Gap-Nacoochee School with its eighteen-hundred-acre farm. He began to converse in Spanish with some of the workers, discussing their methods, and within a few minutes, they had found a common bond.

Fluent in a number of languages, Ledford, in his many travels from Cuba, to India, to Italy, has always been at ease, whether chatting informally with workers in a park, or speaking more formally with such luminaries as Prime Minister Indira Ghandi at her personal residence in Delhi.

William Ransom Ledford was born on May 28, 1923 just outside Franklin, North Carolina to George Ransom Ledford and Lola Gillespie Ledford.

"My parents were mountain farmers," he explained, "and we were a family of ten. I was the youngest male, and had a younger sister. When I was five, my mother died, and I went almost immediately to stay with an unmarried aunt, Eliza Marina Ledford, who lived just a stone's throw down the road from our house."

Throughout his life, Eliza was his champion, his inspiration. Although a fervent Baptist, she had gone to a private Episcopal school– a one-room log cabin in the mountains – and education was important to her. Recognizing William's intelligence, she began to make plans for the boy she called "son."

"I want you to be a preacher, son – a Baptist preacher." At that time, William was going regularly with a friend to the Methodist Church, so he responded, "But Aunt Eliza, I'm Methodist, not Baptist."

"Well, then, be a Methodist preacher," she countered.

Ledford lived with his aunt all through high school and was an excellent student. When he was a senior, he told the principal that he would like to go on to college. The principal gave him an application to Brevard College, which Ledford took home to fill out.

But his father, who had been able to supply only the basics of food and clothing for his family, said, "There will be no money for college. You can not afford that."

Distressed that his hopes for a higher education had been dashed, he confided his dilemma to his neighbor, a Mr. Potts.

"Well, go to Rabun Gap," Potts suggested. "It's close by. You go up there and you work. And you earn your way."

Thrilled with the idea and encouraged by Eliza, Ledford was taken to the school by his older sister and her husband. But after talking with officials at the school, Ledford found that he did not have the necessary money for the dormitory fee – approximately forty-five to fifty dollars. He could barely afford the fifteen dollar quarterly tuition.

Then, someone at the school suggested that he go across the highway to the Dillard House, a mountain tourist home, already renowned for its good home-grown food. Perhaps he could work there for his room and board. And then he could be a day student.

He did so and he was hired. For two years, he worked as a waiter, a busboy, and performed any other chores that needed to be done – whether milking cows, gardening, or harvesting farm produce.

That first August, shortly before school started, Ledford moved into bachelors' quarters, sharing a room with one of the Dillard sons – Henry – in a building called "the dog house."

More like a garage apartment, the building had three or four bedrooms upstairs, complete with wood stove, while down below were the bathroom, the laundry, and storage space.

Henry, the youngest Dillard son, was a merchant – buying merchandise in Atlanta and reselling it in the northeastern corner of Georgia, at Clayton and Rabun Gap, and in Franklin and Highlands, North Carolina. Since he was away a large part of the time, Ledford often had the room and the stove to himself.

By Thanksgiving, when the tourists in the main house had departed, Ledford, with Henry, would move into the main house for the winter. Then in early May, when tourist season began again, both would return to the dog house.

Ledford recalled that he was treated like a member of the family the entire time. He worked hard and was given encouragement, and he enjoyed talking with the visiting tourists, who often told him of their European travels. On occasion, when Dillard House had French-speaking guests, Ledford served as translator, since he had studied French in high school and had received a medal for his outstanding work in the language.

One of the drawbacks of his living off campus was having to walk the mile back and forth to Rabun Gap in all kinds of weather. In the winter, he often arrived wet and cold for classes.

But he loved the classes and the teachers. Highest on his list was Miss Alice Lennon, his Bible teacher, who took a personal interest in him. She often bemoaned the fact that he was missing out on many of the extracurricular activities by not living on campus, but there was nothing Ledford could do about that. Two other outstanding teachers were Miss Tewkesbury, his English teacher, whom Ledford later taught with in Iowa, and Mr. Nicholson, his horticulture teacher.

When Ledford first enrolled, Dr. Ritchie had retired, and Dr. George Bellingrath was president of the school. He remembers that both Dr. and Mrs. Bellingrath were very friendly with the students. "We were a small class, and Dr. Bellingrath knew each one of us personally. I particularly enjoyed his chapel talks."

Once Ledford graduated in 1943, with a certified teacher's certificate, he found himself living on campus—not as a student, but as a teacher in charge of discipline at the boys' dormitory, while Mrs. Knox, the home economics teacher, served as the other houseparent.

Although the community school on campus had a contract with the state of Georgia as a public school, Ledford taught seventh grade at the community school in Dillard. And that was where he met a 1941 graduate of the junior college—his future wife, Kate Marie O'Shields. She had recently received a degree in home economics from the University of Georgia and had come back to the mountains to teach.

The following spring of 1945, Professor E.J. Weekes from Berea College in Kentucky, visited the Rabun Gap campus—looking for transfer students for the four-year college that had a similar work/study program. Meeting Ledford, he said, "You're a perfect candidate. And you've had experience. I can let you do the same kind of work that you're doing here."

Interested in majoring in languages, Ledford went to Cullowhee, North Carolina that summer, to study French exclusively. When he enrolled at Berea in the fall, he had the equivalent of a year's college French.

For the two years and one summer that Ledford was at Berea, he was in charge of one of the dormitories that housed quite a few Cuban students who had come to the United States to learn English at the Foundation School. The dean had told him that all he needed to do was report any out-of-line incidences to him and he would take care of them. In the total time, there were only two reports made to the dean. The students were extremely well-mannered.

And there was a mutual synergy with Ledford. While they practiced their English with him, the Cubans helped Ledford with his Spanish. Two students in particular, one named Carlos Lopez, were eager to help, and Ledford confessed that he learned as much Spanish from them as he did in the classroom.

"Later on, during the Carter administration, when Meredith College took a group of us to Cuba, I relived some of these experiences, although I was unable to contact either of the former students," Ledford said.

"President Carter, who was rather far-sighted, and didn't seem to be so afraid of Communists as some of his predecessors and some who came after him, opened the country to educators, doctors, and nurses. Sandra Thomas, then a dean of students at Meredith College and until recently President of Converse College in South Carolina, took some of the faculty on a ten day trip during Christmas holidays. She had a Ph.D. in Spanish, and she arranged for us to travel all over Cuba.

"We tried to be diplomatic when some of the Communist line

was fed to us by our guides. Some of their assertions were a little hard to take. And they only allowed us to see what they wanted us to see," Ledford said.

In visiting one of the schools comprised of ten to thirteen-year-olds, he observed, "It's amazing how well the students here speak English."

The guide replied, "This is true all over Cuba."

"But I knew that this was a model school in Havana— designed to be shown to foreigners.

"We were also told that there were no prisons in Cuba. But as we passed by a big building that looked very much like a prison, I commented, 'That looks like a prison to me.'"

"Well, we have a few," the guide admitted, "for those that are political delinquents or dissidents."

Wherever they went, they saw both men and women dressed in brown military uniforms—whether working in the cane fields, or serving meals to the visitors.

One day, Ledford struck out on his own, to find a movie. No one on the street would give him directions. "Oh, we don't have many movies here," was the cautious reply.

Curious at this fair-skinned foreigner, one Cuban inquired, "Are you Soviet?" Following up a negative reply, he guessed, "Then you must be German."

Finally, Ledford acknowledged, "I'm an American."

The Cuban smiled. "Oh, I'm so pleased. We don't ever get to see Americans."

There at the street corner, a lively conversation ensued, while men from two different cultures found common ground in speaking about sports and things non-political.

"It's too bad they've had to go through such political trauma," Ledford said.

So Ledford's Spanish experience at Berea in mountainous

Kentucky had translated itself years later onto a brilliant, balmy day in Havana.

In the spring of 1947, before Ledford received his B.A degree from Berea, his advisor told him that he had a graduate teaching assistantship available in the language department of the University of Iowa. He asked Ledford if he would like to have it.

Already engaged to Kate O'Shields, Ledford said, "I'm marrying a Georgia girl, and she might not want to go that far from home. I'd better talk with her first." So he made a quick call to Duluth, Georgia.

"Why not?" Kate immediately replied.

"I couldn't believe it was so easy for her to say, 'Yes, let's do it.'"

In the next two years, Ledford got his master's degree, while his wife Kate did a year's graduate work. And then, with a baby on the way, Ledford found a teaching position at Red Oak, Iowa, in a school that was remarkably similar to Rabun Gap. He taught French in the high school and Spanish in the junior college. It was at Red Oak, where Miss Tewkesbury, his former English teacher, was a colleague. How proud she must have been of one of her star pupils back at Rabun Gap.

After two years, the harshness of the winters, with ice and snow, finally forced the Ledfords to return to the milder climate of the South. While Bill went to summer school at the University of North Carolina at Chapel Hill for six weeks, Kate returned to her parents' home in Duluth. By the fall, Ledford had secured a teaching position in Roxboro, North Carolina, where the family remained for five years. During four of those five years, Kate taught home economics in the public schools.

During a summer break, Kate took their two daughters on a visit to her parents in Duluth. That left Ledford at loose ends in a quiet house. So he decided to revisit the University of North Carolina campus where he had gotten acquainted with several of the professors.

"What are you doing here, Bill?" one of the professors inquired, seeing him. "You're not enrolled."

"No. But I'm just tired of teaching those large English classes in Roxboro. I thought I'd drive over here to see what's going on."

"Well, this just might be your lucky day," the professor announced. "I had a call from Meredith College in Raleigh, and they need someone to teach – essentially Spanish, but also French. And you fit the bill. Why don't you go over there this afternoon?"

So Ledford got into his car and drove to the college for an interview. Within a week, he was notified that he had been accepted. "Back then," Ledford explained, "jobs were readily available if you were qualified."

Ledford was quite proud of his wife's accomplishments as a teacher, also. "She had such excellent training at the University of Georgia, that she was later hired by the Raleigh Public Schools, where she remained for nineteen years as a science teacher. Because of her talents, she received the North Carolina State Teachers Award."

She was also an encouragement for her husband, Bill, who worked on his doctorate in languages at Chapel Hill, while holding his full-time teaching position at Meredith College.

Prior to his return to university studies, Ledford was awarded a Fulbright scholarship to Colombia, South America, where he spent eight weeks. "That was where my Spanish really developed well," he said. "At that time, Colombia was not the drug-related country that it is today. The country was beautiful. We were on the coast for a month, associated with the university there. Then, we went to Bogota, the capital, and finished the last four weeks there, with the same professors at both places."

In 1969, Ledford had received his doctorate, so it was Dr. Ledford who later went on his semester sabbatical to research the

"Quixote" legend in Spain. Upon his return, he introduced the course at Meredith College, where he soon became a full professor and then chair person of the language department.

By the time Ledford received his second Fulbright grant, he was a widower. His Kate had died in 1977. And one of his brothers had been ill. The weekend before he left with a group to India, he went to Franklin to visit his brother, who seemed much better.

The following Monday, Ledford began the twenty-five hour plane trip to India. Waiting for him at the hotel in Delhi was a telegram with the news that his brother had suddenly passed away.

"In my sadness," Ledford recalled, "I took a long walk in the city of Delhi. As I looked around, I thought how my brother would have loved being with me. And in a way, I felt that he was right there beside me, seeing the sights of that beautiful country.

"The lake district was a totally different experience from the larger cities," he said. "In the Veil of Kashmir, in the cool Himalayas, we rode elephants and took day trips and picnics up into the mountains where Hindu priests, with little on, sat by the wayside and asked us for alms.

"The Hindu religion is a very open religion and we were invited to participate in the temple ceremonies. To the sound of bells, we walked around in circles, holding hands, and poured a special milk and rice product that stood for rejuvenation and regeneration onto the shrine. The people treated us with such respect, bowing with their hands folded together and saying, 'Namaste,' which we said back to them.

"But there's so much poverty in that beautiful and wonderful country. In 1982, many were bemoaning the fact that spoken English was rapidly disappearing. Many of the library manuscripts are in Hindi only, and so many Indians, who are not with the government, where some English is required, have reverted to one of the hundred dialects."

At times, Ledford's natural curiosity caused a little consternation with some of the guides, especially when he disappeared from the group. Not particularly entranced with the tough water buffalo that was the meat of choice in the Western dining rooms of the hotels, Ledford would slip into the Eastern dining rooms and eat what the east Indians ate. When word got out that the native food tasted much better, the guide moved the entire group into the Eastern dining rooms.

"One of the highlights of the trip was the visit to Prime Minister Indira Ghandi's almost modest home, where the sixteen of us spent an hour," Ledford recalled. "We had been invited there to discuss our experiences in India and what we had learned.

"Her residence was about a hundred yards from the main street. When we arrived, there were only two Indian policemen, with billy sticks, guarding the entrance to the street.

"We were taken into an impressive hall to await her arrival. The paintings on the walls had been done by Chagall, but were quite shocking to the western eye. She finally arrived, apologizing for keeping us waiting for the few minutes, but we had been taken care of with refreshments—orange juice and trays of sweets.

"She asked each of us questions, and then suggested that we ask some questions of our own. But anything of a political nature was brushed aside. 'Oh, that problem is off in Tamil country. I don't know whether we will solve it or not.'

"When it was time to go, the Prime Minister accompanied us all the way to the street. At the time, I thought how dangerous that was for her to do. Anyone could have shot her from the street. And of course, only a year later, that is what happened. A Sikh policeman—within her own sect—did assassinate her."

Ledford retired from Meredith College in 1991, and although he still teaches Spanish part-time at Wake Technical Community College, he spends each summer traveling throughout Europe. At the moment, his interest is in Italy, where he is making plans for 1998, to meet with friends, who are also traveling with Elder Hostels.

"I do recommend that group. Money-wise, you can't beat it. Both the service and lectures are quite good. The only drawback is that you have to stay with the rest of the group. No veering off on your own."

Ledford is active with Raleigh's sister cities—Compiègne, France and Kingston-upon-Hull in England—in its International Exchange Program. He has also served in various capacities as a member of the Methodist Church. He didn't become the preacher that Aunt Eliza wanted, but his many other accomplishments are listed in such biographical works as *Who's Who in the South and Southwest*.

Perhaps Dr. William Ransom Ledford's greatest legacy is in passing on his thirst for knowledge and his exuberance for life to other generations.

His two daughters, Colette Edwards and Janeen Buckner, are both teachers, with master's degrees. And Ledford's gift for languages and his desire to see the world seem to have passed on to his four grandchildren, Leah Marie and Mark Travis Edwards, and Jenner and Campbell Buckner. His granddaughter, Leah Marie, a student at Berea, has recently returned from Russia, and Campbell, at the age of twelve, is studying Japanese for his trip to Japan.

In pointing out the highlights of his journey through life thus far, Dr. William R. Ledford said, "Long ago, my life was completely changed by attending Rabun Gap-Nacoochee Junior College. The important factors of study, work, and wholesome social life gave me a solid basis for future educational endeavors. I'm very grateful."

Farm Woman Feeding Chickens

Chapter Nineteen

DR. JOE ALLEN MARTIN
UNIVERSITY DEPARTMENT HEAD, RESEARCH SCIENTIST

rom potential high school dropout to president of the American Association of University Professors marks the educational trail that a young man from Bowersville, Georgia began in the summer of 1936 and completed in 1988 when he retired as professor and head of the agricultural economics and rural sociology departments at the University of Tennessee in Knoxville.

Joe Allen Martin's early enthusiasm for school began to flag by the time he finished the ninth grade, and he seriously considered dropping out of school, even though his father, Rod James Martin, was a member of the local board of trustees. His mother, Evelyn Adams Martin, sought some way to keep her son interested in education.

Through a cousin who had attended Rabun Gap-Nacoochee School, Evelyn was able to get a catalogue and application form for the private high school, and persuaded Joe to apply for admission.

"I was accepted," Martin said, "to enter in July 1936. My father and cousin took me there by car, where I was greeted by Dean

Harrell and Dr. Ritchie. I remember my father telling Dr. Ritchie that I had been raised on a farm and had worked on it from the time I was big enough to work. Dr. Ritchie assured him that the school would use my skills.

"Since I was there for four years—two years of high school, and two years of junior college—I gained seniority, so I was able to get the preferred job assignments most of the time.

"These were in the dairy, the poultry enterprise, caring for beef cattle, and building maintenance, such as painting, or firing the furnaces in winter time."

Interspersed with these chores were others so necessary to a well-run farm, such as plowing, cutting timber, cleaning stables, harvesting silage, corn, or hay, and hauling and unloading coal.

"One of my work assignments," Martin recalled, "was to fire the furnace in a chick brooder—which meant adding wood to the furnace twice during the day and twice at night." One night, "we had a snow storm, and it was very cold."

Martin tells of forgetting to set his early morning alarm, and two hours later, when he rushed to the brooder, he found the fire dying out and the baby chicks huddled around the bricks for warmth.

"The wood, piled outside by the furnace door was covered with snow and very wet," Martin said. "I added the wet wood to the fire, but nothing happened. A gallon can of kerosene was sitting by the wood pile, so I poured about a pint of it into a tin can, threw the fuel into the furnace, and closed the door.

"In about three seconds, there was an explosion that could be heard over the whole campus. Inside the chicken house, the brick brooder and small chicks huddled around it were blown all over the chicken house."

Fortunately for Martin, most of the chicks merely had their downy feathers singed, and he was not asked to leave the campus. But he remained uneasy, for he realized that the "poultry enterprise was very important to Mrs. Ritchie, and was also a source of much good food to the dining hall." Yet, from that experience, he learned a valuable lesson about the proper mix of wood and kerosene.

Two other valuable lessons Martin learned in his work experiences were the necessity of taking a bath with strong soap to rid himself of chiggers after picking blackberries, and staying a step ahead of some of the pranksters on the milking team.

"For several months I worked on the milking crew with three other boys," Martin explained, warming to the story of a prank-filled morning. "The milking was done by hand, with each worker milking ten to twelve cows twice a day"– at four-thirty in the morning, and four-thirty in the afternoon.

"The milking crew had one alarm clock, with the junior member of the team assigned to the clock. It was his duty to wake up the other members of the team, then go to the barn, get the cows up, take eight into the milking parlor and feed them, so that they would be ready when the other members of the milking team arrived."

Unknown by the keeper of the clock, one of the crew had reset the alarm from four A.M. to one A.M. When it went off, the junior member got up and proceeded with his regular schedule. But Martin and the others, aware of the prank, rolled over and went back to sleep for another three hours.

At the barn, the cows protested at being awakened at such an early hour. "The dairy herdsman, who lived in a cabin a short distance from the barn," Martin remembered, "was aroused by the student shouting at the cows. He, of course, came to check on the noise and, informing the young man of the real time, he suggested that he should leave the cows alone and go back to bed."

The one work experience that could have resulted so easily in tragedy is one that Martin also remembers.

"The school had just bought a pair of young mules that were broken to work, but were very high spirited and easily excited. In those days, the campus was mowed with a common hay mowing machine, which makes a lot of noise."

Hitching the mules to the mowing machine, Martin proceeded to mow the slanting hillside lawn that surrounded the main building. Excited by the loud noise of the machine, the mules were difficult to handle, since they wanted to run, rather than walk. Just when Martin had succeeded in calming them, a farm truck, without a muffler, passed by on the nearby road, and despite Martin's attempt to hold them back, the mules broke and ran. Dragging the mowing machine, with its sharp cutter behind, the runaway mules hit a deep ditch, the jolt knocking Martin off the seat and several feet into the air. In that split second, Martin realized the immediate danger. "I had enough presence of mind to know that I was going to come down in front of the cutter bar. I hit the ground on my feet, and sprang like a jumping Jack, just as the cutter bar went under my feet."

Martin admits that it took him longer to recover from the experience than did the pair of mules. "I know that a guardian angel was taking care of me on that day."

As is true with many other students, Martin met his future wife at Rabun Gap-Nacoochee School. But he found that "courting on campus required a lot of discipline and ingenuity, with such a strict code of conduct to adhere to. It was not easy to steal a kiss or experience the thrill of a good hug," he confessed.

"What made such things possible was poor lighting. At night, when you moved with your date from one building to another, frequently it was in total darkness. Oh, what fun!"

Passing love notes, according to Martin, was an old tradition at Rabun Gap, and was "one of the major instruments used in courting.... To facilitate secrecy of passage from one person to another, the note was folded in a precise way." A standard sheet of paper was "folded so that it locked together in the form of a triangle, of which the short sides were about two inches and the long sides about three inches." Some sixty years later, using his memory of earlier days, Martin reconstructed one. However, his wife Mary is certain that she has a few authentic ones that are still hidden in a very special place.

In June 1940, after four years at Rabun Gap-Nacoochee School—first as a high school student, and then as a junior college student—Joe Martin graduated. He is the first to admit that "the school rescued me from the life of a school dropout and set me on the road to a rich and wonderful life of service to others and rewards and happiness for me."

Enthusiastic about continuing his education, Martin enrolled in the College of Agriculture at Clemson, and attended that school from September 1940 to June 1941, when he was called into military service.

After spending three months in rugged training as a combat engineer at Fort Belvoir, Virginia, Martin, with his regiment, left for the West coast, for embarkation to the Philippine Islands.

During 1941, over one hundred and twenty-five strikes called by union leaders in the United States had been able to

JOE MARTIN AND FRIENDS

slow down work in factories that were committed to defense projects. Equally harmful were the International Longshoremen strikes called by communist sympathizer, Harry Bridges.

While enroute to the West coast, Martin, with his regiment, learned that Bridges had called a maritime strike, not only on the West coast, but also in Hawaii. Because of this, the regiment's orders were changed to go to Hawaii, rather than the Philippines.

"About seven weeks after I arrived on the island of Oahu," Martin said, "the Japanese attack on Pearl Harbor came. I remained in Hawaii until February 1943, when I returned to the States as a staff sergeant in a cadre to train a unit to go to Europe. The unit was formed as the 159th Combat Engineer Battalion in April 1943, at Fort Meade, Maryland."

Two months later, on June 12, 1943, Martin and his former classmate, Mary Addington, were married in the chapel at Fort Meade, with forty-five recruits from his platoon witnessing the ceremony, along with Mary's mother and her cousin, Irene Hackney, a teacher at Rabun Gap Community School for many years.

For a year, Mary made a home for the couple in makeshift quarters, following her husband from one assigned base to another until June 1944, when the 159th Combat Unit left for Europe, aboard the U.S.S. *West Point*, headed for Scotland.

A week later, Martin, promoted to First Sergeant, and his group were loaded on "a tub to cross the English Channel. We spent seven days on the Channel, waiting to get onto Utah Beach."

War historians are aware of that potentially disastrous period, when ships loaded with troops, tanks, and guns, left England in a secret armada for the Normandy invasion, only to be forced to return to port because of a sudden storm in the Channel. With the added danger of being discovered by the enemy, they waited out the storm, until the signal was given to proceed for the D-Day invasion.

Unknown by Allied intelligence, the Germans were having army maneuvers at Utah Beach, so as the first wave of Americans landed, they were met with ferocious resistance.

For Martin and the 159th Combat Engineer Battalion waiting in the Channel, it was a time of limbo, while they listened to the clash of battle on the Normandy beaches. Their assigned task was to repair roads and clear land mines. "Everyone was ready to fight the Krauts, if we could just get off that tub.

"Those seven days were the worst living experience I had while in the army," Martin commented. "We slept in two shifts: one-half down in the dark, airless hold, while the other half was up on a hard and dirty deck. There were no food facilities on the boat. The only C rations we had were white beans."

By the time they reached the beach, the wreckage from D-Day was strewn everywhere. "We could hear the noise of artillery as we unloaded." And casualties in the combat unit were immediate.

By the second of August, the battalion of engineers was part of the Third Army under Patton, with the objective of driving straight through enemy territory to the city of Brest. Seven weeks later, the city fell.

"The joy of the people of Brittany was a sight to behold," Martin recalled. "They greeted us with open arms, kisses, long loaves of dark bread, and bottles of Calvados, the nectar of the apple."

After drives into Belgium and Luxembourg, they were again assigned to the Third Army, headed for Bastogne, to give relief to the 101st Airborne Division in the December Battle of the Bulge.

"Through the heart of Europe, there are several large rivers," Martin said. "Rivers create a job for combat engineers. We put the infantry across rivers in small row boats, hopefully under the cover of darkness. Then we put the tanks across on pontoons in the same manner. After a bridgehead is established, we build a bridge."

Their progress was rapid. By the time they reached Buchenwald, near Weimar, Martin saw his first Nazi concentration camp. "It was clear to us then why we were in Europe."

By the time the war ended, Martin had spent forty-nine months in military service, while his education had been put on hold. Discharged on August 30, 1945, he resumed his education at Clemson a few days later. With new maturity and focus, Martin became an excellent student and graduated in May 1946 with a B.S. degree in agricultural economics, and completed requirements for his master's degree in August of 1947.

One month later, with a recommendation from his alma mater, he was appointed to the faculty at the University of Tennessee.

Yet, the interview with the department head was almost as hazardous to his wife Mary, as one of Martin's earlier experiences at Rabun Gap.

"Unknown to me, the department head had a well established reputation ... as a pack rat," Martin confided. Describing the thirty by forty foot office, he continued, "It accommodated not only the department head and his clerical staff of five ladies, but also six or seven staff members who composed the research faculty of that department. Research records and files were stacked on shelves that reached from the floor to the eight foot ceiling. Over the many years of the department head's tenure, tons of paper had accumulated, along with much dust."

Sitting quietly in a chair reserved for guests—with her back to one of the stacks—Mary waited while her husband was being interviewed.

Directly behind the department head's desk was an open window, through which a rather stiff breeze was blowing. As the conversation between Martin and the department head was in progress, the breeze picked up, sending several sheets of paper from the top of the shelf, onto Mary's head. The stronger the breeze, the more sheets of paper and dust rained down. "At the peak of the paper and dust storm," Martin said, "I could scarcely see my wife, sitting less than ten feet away.

"After I joined the faculty, some of the staff members who had observed what had happened and were embarrassed by the event, commented to me that they were surprised that I had accepted the position. But of course, I had been informed that the department head would be retiring soon."

Martin's rise in the department was rapid. By 1950, he was

granted a year's academic leave for graduate study at the University of Minnesota. And in that time, he completed all requirements except for the dissertation of the Ph. D. degree, which he completed in 1955. When he returned in 1951 to Tennessee, he was promoted to associate professor, and to professor in 1956. In 1972, he became department head and remained in that capacity until his retirement in 1988.

"My field of specialization was natural resource economics," Martin said, "dealing with the problem of development, use, and conservation of natural resources, such as land, water, air, environment, and so on. My official duties were divided about one-third time in teaching and two-thirds research."

During the years he was actively involved in research, Martin was author or co-author of at least forty technical publications. He was also mentor or major professor to a number of Ph.D. and master's candidates.

"My forty-one years with the university was a time of such pleasure, fun, and satisfaction, that I was bewildered when I realized that I had completed my act upon that stage of life." With wit and a sense of humor, he mused, "When I looked at the young faculty I had been fortunate enough to attract—so full of new ideas and plans for the future—it was obvious that the circle had been completed. Just as I had found an old fogey that needed to be moved out of the way when I came aboard, so it was time for this old fogey to move on."

Optimistic about the future of food production for an exploding population, Martin cites the "emergence of genetic engineering that is developing plants resistant to pests and disease, and the growing interest in aquaculture."

Honored by his peers, Martin received the Distinguished Alumnus Award in 1988 from the Clemson University College of Agricultural Sciences. A member of Phi Kappa Phi and Gamma

Sigma Delta, he is also active in his church and community.

He is an ordained elder, and for ten years served as Clerk of Session at Second Presbyterian Church in Knoxville. A volunteer with Meals on Wheels, he also helps low and modest income senior citizens with tax preparation, and with his wife Mary, he is a member of Fish, an emergency food organization to help the needy.

Other community endeavors through the years include the presidency of the PTA, a member of the Cub Scouts Council, and Board of Directors of Clinch Powell River Valley Association. For several years, he and Mary were the University of Tennessee representatives for the Danforth Foundation.

The Martins have four children: two daughters—Mary Jo Randall and Ann Elizabeth Ogle, and two sons—Douglas Allen and Gary Rodney Martin.

On June 12, 1993, the couple celebrated their fiftieth wedding anniversary—surrounded by their children, seven grandchildren, and many friends.

Since retirement, Martin can be seen on the golf course three times a week. Lately, he has made several holes-in-one. He also enjoys working in his garden. And both he and his wife Mary find pleasure in watching their children and grandchildren grow and mature.

In looking over his long career in education and administration, Dr. Joe Allen Martin said, "The biggest reward of education is being involved with young people and witnessing the role they're playing in the world.... There are many success stories out there that I'm proud to be able to witness."

His own success story is one that began in the mountains of Georgia and continued to flourish for nearly a half century, while he encouraged new generations to achieve their best.

Chapter Twenty

HAROLD McSWAIN MAULDIN
DEPUTY DIRECTOR, IMMUNIZATION BRANCH OF COMMUNICABLE DISEASE CENTER

n 1973, Deputy Director of the Immunization Branch of the Communicable Disease Center, Harold M. Mauldin, received the Superior Service Award, the highest honor conferred by the United States Public Health Services and Mental Health Administration.

Five years previously, he had also received the coveted Silver Anvil Award presented by the Public Relations Society of America, on behalf of his unit's "Measles Eradication 1967," the intensive national effort that had brought a nation together to protect its children from a disease that annually took its toll on over four million school children.

As a member of a large family of five brothers and three sisters growing up on a farm at Middleton, Georgia, Mauldin was the only one of the siblings to go to college. Born on May 31, 1923 to Marvin and Claudia Bruce Mauldin, he graduated from the local high school in 1940. The assistant principal, Smalley, encouraged him in his ambition to continue his education by helping him to apply for entrance to Rabun Gap-Nacoochee Junior College.

The only route for Mauldin at the time was a work scholarship, which helped him offset the cost of tuition and board. Going to the school in the north Georgia mountains that summer before the fall term began, Mauldin worked primarily in the dairy, milking and feeding the cows, with Joe Craft and Fred Kelly as supervisors.

"The school raised a lot of crops—rye and corn, particularly. A world of corn. That's what we fed the cows," he said.

That first summer, with a limited number of students on campus, "we sold the extra milk to the CCC camp. But when the fall quarter began, most of the milk was then consumed by the students."

Once enrolled in fall classes, Mauldin's work load on the school farm was reduced to two days a week, with classes reserved for the other four days.

"I lived in the boys' dorm," he said, "with Sam King and Bill Lovett. For about a six-month period, I roomed with Charles McDaniel, who later became Georgia State School Superintendent. There were usually four boys to a room."

The work experience was the same as on any other working farm. "We slaughtered a couple of hogs each week in the winter," he pointed out, "and a cow periodically. We ground our own beef, and I helped with that, too."

One of Mauldin's most vivid memories of those early college days was "the terrible snowstorm at Easter in 1941. The snowdrifts were so high that not even the mail could be delivered. So many of the students who had gone home for the holidays were stranded. Since I had remained at school, I remember working a little harder, since dairying is a seven-day-a-week commitment."

Shortly after that, a lot of excitement was generated on campus when people from *Life Magazine* came down to take photographs and do a story on the work/study school. They stayed a number of days, but the story was never published. It was preempted by another major event that Mauldin remembered.

"On December 7, 1941, we were in the dining hall, finishing our midday meal, which we called dinner, when the announcement was made that the Japanese had invaded Hawaii."

That announcement affected not only every able-bodied male student, but the history of the school, itself. For within the next four years, with young men drafted into military service, there were few left to work on the multi-acred school farm. So the junior college department was dissolved by the trustees in 1945.

Dr. Andrew Ritchie and Dr. Coit had both retired in 1939. By the time Mauldin arrived in 1940, Dr. Bellingrath was head of the school, with Dean Fry still playing a principal role on campus, as well as directing the Farm Family program.

"I was aware of the importance of the Farm Family program," Mauldin said. "Classmates of mine came out of that background. And I was also aware of the teaching that was done in the farm family setting by home economists. Ruby Nell Taylor, who later married our coach, Jack Acree, held classes in sewing and food preparation for farm families in the evenings."

As to enjoyable leisure time, Mauldin spoke of the periodic picnics and the hikes that many of the students took up to the waterfalls within walking distance of the campus.

By 1942, Mauldin, armed with a two-year certificate from Rabun Gap-Nacoochee Junior College, enrolled at Lincoln Memorial University at Harrogate, Tennessee, sixty miles north of Knoxville in the Cumberland Gap area. He had learned that this school also provided, along with Berry College in Rome, Georgia and Berea College in Kentucky, an opportunity for a four-year degree, if the student were willing to work.

So in the same tradition, Mauldin arrived at Lincoln Memorial in the summer, on a work scholarship. He was immediately assigned to the dairy because of his considerable expertise.

"Actually, I ran the creamery," he added. "The dairy was a smaller concern than Rabun Gap's. We milked about sixty cows, and I did everything from making butter to bottling milk."

Mauldin was not destined to finish his education there. Having volunteered for the U.S. Army Air Corps in 1942, he was finally called up in April 1943.

"A lot of B-2 and B-12 programs were going on at that time." After basic training, Mauldin entered the cadet flying school. He attended the University of Tennessee for the next three months, but when getting to the end of his successful pilot training, the majority of his class was suddenly reassigned. The air corps needed more radio operators and gunners instead, so Mauldin was transferred into that area of training, and went overseas, flying in B-17s as a radio operator in the U.S. Eighth Air Force, with its strategic bombing missions over Germany the costliest of the missions in the European Theatre.

"The Eighth Air Force were the day bombers," Mauldin explained. "The British flew at night. Sometimes, we'd see them going out as we came in. The U.S. Air Force had a higher casualty rate than the Navy and Marines together, although we had only about 350,000 men to begin with, compared to several million in the Navy and Marines."

Flying thirty-five missions, Mauldin was witness to numerous holes in his aircraft from enemy fire and several touch-and-go emergency landings. But he was never wounded, and he arrived home safely, to be discharged on October 19, 1945.

But sadness awaited him upon his return to family. Only ten days later, his father died. So his career plans—his ambition of finishing his education—were put on hold, while he remained at home to help his mother.

By the fall of 1946, Mauldin entered the University of Georgia where he received his B.S. degree in chemistry in December 1948.

And in February of 1949, he joined the Georgia Department of Public Health, where he worked for eighteen months, before going with the United States Public Health Service, where he remained until his retirement in 1979.

Mauldin at first was assigned to venereal disease control, a problem all over the United States at that time in the 1950s. "Although there was still some carry-over from the old 'arsenic and bismuth' days, penicillin was the treatment of choice."

From Louisiana, Arkansas, Michigan, North Carolina, Texas, and Puerto Rico, Mauldin took on increasing responsibilities. He assigned a number of investigators and set up the screening process of individuals in the various areas. In one state alone, he supervised fifty on his staff who were involved in the identification of this infectious pathway that threatened the health of a large segment of the population.

Because of his vast working knowledge and his contacts with both local and state public health departments, Mauldin was then selected to head up field operations for another program that would catapult him into an even wider nationwide campaign.

He had already participated in Chicago, Detroit, and a number of other cities in the smaller Sabin-on-Sunday campaign, the S.O.S. program to eradicate polio. Part of that program was still in place.

Now, with the passage of the National Immunization Act, the focus turned to newborns and school children in the other major childhood diseases. It was up to Mauldin to get this project off the ground, and to develop terms and conditions that were legal. One of his first duties was to select a field staff of one hundred and assign them to every state and major city in the United States.

Many problems presented themselves in such an undertaking. The program not only had to be launched in an effective way, but once in place, it had to be continued and sustained.

"In the advertising industry," Mauldin said, "if a company is selling a product, they're quite willing to get a market share of from two to five percent. But in public health, you can't settle for anything less than ninety-five to ninety-eight percent. That is a given."

The population that he hoped to reach consisted of three components. "About one-third of the population went to physicians regularly and were well cared for; one third sought public care at one time or another; but then, there were those that we called 'the submerged third,' that we had to identify and bring out. That was tough.

"We did this with a whole range of school initiatives. We worked very closely with medical societies, particularly pediatricians. One of the joint efforts that I was extremely proud of was the coalition that I had conceived of and developed with the pharmaceutical industry and medical groups, as well."

Mauldin's innovative ideas came under fire by the press and some of his colleagues. He had to surmount many obstacles in a ten-step public relations plan that encompassed the Federal Government, local and state public health departments, the medical profession, volunteer and civic organizations, and school systems.

"Conceptually, it was to be able to focus massively for one month out of the year, when we could pull out all the stops," Mauldin said. "You could get a tremendous number of volunteers for a short period of time. It would be much harder to find those willing to volunteer for twelve months out of the year."

Receiving the Silver Anvil Award for this "Measles Eradication 1967" campaign, Mauldin is proud of the significant aspects that went far beyond the campaign.

"We conducted surveys all over the country—about laws that affected school entrance requirements. I was one of the chief proponents of establishing such laws. A lot of the time, I had to work in the background. I quietly met with union leaders and elected officials."

Mauldin is also proud of his impact on legislation and the coalition effort that such a successful campaign took. "I think that to have recruited and gotten on the way programs in every state and major city was a milestone. We set some new patterns, such as the use of statisticians for something other than the recording of marriages, divorces, births, and that sort of thing. We put them out front, by design, to assist in developing programs, so we could convey the improved information.

"Secondly, we broke ground in the use of non-professionals. Even if we could have recruited enough nurses, we would not have had the money to pay them. So we trained volunteers, non-professionals, not only in epidemiology and surveillance, but in management. Many of the health departments did not have management capability. Later, nearly all concerned became just as proud as we were with the results."

With seven million children vaccinated that year, there was a phenomenal ninety-five percent reduction in the numbers of measles cases for that same period in 1968.

Two years after Deputy Director Mauldin retired from the U.S. Public Health Service, he went into business with a longtime friend, Chuck Harding, a former FBI agent. They organized a firm doing institutional development and fund raising for colleges and universities in the Southeast.

"Usually, the schools wanted to increase support for staff, develop new facilities or scholarships, or endow a chair.

"We assisted the Director of Development at various schools, helping to set up foundations, identifying and recruiting people to serve on the foundation, planning and many times personally conducting the fund raising of anywhere from four to ten million dollars."

Ten years later, in 1989, Mauldin retired for the second time.

Yet, his tremendous energy has not flagged. He is an active member of the Methodist Church and volunteers regularly at the Methodist Children's Home in Decatur, Georgia. He is also on the Board of Directors of his Army Air Force Bomber Group's Historical Society.

Married to the former Charlotte Floyd of Madison County, Georgia, he is the father of four children, a daughter, Kathie Lynn, and three sons– Harold M. Mauldin. Jr, DVM; Kenneth, and Vernon.

Nearly sixty years ago, as Harold McSwain Mauldin left the small town of Middleton, Georgia, to receive his first taste of higher education at Rabun Gap-Nacoochee Junior College, he carried with him the desire and determination to make a difference, not only in his own life, but in the lives of others. How fortunate for all of us that his sixty-year journey has culminated in such a positive impact on the public health of the nation.

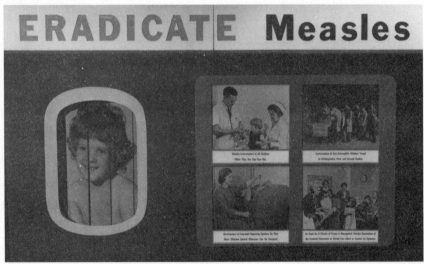

NATIONAL MEASLES ERADICATION CAMPAIGN 1967

Chapter Twenty-One

GENEVA GINN MAYFIELD
SURGICAL AND PEDIATRIC NURSE

 hen Geneva Ginn Mayfield was president of the Rabun Gap-Nacoochee Junior College Alumni, the group got together only occasionally for social events. It was after one of these gatherings that a number of the members, including Geneva, Sue Chandler, Harding Cain, and James Haynes, came up with the idea of starting a worthwhile project—giving an alumni scholarship to a deserving high school graduate, headed for college.

It would be appropriate and have meaning, they thought, especially since they had all received help with their own education.

So Geneva, who wrote the first check for the scholarship fund, went home to Atlanta and coordinated the project. Letters were sent out, explaining to the junior college alumni what they hoped to accomplish. The project escalated into what it is today—a scholarship fund of $60,000. Each year two outstanding seniors from Rabun Gap-Nacoochee School receive one thousand dollars each from the small group that has such an interesting ten-year history in the life of the school.

Geneva well remembers when she left Washington, Georgia on a Greyhound bus, with her suitcase and a carefully wrapped ham biscuit to stave off her hunger until she reached Rabun Gap and the school that had accepted her as a junior college student.

On that morning, she had said good-bye to her farmer father, Jay Gordon Ginn, her mother, Mattie Price Ginn, a former teacher and seamstress, and her eleven brothers and sisters. The bus stopped once — in Athens — to pick up another passenger, but since no one appeared at the station, the bus driver finally pulled out and continued on the winding trip to the north Georgia mountains, with Geneva as the only passenger.

Born on February 23, 1917, Geneva had graduated from Washington High School, and she was following in her older sister's footsteps. Gladys Ginn had attended the Nacoochee Institute in Nacoochee Valley, where Dr. John Knox Coit had been president, until the school burned down and later merged with Rabun Gap Industrial School.

Gladys had earned her tuition by working in the Coit home for the entire four years she was a student. Now, Geneva would be doing the same thing, only this time on another campus, where Dr. Coit was vice-president.

"I got off at the entrance to the boys' dorm, and I had my big suitcase with everything I owned in it," Geneva said. "I didn't know where to go. But a nice lady, who'd been shopping, came along in a car and asked me where I was going. I introduced myself, and she immediately said, 'Oh, you're to stay with Dr. and Mrs. Coit.' I answered, 'Yes. That's where I'm going.' And she said, 'Well, get in, and I'll take you there.'"

Once Geneva arrived at the Coit's brick home, Mrs. Coit was happy to see her. With a sense of humor, Geneva described that first encounter.

"I'm glad you're here, Geneva. I don't have anybody to fix dinner tonight."

"Mrs. Coit never cooked," Geneva said. "So I went to work immediately. I remember that first meal very well. She had a big roast beef, and I didn't know how to cook a roast. So I put it on top of the stove and boiled it. Then, I thought they'd have to have something else to go with it, so I asked Mrs. Coit what else she planned to have with the roast.

"At home, I was used to going out into the garden and picking fresh lima beans, or green beans, or something else.

"She said, 'Look in the refrigerator.'

"We didn't have an electric refrigerator at home. Only an icebox. We both looked in the refrigerator and came up with some cauliflower, which the family loved, and some peas. Not knowing how to make any sauce to go on the cauliflower, I just used the beef gravy.

"Mrs. Coit also wanted to know if I could make biscuits. I told her I could, but I wasn't sure how good they'd be. I'd watched my mother at home, but I had no idea of the amount of ingredients, so I just guessed."

From that time on, Geneva's cooking skills improved considerably, and she soon became indispensable in the Coit household, while she worked that entire summer for her tuition for the fall quarter.

"Besides the Coits," Geneva recalled, "Dr. Galloway, who was Mrs. Coit's father, and Mrs. Galloway, her stepmother, lived with them. They were all in the bedrooms upstairs, except for Dr. Coit, who slept on a little porch. They had one son, who was away at school, and it was common knowledge that Mrs. Coit did not want to have another child.

"My roommate, Fairey Annette Moore, and I shared a twin bedroom downstairs, in the area where we worked, just off the kitchen."

From the viewpoint of the teenager, Geneva described the family. "Dr. Coit was slightly short, and a little bit dumpy, but he had the sweetest expression on his face. He always had something positive to say. Occasionally, he would ask me to represent the school and ride with him to Atlanta, when he'd be seeking money for the school. Mrs. Coit would always ask me to keep him awake and not let him drive too fast.

"He had a second-hand Ford, but a late model. The way he drove—very fast—it took only two hours to get to Atlanta.

"He was speaking at various places. The time I remember most of all was meeting with the representative from the Coca-Cola Company. They gave a pretty good donation to the school that year. We had lunch at a restaurant and the representative was very nice to me. He would ask me about the school. Of course, I was young then, and I enjoyed talking with him.

"Mrs. Coit was Canadian—and slightly heavier than Dr. Coit. Everybody thought she was rather hard to get along with, but I never found that true. My sister Gladys had given me plenty of pointers.

"Mrs. Coit was a stickler for etiquette, old fashioned, and a very strict disciplinarian. She told Annette and me exactly how she wanted things done. Dr. and Mrs. Coit almost always had guests, either ministers, or people from whom they were soliciting funds for the school.

"She had two sets of silver and two sets of china. When the people they hoped to secure contributions from came to dinner, she used one set. When the ministers came, she used the other set.

"We had to have napkins, silverware, and sometimes finger bowls, and the water glass placed just so. And it was our responsibility to keep the white linen tablecloths washed and ironed.

"Then I was also responsible for arranging any flowers for the table. Since she had some pink roses growing on a fence, I'd always use those for a low centerpiece, if they were in bloom. I can't look at a pink rose today without thinking of Mrs. Coit.

"Dr. Galloway, her father, was just the grandest guy. He always wrote religious pamphlets, and he preached every third Sunday at the Presbyterian Church. Mrs. Galloway was quite friendly and nice, and good to us.

"One time, when she was sick, Dr. Galloway asked me to go with him to a revival, where he was preaching in both the morning and the evening services. He asked me to talk with the people, too. I remember the big lunch they fed us—fried chicken, turnip greens, and lots of other good things."

In describing a typical day as a junior college student working her way through school, Geneva said, "We got up in the morning about six o'clock, dressed, got ready for school, and then cooked breakfast for the Coit family. We served breakfast at seven o'clock, so we only had an hour to clean up and get to class by eight. For lunch, another girl would go over to the dining hall and bring back lunch and serve.

"We had four classes a day—two in the morning and two in the afternoon, four days a week. We worked the other two days. When we had study period, that was the only time we had to study that day. Then, we'd come back, fix dinner for the Coits and their guests, more often than not, and serve it promptly at six o'clock.

Describing the procedure, Geneva said, "Mrs. Coit had a little serving cart on wheels. We'd put the food on that, and she'd serve from there. She had a bell under the table, and when she needed something, she'd use the bell. Once the meal was over, Annette and I would sit down in the kitchen and enjoy our dinner by ourselves. Neither one of us ever ate in the dining room. But we much preferred the kitchen, because we knew we'd have to behave if we ate in the dining room.

"Two hours each Sunday afternoon, we were allowed to socialize and have dates. We never entertained in the living room. Instead, when the weather was nice, we would sit outside under the trees. When it rained, we didn't have dates.

"Dr. Coit enjoyed the funny papers and magazines, but Mrs. Coit frowned on them, and didn't want Annette and me to read them, or the newspaper on Sundays. Sometimes, when we were cleaning the rooms, Annette would keep watch while I was on the porch, reading his books and funny papers. Then, I would do the same for her. Later, I had another roommate, and she and I also covered for each other.

"Nearly every night, Mrs. Coit would come downstairs and have prayer with us. Sometimes, the prayers were quite lengthy. We had so little time to study before going to bed. And I remember one time, when we were having both a history and a chemistry exam the next day.

"We heard her coming down the stairs. So I dropped down on my knees beside the bed and began to pray. She opened the door very quietly and said, 'Oh, I didn't mean to interrupt prayer time.' So I stayed on my knees until she left. Then, we pulled the curtains and studied until two A.M.

"After that, Mrs. Coit would say, 'Geneva certainly spends a lot of time praying.'"

Later, a more mature Geneva realized how dedicated the Coits were, to the school and to the students under their care. They were also devoted to their son. "When it was time for him to go to college," Geneva recalled, "the Coits went to Atlanta to buy new clothes for him.

"Mrs. Coit mentioned, when we were getting his clothes ready, that she would like for us to put a little starch in his pajamas to make them look neat and nice. I put in too much, but you couldn't tell when they were folded. They looked quite nice, and Mrs. Coit was pleased.

"But that night, when he tried to put them on, they were so stiff, that they stood up by themselves. The next day, he called his mother and said, 'Tell those girls not to put starch in my pajamas anymore. I had to sleep in my underwear last night.'"

When Geneva graduated, she continued her education. Following in the tradition of her sister, who had gone to Birmingham to train as a nurse, Geneva was accepted at the University of Georgia.

"They had night school there, with only one class required in the day," she explained. "During the mornings, I worked for an insurance company. And when I didn't have a night class, I typed for a lady and kept her books for her. So it was still a work/study program."

Trained as a nurse, Geneva began working in the emergency room at Georgia Baptist Hospital. With World War II in full force, so many of her classmates had been called into service, since they desperately needed nurses. Geneva had tried to sign up also, but she was turned down because of a heart murmur.

"It really upset me that I wasn't in service with my friends. They were out on the West Coast, while I stayed at the hospital, sometimes doing double duty because we were so short of nurses there."

It was on one of those double shifts that an event occurred that would affect Geneva in a way she had not anticipated.

"One night, when a nurse was sick on the medicine floor, I worked her shift, also," she explained. "I was in one of the wards, when an orderly came in and said, 'Patient in the hall.' That was a no-no, so I went to check, to make sure it wasn't one of the patients from my ward.

"I saw that a man had fainted, so I told the orderly to pour some water on him—the general procedure at the time. That caused him to come to."

Geneva didn't think anymore about it. She had her own

patients to take care of. Finally getting off duty, Geneva walked across the street from the hospital to the boarding house, where she had her room and meals.

"A man was sitting in the dining room," she said, "when I went in to eat dinner. He picked up his plate and came to sit beside me. I thought he certainly was bold. He said, 'Didn't I see you at Georgia Baptist Hospital this afternoon?'"

"I don't know, but I do work there," Geneva answered.

The man explained, "I fainted in the hall and you poured water on me."

Geneva replied. "Now I remember you. But no, I didn't do it. It was the orderly who poured the water."

The man's name was James Harold Mayfield, who worked as a sales supervisor for Atlanta Linen Company, during the days when hospitals were a linen company's biggest customers. He had been so busy that day that he had not taken time to eat, so had fainted from a low blood sugar.

On May 6, 1998, Geneva and Harold Mayfield celebrated their fifty-fourth wedding anniversary.

When Harold joined the air force during World War II, he was sent to Fort Myers where he was told he would spend the duration of the war. Geneva joined him one month before D-Day in Europe. When the war escalated, Harold was sent to England for two years and Geneva returned to Atlanta, picking up where she had left off in surgical nursing.

Once her husband returned, she changed from surgical to pediatric nursing, so that she could be at home more. Geneva Mayfield, R.N. recently retired after forty-three years in pediatrics.

Geneva and Harold have three children – a son and two daughters who have all done well. She's particularly proud of their three grandchildren – Andrew, an actor, who is at Yale; Stephen, who owns a music store, has a band, and plays the organ at his church;

and David, an industrial psychologist.

Geneva is active in her church and community. Her home is filled with her creative handiwork. The ubiquitous pink roses of her college days are quite beautiful, captured on her handpainted set of china resting in a glass cabinet. All of the pictures on her walls – the oils and acrylics, as well as the china lamps in their living room, were painted by Geneva.

As for the real roses, Geneva Ginn Mayfield, junior college class of 1939, leaves the outdoors to her husband Harold.

PRESERVING THE HARVEST

Chapter Twenty-Two

DR. CHARLES P. MCDANIEL
STATE SCHOOL SUPERINTENDENT

ccording to his friend and educational colleague, Foster Goolsby, the late Charles Pope McDaniel, who had served as a Marine Corps officer in the Pacific during World War II, "had been shot all to pieces in the battle on Saipan, and he struggled for several years to recuperate." Goolsby added, "Any other human being would have died."

Instead, McDaniel's determination to survive pulled him through—that same determination that had brought him to Rabun Gap-Nacoochee Junior College in 1940, to work for an education denied to him elsewhere.

He was a serious, brilliant student. Honored by his classmates who elected him president of the student council and affectionately called him "Charlie Mac," he nevertheless felt that he had little talent for small talk or forming close personal bonds at that early age. Years later, he once lamented to Goolsby, who became a great personal friend, that he had always envied his ability to relate so easily to people.

McDaniel, who had enrolled at Mercer University prior to the war, returned there afterwards to resume his studies, graduating with an A.B. degree and master's in education. Then, he continued at Columbia University, with a master of arts degree, and from there, he received a doctorate in education from the University of Georgia.

Thus began an illustrious teaching and administrative career, culminating in his being appointed by Governor George Busbee to fill an unexpired term as state school superintendent for Georgia in 1977, and then winning in the next year's election and again in the campaign of 1982, by a vote of seventy-six percent.

Jack Acree, one of McDaniel's former teachers at the junior college, at that time was the executive for the Georgia School Board Association, and had worked closely with various governors in educational commissions and conferences.

"One day, Governor Busbee called me at my office at the old Biltmore Hotel," Acree said. "Since the previous state school board superintendent had resigned and walked out of his office," it was up to the governor to appoint someone to finish his unexpired term. In the conversation, the governor asked, "What would be your reaction if I were to name Dr. Charles McDaniel?"

McDaniel had been a teacher, counselor, principal in DeKalb County, and local school superintendent for both Clarke County and Thomasville, and had served as president of the Rotary Club in both Athens and Thomasville. In 1966, he was named Thomasville-Thomas County Man of the Year, and later received the Mercer University Distinguished Alumni Award. He was also recognized as an outstanding alumnus of Rabun Gap-Nacoochee School and the University of Georgia School of Education.

Turning over Governor Busbee's question in his mind, Acree said, "I knew Charlie was not a political man, but he'd done a great job wherever he'd gone. So I replied, 'Well, Governor, if you can get him, I certainly would support him as state school superintendent.'

"Charlie refused at first, but then Governor Busbee had McDaniel and his wife Beatrice at the mansion for a weekend and convinced him."

From 1977 to 1984, McDaniel presided over a $1.6 billion budget. Under his supervision were almost 2,000 elementary and secondary schools, 60,000 teachers, 40,000 other school professionals, and enough department of education employees in the east tower of the Sloppy Floyd Building to warrant a sign in the hallway that read: "Do you know who your supervisor is?"

But McDaniel had another important assignment that took fifty percent of his time — to serve as a liaison between the state and the public and local school boards, whose opinions helped to shape educational policies. So that involved his traveling around the state, to speak to civic groups and other organizations interested in the welfare of the educational system.

One of the concerns that McDaniel had to address, besides the tremendous population growth with its inherent problems of additional classroom space for students, was the burgeoning discipline problem in nearly all of Georgia's schools.

"This is not a new concern at either the state or the local level," he confessed. Local school boards already had in place rules relating to suspension and expulsion of unruly students. But he felt that the state should have some standard to help guide the local school boards.

With a statewide standard, he said, "the state has provided some general direction while at the same time recognizing local control. In addition, the department of education ...has provided information...on relevant court decisions concerning suspension, expulsion, in-school suspension, and alternative schools."

Dr. McDaniel set up seminars and workshops, and worked closely with the Georgia Legislature on these matters. But in the long run, it would be up to local people to implement these policies.

"Leaving such matters to local officials also allows them the right to refuse admission to a pupil if they believe the pupil will not correct his or her behavior."

Governor Busbee, during his administration, made education a major political priority. At that time, Georgia ranked forty-fourth in money spent per child, and test scores were well below the national average. It was his interest that spurred officials to revamp the educational system, to bring higher standards to Georgia.

When McDaniel took office as state school superintendent, he vowed to work towards stricter teacher certification standards and stronger requirements for high school graduation, including the passing of an exiting test.

He was well on the way to achieving these goals when he suffered a fatal heart attack.

Jack Acree, who had been at the capitol the previous day for a ceremony, told of seeing McDaniel in the hallway with a group of legislators. Seeing him, the superintendent said, "Jack, I'd like to talk with you about something."

"When? Where? Name it."

"How about one o'clock in my office?"

"So I went over. He told me something that he was being pressured into doing. Wanted to know my opinion. I told him very straightforwardly what it was—counter to what he was being pressured to do.

"The next morning, he was dressing to go to his office, when he had the fatal heart attack. I had just seen him the day before."

In tribute to Dr. Charles P. McDaniel, his former teacher, who had watched the serious-minded young student become the most powerful man in Georgia public school education, said, "He was a terrific guy."

Chapter Twenty-Three

MARVIN REX NEAL
COMPANY VICE-PRESIDENT AND INDUSTRIAL ARTS EDUCATOR

 arvin Rex Neal was born on August 25, 1923 at Hiawassee, Georgia, in the Blue Ridge Mountains. When Rex was four years old, Dr. Andrew Ritchie came to the family farm and invited the Neals to move to Rabun Gap-Nacoochee School as part of the Farm Family Settlement Program.

It did not take Wesley Calvin Neal, and his wife, Carrie Kimsey Neal, long to decide. Here was an opportunity of a lifetime. Not only would they be given land to farm and a house to live in, but their nine children would be able to get an education, a scarce commodity at that time in the isolated area where they lived.

On the day the family left, Calvin hitched his mules to the wagons, loaded their pieces of furniture, and tied the milk cow to the back of one of the wagons. Then, the seven boys and two girls climbed aboard and began the arduous two-day trek through the mountains.

As distances go, the journey was not a long one, but the route followed the spine of the Appalachian Highlands, so the progress was slow, with stops to rest and water the mules, and the children to be fed with the food that Carrie had prepared for the trip. That night, the family slept in tents beside Lake Burton.

The next day, the wagons passed through the Gap. The Neal family had finally arrived at the place they would call home for the next five years.

For Rex, each day was an adventure. He not only had brothers and sisters to play with, but friends from the other farm families. Rex remembers those days and the sense of community. "The farmers all knew each other, and the wives would get together for cooking, cleaning, and sewing. If a farm family experienced troubles, all the families would pitch in and help. All of us attended Sunday School and church every Sunday."

At the age of six, Rex entered the community school. But even at this early age, he was expected to do his share of chores on his family's acreage. Sensitive to his surroundings, he loved the smell of freshly mown hay, and the "beautiful sight of the rain in the mountains. The rainbows always came late in the evenings. The weather was about as perfect as one could find. Beautiful springs, when the mountains were green; mild summers, colorful falls, and snow in the winter."

Of course, everything was not idyllic. Rex remembers too, the lack of running water, indoor bathrooms, central heat; the meager transportation, and the struggle in the family of eleven for adequate clothes.

But the pleasant experiences far outweighed the inconveniences. Movies on a Saturday night in Clayton; riding on the Tallulah Falls train; staying up until midnight—making sorghum syrup at the mill—were some of the special treats.

"Dr. Ritchie was a great inspiration to me and my family," Neal said. "We owe so much to Dr. Ritchie for his love and his caring about the welfare of the farm families.

"The farm family work program as well as the study program gave us a lot of thought about our future. This work-study ethic carried on through our lives."

By the time Rex entered high school, most of his work duties were still on the Farm Family Plan, except for a few days of part-time work at the school. His last year in high school, he left his farm family and lived at the school as a boarding student.

In reminiscing about his teachers, Rex said, "One thing, and one thing only carried me through school. And that was the basketball program. Jack Acree was my coach. At one time, three of the Neal boys were playing for the same team for Rabun Gap. My senior year in high school, Jack, who was also the coach for the junior college, took me to a junior college tournament in Tifton. I had never been that far away from Rabun Gap. It was a thrill of my life. As a high school student, playing with the college boys was an unbelievable experience.

"Mr. Fry was my agriculture teacher, but I wasn't a very good student. At an early age, I knew that I did not want to remain on a farm. And I thought math was boring. Later, at the University of Georgia, I became more adjusted to math courses.

"Miss Clayton was a good teacher. And Miss Lennon, who taught Bible, had a great impact on the development of my character. Mr. Walker, my shop teacher, was the man who started my career in the industrial field. I worked with him in the school farm shop, which was a very valuable experience that helped me in later life."

Rex attended the junior college for the fall quarter of 1941 and left after the 1942 winter quarter, due to World War II.

He entered the Anderson Aircraft School in Nashville, Tennessee. "From the experience and work habits at Rabun Gap, I graduated third in my class, which gave me a job at Tyndall Air Force Base in Panama City, Florida."

In 1943, Rex joined the U.S. Navy. After basic training in Bainbridge, Maryland, he was transferred to the Navy Aircraft Training School in Norman, Oklahoma. Then, he was transferred to the Naval Air Station at Pensacola, where he spent the rest of the war, helping to train navy pilots.

After the war, Neal went back to Tyndall Field for about eighteen months. When he left Tyndall for the second time, he enrolled at South Georgia Junior College in Douglas, Georgia and from there, went to the University of Georgia where he graduated in 1950 with a B.S. degree in education.

For three years, 1950-53, Rex taught industrial arts at Lanier Senior High School for Boys in Macon, Georgia.

His road to personal and financial success escalated when he accepted a job with Brodhead Garrett Company, Cleveland, Ohio. As district manager, Neal traveled in eight Southern states, working with school systems in their vocational programs. He was well qualified for the job. In 1975, he became regional manager and vice-president of the company, in charge of the Southern division. "I spent thirty-five years—the best thirty-five years of my life—with the Brodhead Garrett Company."

Rex guided and gave inspiration and encouragement to numerous industrial arts teachers—both in-service and pre-service—in the Southern states. He looks back with pride at his accomplishments and the honors that came his way. In Georgia alone, he supported all of the state's industrial arts clubs, giving approximately fifty trophies each year for various club activities.

For ten years, he served as chairman of the Vocational Advisory Committee for Bibb County Schools in Macon, Georgia. "We reviewed the programs and budgets in each school," he said, "and worked very closely with the industrial community to be sure that our high school and technical school graduates had the correct training to fill the needs of the various industries. We also worked with the vocational supervisor to be sure that the correct programs in industrial education were being taught."

Because of his commitment to these standards of excellence, Marvin Rex Neal received an award of merit and life membership in the Georgia Industrial Arts Association and a life membership in the Georgia Vocational Association. In 1966, he qualified for the honor and was duly initiated into the Beta Omicron chapter of Epsilon Pi Tau, Inc., the international professional fraternity in industrial arts and vocational education.

The highest award from that esteemed organization came in 1971, when Neal was awarded its Laureate Citation—for the breadth of technical and professional preparation, his encouragement to teachers, and his outstanding leadership in the industrial vocational associations.

During those thirty-five years, from 1953-1988, Rex admits that he was so busy that he did not have much time for civic clubs and volunteer work, but his record belies that assertion. For the past eighteen years, he and his wife, the former Gloria Woodard, whom he married in 1961, have been active members of First Presbyterian Church in Macon, where he has served as Sunday School class president and a member of the board of deacons.

A golfer, Neal participated for several years in the Nike Golf Tournament, held annually in Macon. As chairman of volunteers, he organized up to six hundred volunteers to help in that event. He has also been chairman of the cancer tournament and other golf tournaments in Macon.

Now, Neal has a new interest, in which he is throwing his wholehearted support. But it began all those years ago, when his family came to Rabun Gap-Nacoochee School as part of the Farm Family Settlement Program.

"Words can't express what Rabun Gap has meant to me and my family. The lessons and work habits that were taught at the school have stayed with my entire family through their lives. The education received there has helped us all to become successful in our life's work."

For this reason, Marvin Rex Neal is playing a major role in the school's proposed Alumni Heritage Center, honoring the Ritchies; and the establishment of the Farm Family Museum, a part of the school's history, unique to adult education in Georgia.

Chapter Twenty-Four

DR. WALTER E. NEVILLE, JR.
UNIVERSITY PROFESSOR OF ANIMAL SCIENCE

f Dr. Walter E. Neville, Jr. had been around, one hundred years earlier, perhaps the colorful Marquis de Mores would have made a go of it in his attempt to build a cattle empire in the West in the 1880s. Too late, de Mores discovered that Chicago meat packing companies and Eastern consumers were no longer interested in buying range-fed cattle.

Neville, who was born on May 5, 1924 on a farm in Rabun County, Georgia, remembers the scarcity of information even by mid-twentieth century that would directly benefit farmers in the production of livestock and crops. So he later made it his life's work as an animal research scientist – to provide information that would directly affect and educate both commercial producers and consumers.

As one of the two native Georgians in the Animal Science Division of the University of Georgia Experiment Stations, he authored or co-authored over eighty-two scientific manuscripts published in professional and scientific journals and popular press over a forty-year career.

Neville, the son of the former Kate Haulbrook and Walter E. Neville, Sr., of Rabun Gap, began his college education as a day student at Rabun Gap-Nacoochee School, as did his two brothers, J.W. and S.B.

"I remember Dr. Ritchie as being very dedicated toward the development of an outstanding educational system for high school and junior college students," Neville said, "as well as for adults in the farm families. Dr. Coit and Dr. Bellingrath both worked toward the fulfillment of Dr. Ritchie's objectives."

Neville considered the school's work program, the classes taught by dedicated teachers, and the required attendance at church services major assets in shaping the lives of students.

He gave high grades to his teachers—Misses Lennon, Clayton, Tewkesbury, Sledd, and Messrs. Nicholson, Walker, Shotts, and Acree.

I especially enjoyed making and repairing things in the wood and metal workshop," he said, "under the instruction of Mr. W.D. Walker."

That early student experience later translated itself into a retirement hobby in his own woodworking shop.

As a young man growing up in a rural community, he "accepted the rain, sleet, snow, mud, cold and heat as normal," just as he accepted the necessity of doing his share of chores on the family farm. But it was precisely this necessity that interrupted his graduation at the junior college. With World War II in progress, few able-bodied men were left at home to work. So the priority at that time had to be taken from study and classes and directed full time to the preparation of land for planting and the harvesting of crops on both the family farm and other farms in the area.

By fall of 1943, Neville was in school again, at the University of Georgia. Then, he went into the U.S. Navy. Later returning to the university, he received his B.S. degree in 1947.

For the next year and a half, Neville was employed as an assistant agricultural agent for Chatooga County. But realizing new goals, he obtained an M.S. degree from the University of Missouri in 1950.

Now began his career path in research. At the University of Georgia's Experiment Station in Griffin, Georgia, he conducted agricultural research with farm animals by day, while he audited courses at night at Georgia State University in Atlanta. Co-authoring articles on subjects as diverse as mouse crosses for the *Journal of Animal Science*, and the digestibility and deficiencies of seven Southeastern hays in the *Journal of Dairy Science*, Neville was also called upon as a speaker to present his findings before professional groups.

Then, by 1954, with a six-month sabbatical provided by and funded in part by UGA, Neville went to the University of Wisconsin to begin work on his doctorate in animal genetics and animal husbandry. He received his Ph.D. degree in 1957.

"I have never seen a campus so research oriented," he said of that school. "I was very inspired by this fact and the knowledge that the university not only wanted to teach us but to learn from us, as well."

He still has on his shelves a book written by one of his professors, the eminent bioenergeticist, Samuel Brody. "He had a real influence on me, as did my major professors, G.E. Dickerson, A.B. Chapman, and A.L. Pope."

In February of 1957, Dr. Neville returned to the Experiment Station in Griffin, where his research projects were centered on beef cattle and sheep.

"People thought sheep were for the mountainous regions," he said. "They didn't realize that they could be grown profitably in central Georgia."

Neville soon disproved this fallacy, and also addressed the parasitic diseases prevalent in the ovine community.

Consequent results began to appear in professional journals concerning energy requirements for maintenance, weight gain, and milk production in beef cattle, the value of milk for beef cattle growth, ovine diseases in the Georgia Piedmont, and hormone techniques used to increase the number of lambs alive twenty-four hours after birth.

Serving on committees to make long-range studies of Georgia's beef cattle industry, Neville also served as secretary and later, chairman of the Beef Cattle Commodity Group of the Animal Science Division.

In 1975, after leaving Griffin for the Coastal Plain Experiment Station in Tifton, Georgia, Neville received the University of Georgia's Sigma Xi top research award for his paper published in the *Journal of Animal Science* on the energy requirements of lactating and non-lactating Hereford cows.

One of the programs that had been started as early as 1951 at the Coastal Plain Experiment Station involved the Rogers Correctional Institute at Reidsville. Shortly after moving to Tifton, Neville began working with personnel at the prison on the cooperative breeding program.

"This program with Reidsville," Neville said, "has been one of the most effective and practical beef cattle breeding programs ever initiated." Designed to find procedures that would improve efficiency of beef production, the program "has provided results that are very beneficial to the producer as well as the consumer."

Neville's activities as a member of numerous research, college, regional, and national committees, and as a judge at Southwest Georgia Regional Science Fairs, were combined with his research work and publication of his findings. For sixteen years, his primary focus turned to the reproductive performance of bulls, and the early weaning of beef calves.

"Throughout the years, I have had a continuing interest in quality research that would directly benefit livestock producers. Most of my research studies were conducted in areas that either had not been investigated or had limited or inadequate investigation."

The response and appreciation of livestock producers to this information has given Neville a sense of satisfaction, knowing that others are the beneficiaries of his work.

In 1985, he received a grant from International Minerals and Chemical Corporation for a calf implant study, and in 1986, he was one of three to receive the Outstanding Research Award for extensive cattle breeding experiments, given by the Sigma Xi Chapter in Tifton.

Neville retired on June 30, 1989, as Professor-Emeritus, after a long and profitable tenure as an animal scientist. Besides membership in Sigma Xi, the fraternity devoted to research, he is also a member of Phi Kappa Phi, Alpha Zeta, American Society of Animal Science, American Association for the Advancement of Science, and Council for Agricultural Science and Technology.

Yet, during his career, he also found time to be an active church and community leader.

For years, he worked with the Lions Club, Meals on Wheels, and served as group leader and team captain for United Way. A member of the Presbyterian Church, Neville has served as deacon, elder, Sunday School teacher, president of the Men of the Church, chairman of the pulpit nominating committee, and many other church-related committees.

He and his wife Mary Clark, whom he married in 1948, have two children, Gail Stephens and Harry Neville. He was able to pass on to them some of the valuable lessons he learned at Rabun Gap.

"Our children willingly did their share of chores at home. Both started with jobs outside the home before they were sixteen. After that age, their jobs were in stores, on farms, and in hotels on weekends during high school session, and full time in the summers. Each child put his or her earned money in a savings account. When the two graduated from high school, they opened checking accounts and obtained their own credit cards." Continuing to work in the summers during their college days, each earned a large share of college expenses. Extremely proud of them, Neville commented, "Thus they knew the value of money and the effort it took to acquire it, as well as how to interact positively with people."

Besides woodworking in his home shop, Neville also enjoys working with his flowers, fruit bushes, and trees. And if, in retirement, he chooses to put his professional expertise in genetics to work, perhaps we might see an outstanding article on new and improved varieties of garden plants—written by Walter E. Neville, Jr., Ph.D.

Chapter Twenty-Five

ARTHUR A. SCHLOCK
COUNTY CAREER CENTER DIRECTOR

rthur Augustus Schlock has the distinction of having been the last male Rabun Gap-Nacoochee Junior College student in his class of 1945, and the first Director of the Newberry County Career Center in South Carolina.

In 1943, when his parents, Augustus and Flora, were just getting over the depression that had plagued the nation, Arthur, at the age of sixteen, graduated from the rural high school at Fair Play, South Carolina, near Lake Hartwell. As was the case with many farm families of that era, the Schlock family did not have the necessary funds to see their son continue his education.

It was at the end of May that year, that the former principal and superintendent at Fair Play, Clay Dendy, returned as registrar of Rabun Gap to offer his former student an opportunity for a college education.

Nothing could have pleased Arthur more. With a work scholarship available to him, he became a junior college freshman, arriving on campus to work for the summer.

"My first job was cutting grass and campus maintenance," he said. But in less than a month, Fred Kelly, who was in charge of the dairy, inquired if he could milk cows. For a boy growing up on a farm, the answer was never in dispute. "After that first morning of milking," Schlock remembered, "he asked me to stay on. So I spent the rest of my work time at school on the dairy crew. I thought the world of Mr. Kelly."

He was also impressed with the president, Dr. Bellingrath, the friendliness of students, and with the beauty of the school.

He particularly enjoyed getting to know the people in the community. "You see, as students, we attended church services on a rotation basis—from Methodist to Baptist to Presbyterian. That gave me the opportunity to know more people than the average student. Rabun Gap was not like other schools that were separate from the community.

"I became friends especially with the Dickersons, the Pitts, and the Colemans. Mr. Coleman, who owned the buses and drove them for the school, asked me to drive one of the buses on special trips— taking students to Clayton to the movies, to Atlanta for the Southeastern Fair, to Cherokee, North Carolina, and to Klingman's Dome."

Of course, during that time, Arthur had his eye on the Colemans' pretty daughter, Texas, who was a high school student at the school. After World War II, Arthur and Texas were married and have shared their lives together ever since. "That was the best part of going to Rabun Gap," Arthur confessed. "That, and the friendships formed."

By the time Arthur returned as a sophomore, the war had been going on for several years. Extracurricular activities had been curtailed. All around him, he had seen his classmates disappear from campus, and the enrollment in the junior college had dropped precipitously. His former roommate, Otho Maxwell, class of '44, would later be killed in the battle on Okinawa.

In October Arthur turned eighteen, and immediately registered for the draft. He wondered at that time if he would be allowed to graduate before being called up. That question was answered in December, when he was classified as 1A and told that he was subject to being called anytime within the next three months.

"When it appeared that I was going into service by March, two months before graduation," Schlock said, "Mr. Phelp, a wonderful man, who was my science and chemistry teacher, helped me so that I would not lose all my credits. He arranged to teach me a course in semi-qualitative analysis—just he and I. He also arranged for me to take typing, which helped me later in service. Another teacher who was helpful was Mr. Floyd, and of course, Miss Lennon, who taught Bible. I enjoyed her class very much."

Schlock, reporting to the U.S. Army for basic training in March, went to Stark, Florida. After he had completed training, he returned home on furlough for fifteen days. While at home, the war in Europe ended. For a period of time, he was shifted to various camps—from Louisiana, to Washington State, to California.

"The battalion commander at Fort Ord had been the commandant at Clemson. He came out to talk to our company, which was made up of lots of us from South Carolina. 'Well, the chances are, you're going to be scheduled for amphibious assault training for the invasion of Japan,' he said. But then the atomic bomb was dropped."

Two months later, in January 1946, Sgt. Schlock was in Frankfurt, Germany, as Chief Clerk at Headquarters Command, European Theatre. "My job was the same as office manager in civilian life," he said. "I was overseeing typists and file clerks, who were displaced persons. Looking out my window, I could see General Eisenhower going back and forth to his office."

Schlock was discharged in December 1946. He and Texas

Coleman were married on July 19, 1947, and they went back to the family farm, while waiting for his application to Clemson to be processed.

Not long after that, Berry Floyd, who had become superintendent of Rabun County Schools, asked Schlock's father-in-law, Norman Coleman, what he was doing. When told that he had been put on a waiting list for Clemson, because of the tremendous number of applicants, Floyd sent him a message. "Tell Arthur I could use him as a teacher. If he's interested, come up here."

Schlock taught science and seventh grade math at Lakemont High School for the 1947-48 year. Scheduled to teach another year, Schlock had gone to summer school at Piedmont, when the letter from Clemson arrived, with the news that he had been accepted for the fall of '48. That changed his plans. He and Texas moved to Seneca, South Carolina, and in August of 1950, Schlock graduated with a B.S. degree in animal science.

Arthur had enjoyed teaching. But after he graduated from Clemson, he became assistant manager of a department store in Seneca, where he remained for five years.

"A good friend had been after me to get back into teaching," Schlock said. Making up his mind to do so, he found a job on the second shift at a local mill, and went back to Clemson at the same time, to get a B.S. degree in education.

For eighteen months, he taught at James F. Byrnes High School in Duncan, South Carolina. Offered a job as vocational agriculture teacher at Woodruff, he remained there for eighteen years. In 1974, he received his master's degree in education from Clemson.

Then, an unusual opportunity came to Schlock.

"I was hired by Newberry County Schools to come and work with the school district in planning a career center and the courses to be offered.

"So often, a school of this nature—the plans are given to a

superintendent who's not familiar with this field. But getting in on the ground floor, I was able to work with the architects, help to choose the site, work with purchasing the equipment and the employment of the personnel and teachers – all the things involved with getting the school underway."

During that time, Schlock visited the local high schools to survey the students' interests, "listing the areas that the state felt the students had a need for. We interviewed ninth through twelfth graders, asking, if you had the opportunity to take one of these courses, which would you take? From that, we determined our initial curriculum – based on what was popular and opportunities for jobs in the community."

He also visited other career centers and asked the directors about their equipment – what they needed that they didn't have, and what they had that they didn't need.

Built on the same campus as the largest high school in the county, the center opened in 1977, and Schlock served as its first director until his retirement in 1988.

With an average of five hundred students from three different high schools enrolled at any one time, the center serves as "a connection between the world of the classroom and the world of work." Business and marketing, engineering and industrial technology, health and human resources, environment and agriculture are the areas in which the students can develop the skills for the future. The center serves not only the needs of the students, but the community, as well.

"One of the programs that was very successful and still is, is the LPN – the licensed practical nurse program," Schlock said. "It's a two-year program for both seniors and adults. As seniors, the students can come over for half a day, then come back for the second year, after they graduate from high school. The first year is primarily an academic one. The second is academic, plus in-service training. The students work at hospitals, doctors' offices, and nursing homes. They spend two days per week in the classroom, and three days per week in health care agencies, getting experience.

"Others from the community have also taken advantage of the training. Many said that they had always wanted to become a nurse, but had married and raised a family. Then, they were able to come back and get their LPN. Some finished and went on to get an R.N. degree. That is one of the highlights of the program."

Cosmetology, automotive repair, auto body, building construction, machine tool technology, heating and air conditioning, electrical, computer design, and office systems technology are some of the other courses offered, with well-qualified, enthusiastic teachers.

For Schlock, "seeing the interest of students in coming and enrolling in various fields of training; then leaving and going out into the world to work; becoming employed and getting a top beginning salary," are the rewards for the director, as well as the teachers.

And although it has been ten years since Schlock retired, a walk through the halls of the career center brings immediate recognition, smiles, and conversations between former director and personnel.

Arthur and Texas have a son, Kenneth, and a daughter, Dianne. They also have two grandchildren, two step-grandchildren, and two step-great-grandchildren, of whom they are clearly proud.

Schlock, who has been active in community affairs and his church, has served as a Sunday School teacher, chairman of deacons, and chairman of both the building committee and pastor search committee. In 1964, he received the Honorary State Farmer Degree, and the Honorary American Farmer Degree in 1968. Listed in *Personalities of the South*, he is a Gideon, and served as Rotarian president while living in Woodruff. He has also served as president of Retired Educators in Newberry, state director of Retired Educators, as well as president of the South Carolina Vocational Agriculture Teachers Association, and vice-president of South

Carolina Vocational Teachers. He is active with Meals on Wheels and the Red Cross.

Schlock is currently president of the Rabun Gap-Nacoochee School Alumni Association. Enthusiastic about the new direction taken by the school, he said, "We are working toward coordinating all activities under one umbrella—the Hooverites, the Junior College Alumni Association, the Alumni Association, and the Farm Families."

In speaking of Headmaster Greg Zeigler, he said, "I think we have a man that really has Rabun Gap at heart. And Patti Boyd and her assistant, Janie Owens, are doing wonders as far as the alumni are concerned."

With exciting projects to honor the past while building to the future, the alumni association is experiencing a rejuvenation. No one could be happier than Arthur Schlock, who gives credit to the school for any success he has had.

"Rabun Gap-Nacoochee School whetted my appetite for further education," he said. And of course, the valley was where he met his wife, Texas.

STEGALL AND FRIENDS

Chapter Twenty-Six

WILLIAM CLYDE STEGALL
COMPANY FOUNDER, MECHANICAL ENGINEER

 et me tell you a little story," William Clyde Stegall said, in reminiscing about his work scholarship days as a junior college student at Rabun Gap-Nacoochee School.

"When I got to the Gap in 1938, there were two farm bosses, Mr. Pitts and Mr. Miller. Since I was in charge of the two mules, Emma and Kate, I usually worked under Mr. Miller, who encouraged me greatly. But one day, I got with Mr. Pitts. We were plowing a field when I saw rain coming over the mountain. 'Mr. Pitts,' I said, 'we'd better get out of here or we'll get drowned.'

"Mr. Pitts was rough and tough, but he had a heart underneath that crust. But that day he said, 'Oh no. Keep on working, boys. That's nothing but fog.'

"Sure enough, the rain came and we got soaking wet. Oh, my stars! It was a deluge. From then on, any time it rained, it was called 'Mr. Pitts' fog.' I even taught my children, 'Oh that's not rain. That's Mr. Pitts' fog.'"

Born on December 4, 1921 on a farm near Walhalla, South

Carolina, Stegall, the future founder of a successful company and outstanding civic and church leader, was the only child of Berry and Weedie Stegall.

"I don't know why, but when I finished high school, I had an incessant desire to go to college," he said. "But I didn't know where to look. Clemson was the only college I knew about. But it cost four hundred dollars a year to go there, including your uniforms. Well, I could work in the dining room for a hundred dollars, and the college would give me a hundred-dollar scholarship. But as the son of a tenant farmer, I couldn't scrape up the rest of the money, so I was stuck there on the farm.

"But just across the cotton field from our house, there was a little schoolhouse. A young teacher, Helen Barrett, had been hired to teach there, and she roomed with a neighbor, the Barkers. She was the one who told me about Rabun Gap, where I could get an education by working my way through.

"By then, it was already October, but I applied and was accepted. They told me to come on, even though it was near the end of the quarter. So one of the Barker boys, Lawrence, with his fiancée Helen, drove me over to the school in the middle of November.

"The roads were terrible. From our farm to the school, as the crow flies, it wasn't over twenty or twenty-five miles. But it took three hours on the dirt road from Westminster to Clayton.

"When I got there, I didn't have a dime. Before I could matriculate or go to class, my tuition had to be paid. I was told that I could work that first quarter to get some credits, so I did that and started to school the spring quarter of 1939."

At graduation in 1941, Stegall owed forty dollars. "Now up to that time, my folks had not paid a single dollar directly for my education. I'd had to work at various jobs. My dad came up with the forty dollars. Beyond a few clothes, that was his total investment in my education."

Even then, Stegall spoke of the sacrifice that his parents had made, so that he could remain in school. Homesick when he first arrived, he hitchhiked once or twice a month to see his parents. But for some reason, Stegall did not go home for a visit that next fall until Thanksgiving. That was when he learned of his father's accident. His team of mules had run away from him, and he'd broken his leg and crushed his knee. "But they kept this from me," he said. For if he had known, Stegall would have returned home to help.

"Praise the Lord for that, now. It turned out to be an advantage. Dad had always been sort of the community barber. So he set up a little barbershop and cut hair on Fridays and Saturdays. He earned more money doing that than farming."

And this was how Clyde Stegall also earned money at the school. "A fellow, Alexander, who was a year ahead of me, was the primary barber. He charged fifteen cents, and as secondary barber, I charged ten cents. After he finished school, I went up to fifteen cents. No competition. I'd cut four or five heads of hair a night. At the end of the week, I'd wind up with four or five dollars. So I had money."

He also had caring teachers, who gave him great encouragement. "Remember, I was an only child," he said, "and I needed encouragement and a pat on the back. I was six feet, six inches tall, and gangly. I'd never had a date, never had brothers and sisters or neighbors to play with. And I didn't have much self-confidence."

His charm and vulnerability were evidently magnetic. He especially remembered Mrs. Addie Corn Ritchie, wife of the president, in a motherly role on campus. "I don't know why she picked me out. Mostly, she'd just indicate that she cared. It was more her actions than her words. She'd put her arm around me and say that she hoped things were all right with me.

"Dr. Ritchie, the president, was a great man. He would have wonderful words of encouragement, too. I remember his speeches in the dining hall. Sometimes, he'd go on too long, and the farm bosses would get irritated, since there was work to do in the fields. Dr. Ritchie stressed dependability. He'd say, 'When you say you're going to do something, come what may, do it.'"

Stegall still maintains a sense of pride in his former roommates, Ed and Elbert Bishop and the late Morris Ramey, who all became outstanding men in their fields. "We stayed in the Annex, where the tennis courts are now," he explained, "with Jack Acree as our supervisor. Foster Goolsby was one of my first roommates, and I've had a long-running friendship with him.

"Acree was also our athletic coach, and I played first base on the baseball team. We didn't have a real ball field. Dr. Ritchie gave us part of the cow pasture for the diamond. But we played some good teams during the school year—Young Harris, Piedmont, North Georgia at Dahlonega, and West and South Georgia Colleges. In the summer, most of us stayed at the school to work. We would team up with folks in Clayton to form a Rabun County team in a semi-pro league with some of the nearby mills, like Chicopee and Habersham Mills.

"I really loved baseball. I wasn't nearly as good as I thought I was, but Acree gave me lots of encouragement. He'd deliberately make me mad sometimes. He said I played better when I was mad."

Stegall spoke of the time when Acree bought a brand new Ford automobile. "He'd take half the team to Atlanta one Sunday to see the Atlanta Crackers play baseball. The next time, he'd take the other half. Those were good times.

"I loved every minute of it," Stegall said, recalling his school experiences, "except maybe cutting silage. You had to cut it with a blade in August, grind it up and put it in the silo for animal feed." Besides working in the fields, Stegall was also a fireman, keeping the furnaces going, and taking the mules, Emma and Kate, to haul the logs from the woods, or to the Tallulah Falls railroad siding, to unload the coal that Dr. Ritchie had ordered from Birmingham at five dollars a ton.

Now, years later, he laughs about his first date that turned into a near fiasco.

"There was not much opportunity for romance," he said. "When I went to Rabun Gap, I knew nothing about women. I still don't know anything about them. Somehow or other, I had a date for a picnic in the summer of 1939. Somebody else must have arranged it because I didn't have the nerve, and I didn't have any idea what to do on a date. Anyway, we went up with the group on the bus to Warwoman Dell. There were a lot of paths going in different directions, and this beautiful girl and I took one of the paths. I guess this was the time you were supposed to do a little hand-holding, but we got lost and I was in such a panic to find my way back to the group. By the time we finally found them, the rest of the group had nearly finished eating. We were so embarrassed that we didn't even eat. "

Later on, with his boyish charm, Stegall gained more savoir faire with the opposite sex.

Another teacher, besides Jack Acree, that Stegall is thankful for during his days as a student, is Miss Alice Lennon, the Bible teacher, who introduced him to the spiritual side of the school.

When the Nacoochee Institute, with its Presbyterian heritage, merged with Rabun Gap Industrial School to form a new entity, it was seen by some as a union of faith and works. Dr. Coit became the bridge between the school and the presbytery that helped to support the school, while Dr. Ritchie oversaw the secular workings of the school.

Miss Lennon, a graduate of Smith College and Biblical Seminary in New York, was one of the teachers who moved from Nacoochee, and as a Bible teacher, her goal was to see that the Gospel was presented to every student.

"When I got to Rabun Gap," Stegall confessed, "I couldn't even recite John 3:16. My family said they didn't have the clothes to go to church regularly. We'd go to protracted meetings in the summer, but I had never made a decision for Christ. Miss Lennon really sowed the seeds in my mind. Everyday that I have lived, I've thanked the Lord for Miss Lennon."

Once Stegall graduated, he went to work in a cotton mill that hired good baseball players, since baseball was king at that time. "But those were the most miserable two months of my life," he confessed. "I had bought me a little car by then," he said, "and when I heard that some of my buddies from Rabun Gap were working at R.G. LeTourneau in Toccoa, and that Jack Acree was in charge of the Machinist School, I took off one day and went to visit. Within an hour's time, I had signed up for the training program and joined the undefeated fast-pitch softball team

That was the beginning of Stegall's long association with not only the company, but with the LeTourneaus, whom he affectionately called "Mom and Pop."

"The Machinist School was a two-year program, to train key people in manufacturing operations. After a year—this was in 1942—the government wanted LeTourneau to manufacture 155 mm. shells." Since the company was already manufacturing shell casings, and the site in Toccoa had no more room to expand, R.G. LeTourneau built another factory at Vicksburg, Mississippi and sent twenty-five of the seventy-five young men who were at Toccoa. Stegall was in that group.

"They continued our education there," he said, "but we worked ten to twelve hours a day and went to school at night. We literally built the plant and then started building shells. We started in the spring of 1942, and by Christmas time, we were making shells. We couldn't buy machine tools and big presses. We had to make them. That's why they needed machinists. Some of those presses are still in operation."

It was at Vicksburg that Stegall met his future wife, Ann Welden, who had come out to visit her brother, a fellow worker, while waiting for classes to start at the Crawford Long School of Nursing.

During the time he was working and going to school, Stegall tried to volunteer for every branch of military service. But at 6'6", he was considered too tall for the navy or air corps. Only the army would accept him. But the company kept getting deferments for the workers, since it was a vital war industry.

Finally, Stegall was drafted into the army on June 1, 1944, a few days before D-Day. After seventeen weeks of basic and combat training in the infantry, in extremely hot weather to get him ready to fight in the Pacific jungles, he was sent instead, as a replacement to a mechanized cavalry unit, to Europe—covered in four feet of snow, at the time the Battle of the Bulge was in progress.

On March 5, 1945, he and five other buddies were walking across a field where the old Maginot line pillboxes separated France from Germany.

"I was just a few steps ahead, when a guy behind me tripped an anti-tank mine. Three of the soldiers were killed, and I woke up three days later in a hospital—wrapped like a mummy from head to toe, because of severe burns. I had a permanent injury to my right arm, numerous shrapnel wounds, twisted vertebrae, and most of my teeth knocked out.

"When I opened my eyes, I saw a beautiful girl dressed in white. She was standing by a window, raising the shade. I was in one of those elegant French chateaux, with murals on the ceiling and the walls. My first thought was that I must be in heaven.

"From the hospital in the chateau, we were sent to a beautiful place—like a country club resort—to recuperate. The buildings were six stories high, and there were gardens, pools and lakes with swans.

After I spent six weeks in traction and began to heal, I really appreciated the place, especially since it was flower time. I was so impressed that I knew I wanted to come back in better times."

Awarded two battle stars and a Purple Heart, Stegall was flown back to the States in a prop plane that took twenty-four hours. When he landed in Thomasville, Georgia, he recognized R.G. LeTourneau's private plane and his pilot, Red. "What are you doing here, Red?" Stegall inquired. "The old man is speaking here tonight," was the reply.

"A couple of days later, after we'd gotten settled down in the hospital, I got a call over the loudspeaker. 'Private William C. Stegall, report to Colonel Wilson's office.' Since my arm was in a sling, I washed my face with one hand, combed my hair, and went up to his office. I wasn't sure it was the right thing to do, but I saluted with my left hand. The colonel said, 'Stegall, there're some folks here to see you.'

"I looked over to my left and there were Mom LeTourneau and my mother. Mrs. LeTourneau had driven over to Walhalla from Toccoa, picked up my mother and flown her down. And she had arranged with the colonel for me to begin my furlough that day. I flew back with them to Toccoa."

That was one of many kindnesses that Mrs. LeTourneau showed to the young man who had touched her heart when she first nursed him back to health from a severe bout of flu when he was enrolled at the Machinist School in Toccoa.

Discharged in August 1945, Stegall enrolled at Clemson, the South Carolina college that had been too expensive for him earlier.

"Clemson had such a high regard for Rabun Gap-Nacoochee School," Stegall said, "that they accepted every credit—and also several courses I had taken at LeTourneau, such as metallurgy and drafting."

Needing money and also a physical break, Stegall worked once more at R.G. LeTourneau, but this time in Longview, Texas. After four months, he returned and he and Ann Welden were married. He then went back to Clemson with his wife.

"After we got married, I don't think I made anything but A's," Stegall said. "Ann was a good influence."

Inducted into Phi Kappa Phi and Tau Beta Pi, Stegall graduated, *magna cum laude*, in 1948 with a degree in mechanical engineering. Much sought after as an engineer, he accepted a job with General Electric and he and Ann moved to Philadelphia, and then were transferred to Bloomfield, New Jersey. Even though they loved going to New York City by train and watching the Brooklyn Dodgers play at Ebbett's Field, they decided to come back to the South, to Birmingham, Alabama.

From 1949 to 1960, Stegall, a registered professional engineer and master plumber, rose quickly in his profession from sales engineer to manager of the air-conditioning department at Mason-Dulion Company, to executive vice-president of the Hardy Corporation. In 1960, he founded the successful Stegall and Company, Inc. He retired in 1986 at the age of sixty-five, and sold his company.

"There was no reason to keep the business," he explained. "It had served its purpose. I'd been able to send all my kids to Auburn University. They had all married Auburn people and were out on their own. And I didn't care about the power and prestige."

Through those active years, he was a member of the Birmingham Chamber of Commerce, a director, treasurer, and student exchange officer of the Rotary Club; vice-chairman of United Way, and on the board of governors of the Vestavia Country Club.

He also served on the Salvation Army Advisory Board, Baptist Hospitals Foundation, Alabama Institute of the Deaf and Blind Foundation, and as chairman of the Campus Crusade for Christ. Selected as a trustee of LeTourneau University, a trustee of Rabun

Gap-Nacoochee School and president of the Junior College Alumni Association, Stegall still maintains his interest in these two educational institutions.

As for his church-related activities, Miss Lennon would have been proud. Serving through the years as elder, trustee, Sunday School teacher, Home Bible Class teacher, and numerous committees in Birmingham's Briarwood Presbyterian Church, Stegall said, "I still have my notes from Miss Lennon's Bible Survey course, and in my teaching, I often use the diagram I made back then on how everything in the Bible points to Christ."

Stegall and Ann, after retirement, moved seventeen miles from Birmingham to Shoal Creek, an exclusive golf club community, where they remain as busy as ever. "Ann is a real active grandmother to fifteen grandchildren. She takes that seriously," Stegall said. "That's her ministry. And she spends one day a week at inner-city schools, working with second graders to teach them to read on a one-to-one basis. The success rate of the volunteer program, Better Basics, has been phenomenal."

As for Stegall, besides golf, photography, and fishing, his great love is traveling. "We try to take at least one trip a year," he said. New Zealand, Hong Kong, Alaska, Nova Scotia, the Philippines, and Israel are but a few of his and Ann's past destinations. Yet, Europe seems to beckon time and again.

He made his first trip back to Europe in 1965, using the money he'd saved for twenty years from his small pension for being wounded in the war. He and Ann, with their four children, Bill, Leigh Ann, David, and Frank, visited nine countries, retracing the battlefields of World War II. Uppermost on his mind was the beautiful resort outside the French town, Vittel, where he had recuperated from his war wounds.

No one in the town seemed to know of that special place. After numerous inquiries, one Frenchman suggested that Stegall go to a resort nearby that catered to Americans. "I expect you'll find somebody over there who can give you directions to the place you want to find."

A short while later, he arrived. As soon as Stegall got out of the car, he recognized it immediately. "This is the place," he said in amazement. Once he told his story to one of the staff, he was treated with extreme courtesy. "We're glad to have you," the Frenchman assured him, giving him permission to tour the grounds at his leisure.

In anyone's life, wealth and success can be measured in many ways. William Clyde Stegall particularly treasures the wealth of memories from the past.

Foremost among them are his memories as a junior college student at Rabun Gap-Nacoochee School.

"As we grow older, our recollections may fade a bit," he admitted, "but not so the strong bonds of friendship that still exist between the alumni, staff, and the school. Each passing year, those ties become even stronger. We thank the Lord for them."

Bull Given To School By Mr. Woodruff

Chapter Twenty-Seven

COLONEL WESLEY BENJAMIN WILLIAMS
ENVIRONMENTAL AND CIVIL ENGINEER

ixty years after he arrived at Rabun Gap-Nacoochee School as a sixteen-year-old junior college freshman, Wesley Williams is able to draw such vivid word pictures of those days, that one suspects he has a photographic memory.

Nothing seems to have escaped his natural curiosity, from the landscape to the people to the mechanics of the pipes that brought running water to the campus from the nearby springs.

At that time, no one could foresee that this curiosity and innate intelligence would benefit the water and wastewater systems of major cities throughout the South – plus the new capital city of Nigeria, Abuja.

Williams will always be grateful to the minister of the Conyers Presbyterian Church, the Reverend J. Walton Stewart, who convinced Wes's parents, Lucy Clyde McDonald and John Washington Williams, to allow him to continue his education, once he had graduated as salutatorian of his high school class, in a year, 1939, when the local school board ran out of money, forcing an early closing of schools.

As the eldest son in a family of eight children, Wes had been expected to remain on the farm that had seen hard days with the Depression and the boil weevil devastating the main crop—cotton. Although his mother had inherited the house in Rockdale County, and the farm yielded enough food for the family, no cash was available for college tuition.

"On an early Saturday morning," Wes began, "Reverend Stewart took my parents and me to Rabun Gap in his 1934 Chevrolet. He did this since we couldn't afford bus fare, and principally to introduce us to the school faculty and staff, and to insure that the school would let me stay....

"Neither my parents nor I had ever been to Rabun Gap. We stopped on the way to see Tallulah Gorge. What an awesome sight! Two miles long and nearly one thousand feet deep. To me, this was a most thrilling and adventuresome trip.

"In those days, mountain roads had sharp curves, and the automobile tires squealed when rounding the curves at about thirty-five miles per hour. On one side of the road would be a steep bank, almost vertical, and on the other side, a steep drop-off. My dad was quite uneasy and expressed this, wishing the preacher would slow down. Per usual, my mother traveled on faith." But of course, Wes was thrilled with the trip that to him was akin to his first ride on a roller coaster.

"At the school, we were well received and invited to eat lunch. My father and I were impressed with the rich soil and the thickness of the corn, beans, and other crops. At lunch, Professor Shotts amazed me with his knowledge and brilliance, especially in scientific matters. And the Reverend Stewart knew what questions to ask about the school, to make us feel more at ease."

The tears that Wes had forced back when he said goodbye to his mother had been forgotten by that evening at the outdoor meal with homemade ice cream, and the social that followed at the girls' dormitory. "Everyone was very friendly in welcoming me to the school," he said.

Everywhere he looked, there were new things to see, to get accustomed to—especially the modern conveniences that he had not had at home—electric lights, running water and indoor plumbing, central heat in most buildings, and the cool mountain air that was at least ten degrees lower than the uncomfortably hot summers on the family farm.

"I was assigned to the boys' dorm, next door to the supervisor, Professor Warren, who had a wife and little son. My three roommates were Paul Crowe of Ball Ground, where Warren had been a Baptist preacher and school teacher; L.C. Nix of North Carolina, and Marshall Jones of Spring Place and Chatsworth.

"That first Sunday afternoon, after we'd gone to church and eaten our midday meal, the Warrens invited Paul and Marshall and me on a tour in his relatively new 1938 Plymouth. We rode to Highlands, North Carolina and returned by Franklin.

"Since this was before many 'flat landers' moved to the mountains, I was awed by the homes of the mountaineers and their habits of walking along the highway, some with shotguns over their shoulders. They took the right-of-way over automobiles, so one had to drive carefully, especially around curves. At one place, we drove under a waterfall, since there was a rock overhang."

At Highlands, Wes for the first time saw the summer homes of the wealthy from Atlanta and other areas, and the surrounding well-manicured golf courses. "I immediately wrote home about this wonderful trip."

His close association with Professor Warren continued on subsequent Sunday afternoons, much of the time traveling with a group of boys as Warren, an ordained minister, preached at some of the remote, rural Baptist churches. "He took us along for several reasons," Williams said, "– to increase attendance, to help with the singing and worship, and primarily I think to push him out of the mud or ditch, if and when he got stuck" on the unpaved roads.

During a student practice, Mr. Warren stopped the singing and commented, "Something doesn't sound quite right." Williams said he was then asked to sing a bar or two by himself. "That's it," Warren said, and gently suggested from then on that Wes only mouth the words. Dismissed from the singing group, he was still invited along and was a help in pushing the car out of the ditch.

"I never had any musical training," Williams philosophized, "but I've always loved to try to sing." And he takes comfort in singing in a car when he's alone and in large Baptist congregations, since all Baptists, he asserts, "sing with gusto and my voice is drowned out."

That same gusto was evident on his first coed outing to pick wild blackberries, the fruit that made such excellent jams, jellies, and pies for the dining hall.

Within a short time, he had picked a full bucket of berries. Spurred on by the praise of the supervisor, Miss Miller, he immediately went to work again. He could not understand why others were not nearly so proficient as he, until he saw a quick kiss exchanged by a couple behind a blackberry bush. Then, he realized that mixing a little romance with work made the work, however slower, much more pleasant.

Because of his small stature, Williams was not allowed to plow or work in the fields. He used a sling blade to cut down weeds; he shucked corn, and then his most lasting assignment was taking care of the pigs and hogs. "The school raised a lot of swine for food and some cash sales," he said. "They were mostly a breed called Chester White. Richard Hart from LaGrange and I worked together. We fed the swine and helped build hog houses, retaining fences, and feed troughs, and maintained them.... Sows with pigs were kept separate and given special attention. One task that Richard and I had was to castrate some of the young male pigs when they were about four to six weeks old. Poor pigs! Fortunately, all of them lived.

"Joe Craft was in charge of slaughtering and meat processing of swine and cattle. I helped once but couldn't take it emotionally," Wes confessed. His soft heart forbade him to preside at the demise of some of his favorite animals that he had cared for.

"It was not the cleanest job on campus... and because of it, I can relate much better to the story Jesus told of the prodigal son, even though I had not quite sunk to the depths of the prodigal son."

But a decided advantage to this care of the swine was the time and a half pay. Students were graded by performance and paid accordingly– poor, nine cents an hour; satisfactory, eleven cents; outstanding, thirteen cents. Most students, according to Williams, received a satisfactory rating. He was proud of a few outstanding ratings he received.

"I also had my first experience clearing ground," he added. "The trees were harvested and the stumps blown loose with dynamite, then manually removed and burned." Since students were not allowed to do so, Mr. Esco Pitts was always the one who packed the explosives and set the fuses.

"Mr. Pitts smoked a pipe," Wes remembered. "That day, he struck a match and set the fuse, and with the same match casually lit his pipe. Then he said, 'Run.' But we already had."

Even up through the 1950s, it was the custom throughout the South for college students to stand on a street corner near their schools, and local townspeople, recognizing them as students, would stop and give them a ride downtown. And although in a remoter area, such as the north Georgia mountains, women students were never allowed to do so, many of their counterparts thought nothing of hitchhiking home on a weekend, especially when they had no funds for bus fare.

Wes Williams' hitchhiking experiences were varied, from being half-frozen while riding in the open back of a pickup truck in the dead of winter, to the time he unknowingly caught a ride with a "tripper," a moonshine runner delivering his illicit cargo to Atlanta. At that time, Rabun County was the moonshine capital of Georgia. With revenuers always on the lookout, Wes was extremely worried that this fast-running car would be stopped and he would be accused of the crime.

Equally scary was a ride on the Tallulah Falls Railroad, an experience etched into the memory of many students. "As I recall," Williams said, "I rode the train (nicknamed Total Failure) twice to Cornelia and once to Clayton. The passenger car had both a swaying motion as well as some vertical motion, giving a lot of squeaking. The engine was an ancient steam engine fired by wood. The top speed was probably about fifty miles per hour going downhill. Locally cut timbers were used for the track ties, which tended to warp, and overall track maintenance was poor.

"The numerous trestles were also made of locally cut timbers, except for one or two steel trestles from Rabun Gap to Cornelia. In hot, dry weather, the trestles might occasionally catch fire from engine sparks or perhaps, arson. So every trip in such weather had a potential danger. On some days, the train would not run until the trestle could be repaired or rebuilt. Handcars often went before the train to spot any trouble on the tracks ahead."

During the depression years, farm families raised nearly all their food, and this was the case also with the Rabun Gap-Nacoochee School. The few exceptions were sugar, salt, baking powder, and wheat flour, which had to be purchased. These "store bought" items were carefully monitored in the kitchen to prevent any waste. The frugality of that period also extended to the making of lye soap on campus, using soda ash and animal fat.

Since each Sunday was supposed to be a day of rest from the week's labor, no cooking was done after the midday meal. Instead, as students left the dining hall, each was given a sack supper, with a sandwich, an apple, and cookies. But many times, as is the case with growing boys' appetites, that snack had disappeared long before evening.

Christian Endeavor, the Sunday evening vesper service was not mandatory, so a small group of hungry boys with a little money in their pockets would head for the old stone house, where the elder Mrs. Dillard, of Dillard House fame, would serve a fried chicken dinner for twenty-five cents. The few times that Williams had that amount, he would join them.

When Wes first arrived on campus the summer of '39, Dr. Ritchie, the president, had been away on a fund raising trip. He met him several days later in the dining hall. Dr. Ritchie always kept the students up to date on his activities, and he, in turn, seemed to know everything that was going on, on campus. He greatly encouraged the students, but he also chastised them when they had done something inappropriate.

"One day, the boys doing plowing in the field decided to become cowboys in returning the mules to the barn." According to Williams, "the cowboys were Sherman Wilson, Tubby Wilson, Dean Bannister, and perhaps Rip Chandler and James Martin. They put on a good show, but I don't remember who won the race. The next morning at breakfast, Dr. Ritchie called names and announced that there would be no further mule racing.

"Dr. Ritchie in his talks also commended faculty, staff, and teachers on their accomplishments, programs, and good deeds, and gave inspirational lectures on morals, character, faith, and work ethics."

By the fall of 1939, the Ritchies had retired, along with the Coits, and Dr. George Bellingrath had become the new president. "His leadership style was quite different from Dr. Ritchie's," Wes acknowledged. "He taught me a Bible class in New Testament, on which he had a profound knowledge, but he put the information in understandable terms. He also gave personal attention to individual students." Besides talks that covered school programs, and ethics of character and integrity, he held Christian Emphasis Week, during which a visiting minister would speak at chapel and at meals, and counsel students. The Bellingrath's daughter, Ruth, had arrived on campus with them and attended the high school.

Other teachers who made an impact on Williams were Jack Acree, the athletic coach; Miss Alice Miller, who later became a missionary to Africa; Miss Alice Lennon, a graduate of Smith College, who was on the first USA girls basketball team; and Miss Tewkesbury, "another teacher I dearly loved. She taught me a course in public speaking, but unfortunately did not help me get rid of my Southern drawl," he said.

The man whom Williams considered as the guiding force behind so many students' decisions to go into the educational field was Professor Berry Floyd, who taught educational subjects and some elementary math courses. Floyd later became Superintendent of Education of Rabun County Schools.

Also in the fall of 1939, Claude Nix, a 1937 junior college alumnus, with a recent degree from Berea College, returned to teach agriculture. He and his bride, Martha Roberts, of the class of 1938, became upstairs supervisors in the dormitory suite that Prof. Warren had occupied. "All of us boys next door kept our eyes and ears open," Wes said, "to learn what we could about newlyweds. We really didn't learn too much, but what we did learn was exciting."

As for extracurricular activities, Wes played tennis whenever he could borrow a racket; he took part in plays produced by Miss Tewkesbury. "We performed before a volunteer audience and attendance was never very good." He also looked forward to the square dances, called Big Ring, on Saturday nights – the event termed "folk games" since dancing, as such, was strictly forbidden.

Perhaps one of his most satisfying activities was in working as feature editor of the student newspaper, *The Indian Chief*, whom Emmett Rhodes, class of '41, started with Wes and a few others. Since Williams was selected as the wittiest boy in the class, his features were eagerly read.

By late summer of 1940, Wes' father became seriously ill. From earliest childhood, Wes had been well trained in his role as eldest son. In the absence, illness, or death of his father, he would be the one to assume the role of protector and provider of his family. So he returned home to supervise the gathering of the crops. "Cotton was our principal cash crop, on which the family depended for money for the remainder of the year," he said. "We also had other crops, such as corn, sweet and Irish potatoes, wheat, oats, and fruit. We did sell some of these too, but the income was small compared to cotton."

Once the crops were gathered and his father had improved in health, Wes returned to Rabun Gap, but lacked one quarter to graduate.

In 1997, Rabun Gap-Nacoochee School awarded Wes Williams an honorary diploma as one of its most outstanding alumni. Through the years, he had not allowed this interruption in his education to change his goals. If anything, he worked with new impetus to become one of the most recognized men in his field.

After Rabun Gap, Williams found day jobs in the Atlanta area, while he went to school in the evenings at what is now Georgia State University.

But once again, a situation beyond his control interrupted his schooling—World War II. He was accepted into flight training by the U.S. Navy, but before completion, Wes was transferred to the U.S. Merchant Marine Academy.

"The U.S. Merchant Marine Academy required and still does, sea duty with academics under supervision of ships' officers, as a part of the course," Williams explained. "It's the only service academy that sends its cadets or midshipmen off to war. My sea duty was in the Atlantic to South America, the Caribbean, and Europe. I could relate some horror stories of storms, hurricanes, enemy subs and aircraft, but won't." Merely describing it as "six months of very hazardous duty," he resigned, since he'd discovered that he liked neither sea duty nor the seaman lifestyle.

Transferring to the U.S. (Army) Air Force, he received a direct commission as 1st Lt. and was assigned to a trouble shooting and training crew that visited numerous bases in the USA and, during the latter part of the war, went "island hopping" in the Pacific. After the war, Williams remained in the Reserve until 1979, rising to the rank of colonel.

When the war was over, Williams resumed his education, enrolling at Georgia Institute of Technology, where he graduated in 1949 with a B.S. degree in civil engineering.

His classmates at Georgia Tech included other Rabun Gap alumni—Col. Charles Gay Johnson, who accepted a regular commission in the USAF, John H. Askew, John Naglich, Richard E. Black, and James (Jim) Fry, who became president of a textile business.

Wes Williams' meteoric rise in his profession is recorded in the Seventh Edition of *Who's Who in Engineering*, from consultant engineer with Hensley-Schmidt, Inc., to CEO and President of his own company, Weslyn Enterprises, Inc.

Through the years of his active reserve duty status in the air force, when he was subject to going anywhere in the world in twenty-eight hours after recall, and with numerous weekends, vacations and unpaid job leaves spent on active duty, he served as Director of Facilities Maintenance and Operations at Headquarters, Continental Air Command, and Headquarters, Air Force Reserve. He also became Director of Civil Engineering, Eastern Air Force

Reserve Region, staff civil engineer at U.S. Air Force Headquarters Command, and chief reserve engineer, Headquarters, Military Airlift Command. For his outstanding engineering works, he received the Commendation Medal, Legion of Merit, and other service awards.

In 1951, Williams took advanced studies in sanitary engineering at Tech, and later advanced engineering courses at Air Force Institute of Technology, Air University, and Taft Center, U.S. Public Health Service. In 1974, he graduated from Industrial College of the Armed Forces.

In civilian life, his expertise in civil and environmental engineering with specializations in water supply, water pollution control, and wastewater management had an effect on nearly every major city in the Southeast. In his overall engineering career, he was engaged in either the planning, design, or construction of over three hundred projects of various sizes, that ranged from Miami, Florida; Raleigh, North Carolina; Savannah, Georgia; Columbia, South Carolina, and Nashville, Tennessee to Abuja, Nigeria's new capital city. An earlier work experience included his serving as Director of Water Quality Central Services for the Georgia Water Quality Control Board.

Besides his military awards, Williams has received such outstanding professional honors as the Bedell Award and Service Award (past director) from an international organization, the Water Pollution Control Federation (now called Water Environment Federation); the Past President Award, the Alva T. Storey Award and Honorary Life Membership from the Georgia Water and Pollution Control Association; and Order of the Engineer. As a certified professional engineer, Williams is a life member of several prominent organizations, such as the National Society of Professional Engineers, and the Society of American Military Engineers.

Over the years, his academic posts have ranged from student assistant instructor in Field Surveying and Air Force ROTC instructor at Georgia Tech, to supervisor and part-time instructor and lecturer for Georgia Water and Wastewater Schools.

Co-founder of Georgia Water and Wastewater Institute, he published a number of articles in his areas of expertise, a more serious endeavor than his witty bon mots for Rabun Gap's school newspaper, *The Indian Chief.*

Wes is married to the former Carolyn Wilson, a graduate of Tift College. As a classmate of Mildred McClain Chlupacek (JC '44), she is a former school teacher/librarian. She and Wes have two children, Susan W. Gilbert, an educator with three children—Melissa, Justin, and Andrew; and Wesley Howell, a builder, whose own son, Wesley S. Williams, is the fifth generation to bear the name of Wesley.

Despite his very active travels with his work and his commitments to the Air Force Reserve, Williams through the years remained a leader in the Presbyterian Church, serving as deacon, elder, Sunday School teacher, president of Men of the Church and president of Men of Atlanta Presbytery, commissioner to the Presbytery and General Assembly, and co-founder of the Christian Association for the Retarded.

He has also been active in neighborhood and school organizations, and served as president of the Rabun Gap-Nacoochee Junior College Alumni Association.

Reflecting on his contributions to society, Williams said, "I enjoyed my life's work and I firmly believed engineering was my calling. The Apostle Paul admonished us to be worthy of the calling which we received. Without boasting, I feel that I have contributed to the betterment of the environment and the community, and have served to keep peace in the world." Nevertheless, he regrets the amount of time he had to spend away from his family in work and military service.

Now retired, Williams enjoys his hobbies of gardening, hiking, reading, and traveling. Although he has given up his private pilot's activities, he still works part-time as a consultant for environmental engineering projects.

How gratifying it must have been to serve as a water consultant at his alma mater, where years before, as a boy of sixteen, Wesley Benjamin Williams became intrigued with the pipes that carried water, by gravity, from the nearby mountain springs to the campus of Rabun Gap-Nacoochee School.

Chapter Twenty-Eight

HEROES OF WORLD WAR II

n 1917, a young man from the Appalachian Mountains, Alvin York of Tennessee, was faced with a dilemma. He had been drafted into the U.S. Army, but as a Christian, he felt it was wrong to take another's life.

Although the effects of becoming a conscientious objector would be devastating, he had reached a decision. He would not fight because of his faith. Yet, a talk with his commanding officer convinced him otherwise. The officer showed him the Biblical passage concerning the responsibility of the watchman in the tower against the nation's enemies, and York went on to become the most decorated hero of World War I.

Now, once again, nearly twenty-five years later, the men and women of the Appalachian region were called upon to serve their country in another world war. Also of strong faith, few seemed to have the same hesitation as to patriotic duty. So overnight, the campus of Rabun Gap-Nacoochee School was suddenly bereft of the young men who had plowed, sowed, and harvested the eighteen-hundred-acre farm that was so necessary to the welfare and sustenance of the school.

Young women students learned to drive the tractors, and extra help was sought from men in the local community. But this particular battle was a losing one, and by 1945, the board of trustees voted to dissolve the junior college that had seen such success for the previous eleven years, and return the school to its former status as a high school.

Gathered around the large radios, with their distinctive odor of vacuum tubes, many of the students remembered the "Day of Infamy" speech of President Franklin D. Roosevelt, who addressed the nation after the bombing of Pearl Harbor by the Japanese on December 7, 1941. And many remembered the words of Professor Nicholson, who was a veteran of World War I. "Your lives will never again be the same."

Many young men, not waiting to be drafted, volunteered so that they might choose their own branch of service. At least six of the junior college women, Frances Hayes (Sarzoni), Alice Mae Kitchens (Garren), Lucy Mashburn (Blackwell), Lois Miller (Romanczyk), Ruth Sisk (Williams), and Blanche Suddath (Descani) also volunteered for military service.

The U.S. Army, Navy, Air Force, Marines, and Merchant Marines were well represented by the former students of the school. Many of their experiences are recorded in the profiles of outstanding alumni, who went on to become successes after the war had been won.

From the Nacoochee Institute came Gladys Ginn (Berryman), an army nurse who survived both the infamous Bataan Death March, after Corregidor had fallen, and her years as a prisoner of war. There is also the story of a high school alumnus, Hollis Epps, the commander of the submarine squadron that fished from the sea a young navy pilot, Lt. (jg.) George Bush, who later became President of the United States.

But there are others who were not so lucky—like Capt. Denver V. Truelove and Staff Sgt. Robert Sangster, Jr. who lost their lives in service to their country. Some, such as Staff Sgt. John W. Naglich, Jr., reported missing, survived against all odds, along with those like Lt. Norman Simonton, a B-29 aircraft commander with the Twentieth Air Force in the Pacific. All these men received the Distinguished Flying Cross.

Then, there are the ones who made military service their careers, such as the much decorated Col. Charles G. Johnson, who rose to prominence in three wars and the Berlin Airlift, and was later assigned to the Pentagon—and Col. Albert M. Willoughby, a thirty-one-year veteran of the U.S. Air Force, who flew with the Strategic Air Command for seventeen of those years.

Capt. Denver V. Truelove

In December 1941, a B-25 Mitchell bomber, named for General Billy Mitchell, sank a Japanese submarine off the Pacific coast of the United States. It was not until April 1942 that sixteen B-25s first launched an attack on the islands of Japan.

In that space of time, from Guam, the Philippines, the Solomons, the Dutch East Indies, Malaya, and Singapore, the Japanese had taken control of the Pacific Rim and its sea lanes, and morale in the United States was low.

To give hope to the American people, a secret mission was born—the First Special Aviation Project—the famous Doolittle Raid on Tokyo.

Sixteen B-25s, the conventional twin-engine, twin-tail medium bombers with tricycle landing gears to be used on the mission, were altered. Additional fuel tanks were installed; only the twin .50 caliber machine guns in the upper turret and a single smaller caliber in the nose were kept for defense. Their important cargo was to be the incendiary bombs to be unloaded on the unsuspecting enemy—if the planes could manage to slip through unobserved, at a low altitude. Even if everything went right, the project was still considered a suicide mission. The extra fuel would not be enough to return to the aircraft carrier, so optimistic plans had been made for any survivors to land on airfields in China.

A carefully selected group of eighty men were asked to participate. Each was told the dangers and given the option of backing out, but no one did. In that group was Lt. Denver V. Truelove, a young bombardier from Lula, Georgia, a town of three hundred and fifty people. He was the only Georgian included.

Personable, with immaculate good looks and twin dimples, Denver was the younger brother of Blanche T. Bowen, and he had followed in his sister's footsteps, also graduating from Rabun Gap-Nacoochee Junior College, before continuing his education at the University of Georgia. He was a favorite of Dr. Ritchie and became his student chauffeur while on campus.

Denver went to Eglin Field in Florida to train for the mission. While the pilots learned how to take off from a carrier within an allotted space of five hundred feet, Denver, with the other bombardiers, practiced low-altitude bombing with a Mark Twain bombsight, a special device that had been made from about twenty cents of metal.

In scrapbooks and personal memoirs belonging to Blanche Truelove Bowen, the picture of an enthusiastic young man emerges, with his assurance that if he lost his life, it would be for his country, and he would not regret it.

By April 2, 1942, the sixteen planes and eighty men had gone aboard the U.S.S. *Hornet* and set sail from San Francisco to rendezvous with a task force surrounding the carrier, *Enterprise*. Only when they were at sea was their destination revealed. In the western Pacific, the convoy was spotted by a Japanese patrol boat, who radioed a warning before it could be sunk. Now, there was only one alternative—for the Doolittle Raiders to take off sooner than planned. Vice-Admiral Halsey, the task force commander, gave the order.

On April 18, the group was not sure that it had enough fuel to reach Japan, much less to land on the Chinese mainland afterwards. Perhaps it was just as well they were unaware that no provisions had been made to receive them in China.

Under Lt. Col. Doolittle's command, the group of B-25s reached the Japanese coast undetected. A strong tailwind from a storm had miraculously helped them to conserve enough gasoline to reach their target—Tokyo. Causing far more damage than had been anticipated, Doolittle's Raiders accomplished their mission—to shake the confidence of the Japanese and to give a great boost in morale to the American people, who had seen nothing but defeat up to that time.

The planes now headed for safety. But weather over the Chinese mainland had worsened. There was little visibility, and with no radio beacons to guide them, the planes became lost while the fuel ran low. Four of the B-25s crash landed, including Lt. Col. Doolittle's. The crew parachuted, with some killed, several drowned, while others were picked up by Japanese patrol boats. Out of those, nearly half were executed, the rest made prisoners of war. Out of sixteen planes, only one remained intact. The pilot had flown north and landed in the USSR, where the crew was immediately taken prisoner. The men remained in Russia for a year, until an escape could be arranged.

In the meantime, Denver and the engineer/gunner of Crew Number Five bailed out about the same time and landed in nearby trees in a mountainous region of China. Hanging by the straps of their parachutes, they finally extricated themselves and, after spending the night on the mountainside, they found a friendly village. With the help of missionaries and Chinese operatives, they arrived at their prearranged destination: Chühsien. Several days later, with Doolittle's arrival, the survivors traveled on to Chungking, where they were treated royally by the Chinese. Each was decorated with medals; with the newly promoted General Doolittle receiving the Military Order of China: the Chinese Order of the Celestial Cloud. At a banquet in their honor, where Generalissimo Chiang Kai-shek made a speech, the Generalissimo's wife, Mai-ling Soong Chiang, who had been a student at Wesleyan College in Macon, Georgia, pinned the medals to the airmen's uniforms. Among Denver's treasured possessions was the personal thank you letter by Madame Chiang.

On May 4, 1942, Denver left China for Calcutta. The Burma Road, Jerusalem, and Cairo were some of the places he saw on his indirect journey home. From Port-au-Prince in Haiti, he flew to Miami and on to Washington, where General Hap Arnold was waiting to decorate him with the Distinguished Flying Cross and other medals that befit a returning hero.

Then, he was allowed to return home on furlough, to visit his family and to sell U.S. Government War Savings Bonds. Lula, his hometown, held a parade in his honor, sponsored by the American Legion Post in Gainesville. The press followed him wherever he went. He was the guest of honor in a parade at Ft. McPherson, and gave a speech broadcast by radio. In Atlanta Mayor Hartsfield's office, he sold and autographed fifty thousand dollars of War Savings Bonds to one man. He was photographed on the family farm with twin calves, and with his mother admiring his medals, including the Purple Heart and Air Medal with three Oak Leaf clusters. James Haynes, his junior college roommate, added additional pages to the "Denver" scrapbook.

In September 1942, Denver, now promoted to captain, was assigned to the European Theatre, moving from England to North Africa to begin bombing missions on Italy, prior to the ground troops' invasion. On a bombing run on April 5, 1943, enemy flak hit the plane, setting fire to both engines. In the crash landing into the turbulent sea off the coast of Sicily, a giant wave crushed the burning plane as it hit the water, and Denver and two other crew members lost their lives. Four days later, Georgia's hero would have been twenty-four years old.

In a letter to the Truelove family, his squadron commander wrote that Capt. Denver Truelove was one of the coolest men under fire that he had ever seen, and that "his bravery was an inspiration to his comrades and his life an example of American courage and patriotism."

STAFF SGT. ROBERT H. SANGSTER, JR.

When Robert Hamilton Sangster, Jr. graduated from Rabun Gap-Nacoochee Junior College in 1941, he gave a speech of encouragement to his graduating class.

"...Some of you left a sheltered life upon leaving home," he said. "Your life in the dormitory with fellow students has taught you to live with other people. These fellow students represent the public of tomorrow. If you have learned to live with them, and gotten along in a helpful and happy way, don't worry about living with the public.

"In working for your education, you have an advantage over students of other schools. This advantage depends upon how well your work has been done, and the realization that most worthwhile things are earned, and not received as a gift."

Robert Sangster, Jr. has earned a place in the hearts of all who knew him. Born in Vienna, Georgia on September 11, 1921, he graduated from Vienna High School in 1938 and soon after entered the work/study junior college in the north Georgia mountains. While there, he helped to organize the school newspaper, *The Indian Chief,* and was its business manager. He sang in the Glee Club and participated in many of the religious and student organizations.

On March 20, 1941, having volunteered for the U.S. Army Air Corps, he was assigned to Fort Benning, Georgia for basic training and then sent to other fields. He became a gunner, leaving the United States for England, to a base of the U.S. Eighth Air Force. Sorties into Germany prior to the European invasion were some of the most dangerous air battles in Europe. He acquitted himself well, and received a number of air medals for heroism.

In his possession was an anonymous poem entitled "A Gunner's Vow."

"...It takes guts to be a gunner/ To sit out in the tail,/ When the Focke-Wulf boys are coming/ And the slugs begin to wail...The pilot's just a chauffeur/ It's his job to fly the plane/ But it's we who do the fighting/ Though we may not get the fame...."

He downed a number of Focke-Wulfs, and in his brief career, he was awarded eight medals, including the Distinguished Flying Cross, the Air Medal with three Oak Leaf clusters, the Purple Heart, the American Defense and the Victory medals, the Citation of Honor, and the Presidential Citation. Little is known about his last battle on March 31, 1943, when he was killed in action. He was twenty-two years and six months old.

Buried in Brookwood, a cemetery in England, Staff Sgt. Robert H. Sangster, Jr. was brought back home after the war, and his body reinterred in Andersonville Military Cemetery. During the memorial service in 1948, full honors were extended to him.

"He stands in unbroken line of patriots who have dared to die that freedom might live, and grow, and increase its blessings," his Presidential Citation read. "Freedom lives, and through it he lives in a way that humbles the undertakings of most men."

STAFF SGT. JOHN W. NAGLICH, JR.

The headlines in the newspaper read: Georgian Rescued From Crocodile-Infested Wilds.

John Naglich, Jr., nineteen years old, was a corporal at the time, a gunner stationed at an airfield in New Guinea. He had participated in the American air attack on a Japanese-held airfield on New Britain Island in the Solomons and the B-17 Flying Fortress, with only two engines in working order, then limped for home.

But the pilot, discovering that their landing base had undergone an air raid during their absence, realized the landing would be too risky for the plane and his men. So he diverted the B-17, looking for an alternate landing.

New Guinea, one of the largest islands in the world, was then made up of the Netherlands New Guinea on the west, and on the east was divided into two areas, Northeast New Guinea and Papua, both territories claimed by Australia. With the exception of a few coastal areas, such as Port Moresby, the rest of the island was jungle, or bush country, with sharp-edged grasses that could draw blood at a touch. Leeches and other hazards were prevalent, but perhaps the most dangerous were the crocodiles that inhabited the swamps.

While an adequate place to land was being sought, a squall came up suddenly and bombarded the plane that was already running low on fuel. One engine failed, and then the other began sputtering. The crew had already thrown out any excess equipment to lighten the load. But now, with all engines gone, there was only one alternative—for the men to parachute to safety.

Out of the four officers and five enlisted men aboard, seven landed within a mile and a half apart. A short time later, the seven were able to join up with each other, even though two were injured and unable to walk. The other two members of the crew, including the pilot, had evidently landed farther away and remained missing, despite the crew's looking for them.

With little more than one full canteen of water among them, Naglich and two others volunteered to go in search of water.

In the jungle, as they crossed stagnant streams, and fought their way through the bush, the three became lost. No good water was found, and they had to quench their thirst by drinking from the foul-smelling pools. In those four days, the only food they ate was a raw fish, five inches long.

In the meantime, with his brother Wilhelm serving in the Seabees, and both parents having passed away, Naglich's sister, his closest relative at home, received the ominous telegram from the War Department that their brother was missing in action.

In the jungle, the lost three decided to retrace their steps. By that time, the lack of water had taken its toll. But as they stumbled toward the coast, they heard the sound of a rescue plane. An American pilot and an Australian spotted them and dropped supplies—meat and much-needed water to alleviate their swollen tongues and parched throats. When they were rescued later, they learned that the others had been discovered, including the missing pilot, who had been injured. Bush boys led that group to the coast, where they were picked up by a flying PT boat. Only one member of the crew was never found.

Later, Staff Sgt. Naglich, who had become a radio operator, received the Distinguished Flying Cross for his mission in an unarmed, unarmored troop carrier aircraft to deliver supplies to Allied troops behind enemy lines in Italy.

This alumnus of Rabun Gap-Nacoochee School, who always felt that life at the Gap gave him both a good work and spiritual foundation for later life, enrolled at Georgia Institute of Technology after the war, and graduated with an engineering degree in 1950. Two years previously, he had married Marjory J. Smith. During his career, he worked for Arkansas Power and Light Company, and the Federal Aviation Agency, from which he retired in 1985.

According to his wife Marjory, from that time until his death in 1994, he enjoyed his flowers, his garden, and his variety of birds.

A native of Sautee, Georgia, John W. Naglich, Jr. was the son of immigrants who had settled in the Nacoochee Valley thirty years before World War II. All his life he exhibited his love for God, family, and country.

COL. CHARLES GAY JOHNSON

In March 1943, Charles Gay Johnson of Epworth, Georgia entered the aviation cadet program of the U.S. Army Air Corps. By December, he had graduated and received his wings and the rank of second Lt.

It was not long before he was sent overseas, to the European Theatre where, as a P-51 Mustang pilot, he flew eighty-eight missions over Germany—quite an accomplishment of survival in such a hazardous theatre of operations. During this time, he was awarded the Distinguished Flying Cross with one Oak Leaf cluster, the Air Medal with sixteen Oak Leaf clusters, and the Purple Heart for injuries received.

After the war, Johnson returned to pursuing an education,

enrolling at Georgia Institute of Technology, where he was awarded a degree in chemical engineering in 1948.

Following graduation from Tech, he reenrolled in the air force and was sent to the Air Force Institute of Technology for a master's degree in engineering. From that date on, his years of service were spent in the field of Research and Development, which included a five-year assignment at the Pentagon. His last assignment before retiring after thirty-one years of service was at Hanscom Field in Bedford, Massachusetts, where he was Chief of Staff of the Electronics Systems Divisions.

At that time, in 1974, he held a Command Pilot rating with over four thousand flying hours in both jet and conventional aircraft. And in addition to the World War II Distinguished Flying Cross with Oak Leaf cluster, Purple Heart, and Air Medal with sixteen Oak Leaf clusters, he was also the recipient of the Air Force Commendation medal, and the Legion of Merit.

Born November 17, 1920, Col. Johnson was fifty-four years old when he retired, with too much energy to go fishing for the rest of his life. Thus, he embarked upon a second career. Accepting a teaching position at Sumter, South Carolina High School, with its student body made up of twenty-seven hundred students, he immediately enrolled at the University of South Carolina to begin work on a master's degree in education, while he continued to teach math, physics, and chemistry. From 1980-85, he was chairman of the Science department.

In speaking of his two outstanding careers, he said, "I received great satisfaction from serving in the armed forces of my country during World War II, Korean War, Vietnam War, and the Berlin Airlift. I believe I made a further contribution to my country by engaging in the education of our youth."

His own earlier college education was hard won. But he took the opportunity offered him to work for his tuition as a student at

---

Rabun Gap-Nacoochee Junior College, arriving at the mountain school the summer of 1939. Like so many others, he had come early to acquire the necessary funds for the fall quarter.

"I spent the first six weeks working in the fields as a farm hand," he said. "During the remainder of that summer, I worked at cutting wood in the forest... which we used to heat the school buildings that winter. This was probably the most physically demanding job I had during my two year stay.

"We were on the job from eight to five the entire month of August, with daytime temperatures in the nineties. Our lunch was brought to the work site. After a day of walking behind a team of mules in the corn fields or cutting wood, we were usually ready for bed pretty early."

By the second year, Johnson served as an official courier, a much less strenuous job. He drove the school truck to transport workers back and forth to work sites, and went off campus on school errands. Occasionally, he drove the school bus.

One of his pleasurable memories involved being the manager of the basketball team and traveling to schools in the southern part of the state. These road trips would vary from three to five days. "We traveled by car," he said, "and Coach Jack Acree would drive one car while I drove the other."

Other pleasant memories involved riding the Tallulah Falls train into Clayton; hunting rabbits in the snow; enjoying the wonderful aroma from rolls baking in the oven and the taste of homemade ice cream, the camaraderie with fellow students, and best of all, meeting the coed, Frances Freeman, who later became his wife.

"There were watchful eyes at all times when we were dating. But as young students, we could always find a way to isolate ourselves once in a while," Johnson commented.

The year 1939 was a transition time at the school. President Ritchie, whom Johnson saw frequently during that first summer, had retired when the fall quarter began, and Dr. George Bellingrath became president. Johnson remembers the New Testament class taught by Dr. Bellingrath. He was also impressed with Miss Lennon, Mr. Nicholson, Dr. Shotts, who taught chemistry, and Jack Acree in social science.

"Work in the classrooms was trying at times," he confessed. "When one goes to school for two days, works in the fields for two days, and goes back to class for two days, it can be challenging." But he evidently did well enough to graduate with honors in 1941.

For two years, until he went into the air force, Charles Johnson, as so many other graduates of Rabun Gap, worked at R.G. LeTourneau Company in Toccoa, which held a government contract to make shell casings—essential to the war.

With him, he had brought the strong work ethics and sense of responsibility that had blossomed under the encouragement of his teachers. In later years, after his distinguished military career, he was able to pass on those philosophies to a new generation of students.

"Through my adult life," he said, "I have actively engaged in the programs of my church." He has served as deacon, Sunday School superintendent and teacher, and Training Union Director. He has been a leader in his community—the PTA, the Kiwanis Club, and on the board of directors of Christian Charities.

The son of William V. and Jessie Johnson, he and Frances have one son, David, an architect, and one grandson, David, Jr. "Oftentimes, Frances and I are reminded of our work experiences while at the Gap. We had an opportunity to do new and interesting tasks that young people of today do not have a chance to do."

War hero, educator, and community leader, Col. Charles Gay Johnson represents his alma mater with distinction.

World War II Service Roll
Rabun Gap-Nacoochee Junior College

A: Servicewomen

1. Frances Hayes (Sarzoni)
2. Alice Mae Kitchens (Garren)
3. Lucy Mashburn (Blackwell)
4. Lois Miller (Romanczyk)
5. Ruth Sisk (Williams)
6. Blanche Suddath (Descani)

B. Servicemen

1. Bernard D. Adair
2. Henry Addor
3. J. T. Alexander
4. Beaman Allen
5. Robert L. Ambrose
6. J. Manuel Ammons, Jr.
7. Marion Arnold
8. John Henry Askew
9. Curtis R. Ayers
10. Robert Lee Babb
11. Earl Dean Bannister
12. Edwin Bannister
13. Wilton Bell
14. George Bennett
15. Edwin Bishop
16. Elbert Bishop
17. Richard E. Black
18. Thomas J. Blair
19. Jim Ed Bleckley
20. Thomas Bleckley
21. L.G. Bowen, Jr.
22. Walter Bowen
23. Joe Braddy
24. Russell Bradford
25. Neil E. Brantley
26. Charles C. Bridges
27. Eugene Bryant
28. Ralph Buchanan
29. James Harold Buffington
30. Joseph Harding Cain
31. Thomas Callaway
32. Marlar L. Carpenter
33. Edwin Ross Cathey
34. Richard Chandler
35. William Rogers Chandler
36. Frank L. Clark
37. Joe Clark
38. Lloyd Cowan
39. Joe Raleigh Craft
40. Paul Crowe
41. Arnold Darden
43. Jackson C. Davidson
42. Herschel Davis
44. Hugh Davis
45. James F. Deal
46. Mark Deal
47. Lee Roy Deaton
48. Robert S. Dickerson
49. Earl John Dillard
50. Emmett Urcey Dillard
51. Darrell Dollar
52. Ellis Jaudon Dollar

53. Albert Dorsey
54. Dolphus Duckett
55. Irwin Allen Dyer
56. William Turner Enloe
57. Sam Fant
58. Joseph Hansell Farmer
59. E. Frank Ford
60. Elmer Lee Fry
61. Walter Fuqua
62. J. Foster Goolsby
63. O'Gilvey Gosnell
64. Albert F. Greenway
65. Archie Lamar Gregory
66. James W. Griffin
67. George A. Grist
68. James Lester Grist, Jr.
69. Charlie O. Gunn
70. Curran T. Gunn
71. Marion Holman Haley
72. Roy S. Harper, Jr.
73. Fred Z. Harris
74. Doris Hart
75. Richard M. Hart
76. Jackson Ashley Hayes
77. Jesse Abel Hayes
78. Nelson Hayes
79. James F. Haynes
80. Glenn Hopper
81. Herman E. Hopper
82. James Etsel Hopper
83. Jack Vernon Hulme
84. Earle Irby
85. Charles Gay Johnson

86. Donald Johnson
87. Kenneth Johnson
88. Luther Gentry Johnson
89. Oscar Lloyd Jollay
90. Howard Jones
91. Marshall Jones
92. McKinley Jones
93. Howell King
94. W.E. Kirkland, Jr.
95. Watson Ray Lankford
96. Raymond Paul Leonard
97. William Lovett
98. Walter Lloyd
99. Thomas Aubrey Mann
100. James Martin
101. Joe Martin
102. John Beck Mauldin
103. Harold M. Mauldin
104. Quentin May
105. Otho Maxwell
106. Delma McAfee
107. Charles McDaniel
108. Fayette M. McElhannon
109. Charles E. McRae
110. Willie Mize
111. James F. Moore
112. Woodrow Morrow
113. John Naglich
114. Marvin Rex Neal
115. Roy Neal
116. Walter Neville, Jr.
117. W.A. Newman
118. Ralph Nicholson

119. Claude A. Nix
120. L.C. Nix
121. Victor Nix
122. Wilson Goodwin Nix
123. Charles Ogletree
124. William Osborne
125. Robert Oswald
126. Russell Perkins
127. J.S. Perry
128. Joseph Peterson
129. Johnny Phillips
130. Lamar Pickens
131. John Cecil Porter
132. Ray Porter
133. Truett Porter
134. Charles A. Puette
135. Samuel C. Pursley
136. Emmett L. Rhodes
137. Randall Rice
138. Byron Rich
139. Owen Robson
140. L.E. Rodgers
141. Edwin Roe
142. Carl Rogers

143. Bartley Jack Sanders
144. Robert Sangster
145. Arthur Schlock
146. Norman Simonton
147. Reo L. Simmons
148. Eric Smith
149. Raymond Smith
150. Roy Smith
151. William Smith
152. Glenn Southers
153. Herbert Spears
154. Montelle Stamey
155. James Sutton
156. Edsell Taylor
157. Guy Taylor
158. Andrew Edwin Teasley
159. Warren Thornton
160. Denver V. Truelove
161. Virgil Wellborn
162. James Williams
163. Wesley B. Williams
164. Albert Willoughby
165. Sherman Wilson

Top Row: J. T. Alexander, Jr., Marion Holman Haley with B-17 Crew, Jimmy Deal, Marion Holma[n]
Cannon (Watrous), John W. Naglich, Joe Martin, Marlar L. Carpenter, Bottom Row: Claude Augustu[s]

HALEY, ALICE MAE KITCHENS (GARREN), MIDDLE ROW: HARDING CAIN, L. G. BOWEN, JR., MARY JACQUELINE NIX, GUY L. TAYLOR, NORMAN SIMONTON AND CREW, LUCY MASHBURN (BLACKWELL), DENVER TRUELOVE.

Chapter Twenty-Nine

MINISTERS AND MISSIONARIES

ALICE LENNON, ANNA LEE JONES AND ALINE CLAYTON

he Christian atmosphere of the Rabun Gap-Nacoochee School campus during the '30s and '40s was reinforced by both the dedicated Bible teachers and the idea that each task well done was an exercise in spirit and faith.

For impressionable young people, the examples of their teachers were a powerful force in the development of work, worship, and study ethics. For some, it was a new experience. For others, it was a continuation of the Christian values at home.

Citing his remembrance of Miss Alice Lennon's New Testament class, one of her former students said, "It was rumored that she could recite the entire New Testament." But perhaps her most memorable achievement was in the care and nurture of her students.

During the junior college era, other outstanding Bible teachers were Dr. George Bellingrath, Dr. and Mrs. Coit, and her father, Mr. Galloway, who often served as chaplain, according to Geneva Mayfield.

It is always difficult to measure scientifically the impact of caring adults on young people, but from the examples of hundreds of former students who went forth into the world to become lay leaders in their churches, there is no denial that the Bible classes, combined with the careful, personal nurturing of faith, had a remarkable influence, not only on the students, but on society, as a whole.

In that period from 1934-45, at least four of the students made commitments to full-time service as ministers or missionaries— Curran T. Gunn, Morris Jesse Ramey, Georgia Alice Miller, and Margaret Folsom Taylor.

The Reverend Curran Thorton Gunn

When Curran Thorton Gunn, class of 1941, arrived on campus in the summer of 1939, he was a typical young man, with a thirst for higher education.

"I was born in a Georgia sharecropper's house," he said, "on April 6, 1921. After graduating in 1938 from Byromsville High School in Dooly County, Georgia, I received a brochure from the junior college."

But it was his brother Charlie who enrolled first. Later accepted on a work scholarship, Curran arrived at Rabun Gap by bus, with all his worldly belongings in his trunk. He was just in time to see Charlie graduate in the May 1939 ceremony.

He was also present for the farewell dinner when both Dr. Ritchie and Dr. Coit retired, with Dr. George Bellingrath becoming the new head of the school. "Tears flowed that night," Curran remembered.

Accepted for the fall quarter of 1939, Curran immediately went to work on the farm crew to help pay his tuition. That first summer, he was paid eleven cents an hour.

"Two days a week," he said, during the fall quarter, "I helped the girls do the boys' laundry." With no heavy duty washing machine, this task required muscle strength. He used an old-fashioned scrub board to wash the overalls, and once the girls rinsed them, then Curran wrung them out. The girls on the laundry team then hung them on the lines to dry.

"I also kept the fire going under the vat where the clothes were boiled," he said. "Then, I worked in the corn fields, cut grass, and did anything else that Mr. Miller asked me to do.

"My second summer, I worked as a janitor in the boys' dormitory, and in the fall, when school started, I continued to work there on Fridays and Saturdays."

For the short visits home, one week in summer and during Christmas holidays, Gunn hitchhiked from Rabun Gap back to his rural home outside Vienna. A more certain transportation was provided by the school for social outings off campus, such as the trip to Cherokee, North Carolina, which Gunn enjoyed. Also enjoyable were the social events on campus—especially the folk dances or "Big Ring" on Saturday nights.

For one hour and a half on Sunday afternoons, the girls' dormitory was the scene of much social activity. "I dated some," Gunn said, remembering a certain young lady in the class of '43. Besides Sunday afternoons, "we would walk to the planned social gatherings and back to the girls' dorm. Some days at noon, we would get to walk together to the dining hall from the administration building and back after lunch."

Except for that brief time reserved for dating, Sundays were a day for religious activities and rest, if one were not assigned to the caring and feeding of animals.

"During the school year, I went to Sunday School in the administration building every Sunday morning," Gunn said. "On the first Sunday of each month, we were required to attend church services at the local Methodist Church. On the second and fourth Sundays, we went to the Baptist Church; the third to the Presbyterian, and any fifth Sunday, Dr. Bellingrath preached to us at the Presbyterian Church."

Up to that time, Curran had not joined a church, had not been baptized, or made a serious religious commitment. All that changed during the religious emphasis week that first year. "I accepted Jesus as my Savior," he said.

"I united with the Head of Tennessee Baptist Church and on the second Sunday in May 1940, I was baptized by Rev. J.F. Marchman of Dillard in Betty's Creek, where the road starts up the hill to the church. The Lord began dealing with me to serve him full-time, and as I entered my second year, I felt the call to the ministry."

Gunn enrolled at Mercer University in Macon to continue his education. But after one quarter, World War II intervened. He worked as a storekeeper at Warner Robins Airfield for three years before entering the U.S. Army Air Corps. For eighteen months, he served as a rawinsonde operator, tracking weather balloons in the upper atmosphere.

Returning to Mercer after the war, Gunn graduated in 1949. From there, he entered New Orleans Baptist Seminary and completed his bachelor of divinity degree in 1952.

"The summer of 1950, I was appointed by the Home Mission Board to serve for ten weeks at Thibodaux, Louisiana. There, I met Nina Belle Holaday, who was a Home Mission appointee to the people of French descent. After a short courtship by mail, interspersed with visits, I asked Nina Belle to marry me, and she accepted.

"Our marriage took place in the New Orleans Seminary chapel, and I became the pastor of a small church in central Louisiana where Nina Belle was working.

"In our nearly ten years there, I learned the French culture and to use a little of the French language during visitation. Our work together consisted of teaching classes, preaching, holding revivals, and visitation. In 1952, Nina Belle and I were appointed by the Southern Baptist Board to serve as 'church planters,' to cultivate and nourish new believers. For thirty-one years, we served in five different locations, working and helping to build three complete church buildings, and educational space on the fourth church building.

"At different times," Gunn said, "I served as Moderator, Vice-Moderator, and Clerk of the Louisiana Association, as well as Clerk in Natchitoches Association." Working in many summer camps for boys and speaking at World Mission Conferences on French Home Missions were also part of his ministry.

"The last four years of our active ministry," he commented, "Nina Belle and I served as Co-Directors of the Grace Rescue Mission in Lake Charles, Louisiana, ministering to the needs of transient and homeless men."

The Gunns retired in August of 1986. Moving to Montana to be closer to their daughter and grandchildren, they had eight retirement years together before Nina Belle died in 1994.

The Reverend Gunn is still active in his witnessing. "I am still going to a nursing home every week to conduct a service and do some visitation. And I'm currently serving on the Executive Board of the Southern Baptist Fellowship of Montana."

His hobbies of reading, gardening, and genealogy also keep him busy.

In remembering those early days as a junior college student at Rabun Gap-Nacoochee School, the Reverend Curran T. Gunn said, "There, I learned to work and take responsibility. The religious atmosphere helped me into a life's vocation that was very satisfying."

THE REVEREND MORRIS JESSE RAMEY

The class of 1941 produced another outstanding minister, but his ministry was cut short by his untimely death at the age of thirty-five.

Morris Ramey lived on a farm at Mountain Rest, South

Carolina. His parents were quite poor, and to enable him to enroll at the Rabun Gap-Nacoochee Junior College, they sold one of their cows for his initial down payment on his education. All the rest he earned in the work scholarship program at the school.

After the two years at Rabun Gap, Morris completed his degree at Furman University and was ordained a Baptist minister. While at Furman, he and the former Lynda Wilson, junior college class of '42, were married. This was during the war, and while Morris was in school, Lynda worked in a bandage factory in Greenville, South Carolina, where the school was located.

When the two moved to Louisville, Kentucky, where Morris worked on his master of divinity degree at Southern Baptist Theological Seminary, Lynda continued her war work as an electrician, modifying planes at the Vultee Aircraft Company.

While studying at the Seminary, Morris pastored two churches in the northeast corner of Kentucky, near Glenco, and upon graduation, he accepted various pastorates in both Georgia and Florida. At the time of his death from cancer, he was pastor of a new mission of First Baptist Church of Gainesville, one of the largest Baptist churches in Florida — situated near the campus of the University of Florida.

For eight years after his death, Lynda worked as a secretary at the First Baptist Church in Gainesville. And then for twenty-two years, she served as associate director of Baptist Campus Ministry at the University of Florida, retiring in 1985.

The Rameys are the parents of a son, Edwin Morris, and a daughter, Katrina Dale.

Lynda remarried in 1969 — to Allen H. Hasty, who passed away in 1995. For twelve years, she has been a volunteer for Hospice of North Central Florida. Ordained a deacon in Westside Baptist Church in Gainesville, and working with senior adults, Lynda continues her interest that she shared with the man she met at the

Rabun Gap-Nacoochee School—Morris Jesse Ramey.

Although his life was cut short, he was an example of the best that came from a school where work, worship, study, and responsibility were words to live by.

MARGARET FOLSOM TAYLOR AND ALICE MILLER

Two other alumni who made a difference in the religious world were Margaret Folsom Taylor, missionary to Brazil, and the late Alice Miller, missionary to Africa.

Margaret Folsom, from Leesburg, Florida, was in the class of 1942. After a year at West Georgia College, she married a Presbyterian minister, Rev. T. Reichardt Taylor. As a student at Rabun Gap, she had particularly enjoyed the Bible classes and Christian Fellowship. In 1946, she and her husband went to Brazil as missionaries of the Presbyterian Church, USA. They retired in 1982 to Black Mountain, North Carolina.

Margaret, who now lives in Virginia, said, "Rabun Gap prepared me for thirty-five years of serving God on the Foreign Field. As a missionary, I filled many positions of leadership in the frontier of Brazil and established churches there."

Georgia Alice Miller, class of '36, had a varied life as a teacher, a nurse, and a missionary.

ALICE MILLER, R.N.

Dr. Ritchie, aware of her ambition to become a registered nurse, gave her employment after graduation, as the supervisor in charge of the girls' work in the kitchen, until she could save enough money to enter nursing school. At that time, he was not aware that his generosity would be repaid by Alice Miller, R.N. Dr. Ritchie passed away on November 22, 1948, and it was Alice

Miller who returned to the mountains of north Georgia to care for him in his final illness.

Later becoming a missionary nurse, Miller was sent by the Southern Baptist Missionary Board to Ogbomosho, Nigeria. One of her classmates, Blanche Truelove Bowen, in her adult work as Girls' Auxiliary counselor, corresponded with her.

"She wrote of traveling by canoe on the river to the villages to vaccinate the children."

While in Africa, Alice Miller contracted a native disease that, within hours, was fatal.

She gave her life in service for others. Surely, no one could have a finer epitaph.

Dr. Ritchie's Final Resting Place

Song of the Valley Dweller

By the crystal Chattahoochee
'Neath the cloud-capped cliffs of Tray,
Where the blue of earth and heaven
Kiss each other every day,
Lies a wide and wondrous valley
Like a smile on old earth's face,
Winsome, witching fair Nacoochee
Full of nature's charm and grace.

Northward swing the hills of Rabun
And Tallulah's crescent range,
Southward Yonah's granite summit
Greets the dawning's purple change.
North and west the rugged Blue Ridge
Skyward holds her sheltering line,
While against the morning twilight
Lynch lifts high her lonesome pine.

Fair Nacoochee, vale of beauty,
Thou hast won my heart of hearts;
All my love is gladly given
For the smile of love thou art.
Lynch, Tallulah, Tray and Yonah,
May thy 'circling summits high
Ever guard this charming valley
As the years pass swiftly by.

Then, if I should fail to hear Him,
And these hands must folded be
And this heart must cease its labor
E'er the Master's face I see
Then may those who know and love me
Come and lay me close to rest
By the bright streams of Nacoochee,
Near the hills I love the best.

John Knox Coit, Sr.

Part Three

Post World War II

DR. GEORGE BELLINGRATH
PRESIDENT 1939-1948

MR. OLIN CONWAY SKINNER
PRESIDENT 1949-1956

DR. KARL ANDERSON
PRESIDENT 1956-1984

REV. BRUCE C. DODD, JR.
PRESIDENT 1984-1992

Chapter Thirty

THE ERAS OF PRESIDENTS
BELLINGRATH, SKINNER, ANDERSON AND DODD

A World War I-vintage song asks the question: "How're you gonna keep 'em down on the farm after they've seen... Paree?"

This was particularly true after World War II. New avenues emerged for veterans. The G.I. Bill was established, enabling many to go back to school.

New vistas opened, beyond the rural life and dawn-to-dusk occupation of farming. New technologies emerged and, suddenly, there were options.

Some, who had previously never traveled more than twenty miles from home, had seen the world and exchanged with their compatriots new ideas and hopes for the future. Their lives, truly, would never be the same.

Neither would the school that had nourished and encouraged them in their earlier years.

Dr. George Bellingrath, who had been president of nearby Piedmont College, had come to the campus upon the retirement of the Ritchies and the Coits in 1939. At that time, there was some discussion of yet another merger between two schools—Rabun Gap and Piedmont.

Bellingrath had impeccable credentials, with a bachelor's degree from Davidson College, his B.D. degree from Union Theological Seminary, and his Ph.D. degree from Columbia University. He had also served pastorates in Chattanooga, Tennessee; Flushing, New York; and Richmond, Virginia. With him came Mrs. Bellingrath and their daughter, Ruth (Mobley), who was a high school student at the time.

For the next few years, everything ran smoothly on campus, until the war clouds thickened. And then, the number of boarding students, made up primarily of junior college age, dropped precipitously. As the war progressed, the number of older high school students also began to drop as the drafting of eighteen-year-olds became significant.

According to Dr. Karl Anderson, Bellingrath, because of the war, had the unfortunate experience of seeing the junior college department dissolved by the trustees in 1945, despite strenuous objections by the community. Yet, there seemed to be no alternative.

Then began the careful rebuilding of the school into a four-year high school program. During the war, a number of much-needed renovations took place on campus. The heating systems of both dormitories and Hodgson Hall were updated from wood to coal, and a filtration system was added to the water supply.

But by December 31, 1948, Bellingrath resigned to become Academic Dean and professor of psychology at Presbyterian College in South Carolina. Later, a girls' dormitory on Rabun-Gap campus was named in his honor.

Mr. Olin Conway Skinner, who had retired from Berry College in 1948, had moved with his wife to Highlands, North Carolina, after a twenty-four-year career in which he had been head of the student industrial work program and representative supervisor of the construction of the four buildings in the Ford Quadrangle on the Berry campus in Rome, Georgia.

A native of Alabama, he had received both a bachelor's and a master's degree, with honors, in mechanical engineering from Auburn University, with subsequent teaching positions in Eufala, Alabama and at Richmond Academy in Augusta, Georgia.

He was persuaded to come out of retirement to serve as interim president, until a successor to Dr. Bellingrath could be found. He remained as president from the spring of 1949 to July 1956.

During that time, he worked closely with Mr. George Woodruff, Chairman of the Board of Trustees. The two launched an impressive building program that included two new wings to Hodgson Hall—the Woodruff Chapel and the library-auditorium; the Arthur Smith Industrial Arts building; and the Addie Corn Ritchie dining hall. Since Skinner had stumbled on the rough pathway one night on his way to a basketball game, he felt there was also a need for paved walkways for all students and faculty. Under his presidency, equipment in the classrooms was updated; the farm program expanded, and other plans put in place for the future.

In those seven and a half years, a search had begun for his successor, and that man had already been brought on board by the time Skinner retired for the second time from a long and distinguished career as an educator and administrator. He was often heard to say in later years that his time spent at Rabun Gap-Nacoochee School had been the capstone to his career.

O.C. Skinner passed away in 1979, and in his honor a new building was named for him—the O.C. Skinner Natatorium, a recreation complex with indoor swimming pool.

In the late '40s, when Dr. Karl Anderson was finishing his graduate work at Columbia University after military service, he attended a church meeting in New York, where the president of Toccoa Falls Institute, also a mountain school in Georgia, was speaking.

From that talk, Anderson became interested in the institute, and when he received his master's degree in business education, he was hired as a coordinator of educational activities at Toccoa Falls.

Anderson did not fit the profile that O.C. Skinner had in mind as his successor at Rabun Gap. Anderson was young – only thirty-one, and he looked much younger. He did not have a connection with the Presbyterian Church. And he was perfectly satisfied in his position at Toccoa. Added to that, he was pursuing his doctoral degree with the idea of becoming an administrator in a junior college – not in a high school.

But Anderson's name kept coming up in conversations Skinner had with various people concerning a possible successor. Finally, the two got together.

Suitably impressed with Anderson, O.C. Skinner arranged a Sunday afternoon visit with the Chairman of the Board, Mr. George Woodruff, at his summer cottage, so he could meet the man they planned to bring on board.

"Mr. Woodruff's cottage," Anderson said, "was much more palatial than the word suggests. And as to Mr. Woodruff, he was in the slang of today, 'a class act.' He was a polished gentleman – gracious, but he was also a hard-nosed business-man."

That graciousness was also evi-dent in Mrs. Woodruff (Irene), who entertained Anderson's wife, Elizabeth, and their young adopted daughter, while the men talked.

MR. GEORGE WOODRUFF, BENEFACTOR

Anderson was hired as the school's business manager, with the proviso that, if things did not work out for his assuming the presi-dency of the school at Skinner's retirement, he would still be kept on as business manager.

For four years, from 1952-1956, Anderson worked with O.C. Skinner, and upon his retirement, Anderson became president—and remained at Rabun Gap for thirty-two years, until his own retirement in 1984.

In explaining the public and private aspects of the school, Anderson said, "You'll have to go back to the early '20s. Andy Ritchie had started the school on the hill. And a good many young people walked in or rode in as best they could. Then, as time went by, the boarding department began to grow more important, and some people in the community felt left out. One of the things Ritchie did was to raise money to build a school in Dillard, called Rabun Gap Community School.

"When the junior college got underway, children went to the community school through the ninth grade, and then came to the main campus for the tenth and eleventh grades. For many years in Georgia, high school education ended in the eleventh grade. So it was in effect what California had, which they called a four-year junior college.

"In the community school, the county took care of the hiring of teachers and provisions for county students, and helped also with community students in the tenth and eleventh grades on the Rabun Gap campus.

"In 1945, when the junior college was closed down, it was decided to move the eighth and ninth grades onto the campus, to make a four-year school, and the community school became an elementary school.

"On the basis of enrollment, Rabun Gap-Nacoochee School provided the facilities, and the county hired the teachers.... Rabun Gap added to those teachers, to accommodate the boarding students. What the community liked were the basically smaller classes.

"There was not a distinction between the boarding students and day students. So that was the basis for the county contract that lasted until 1977, when the new consolidated high school was built."

After 1977, Rabun Gap-Nacoochee School once more became a private school.

It was during these public-private years of the '60s that the Foxfire Books were published. Giving credit to the young English teacher, Elliott Wigginton, Elizabeth Anderson said, "Wig was interested in getting the kids involved in writing through his English and journalism classes. He had been familiar with this area from early childhood, and he knew the folklore...."

Anderson took up the story. "He was a young beginning teacher, but he was not succeeding as he wanted to. So he said, 'If we get kids to write about something they know'—He simply had them talk to their own parents and grandparents. That was how it started."

These efforts were tremendously successful, and once more Mr. George Woodruff, Rabun Gap's primary benefactor, gave a personal gift to help in the publication. The students also raised money through the local merchants and other interested citizens. "When they printed the first edition," Anderson commented, "the books sold like cotton candy at a fair."

During Anderson's thirty-two years of stewardship, many changes took place. Dormitories were upgraded, with carpeting, and new furniture—some of which was made in the industrial arts classes.

The plans for many new buildings were already in place, when Skinner retired. These were built in Anderson's time—the Irene Woodruff and Karl Anderson dormitories; the natatorium, the new administration building, and the gymnasium, named for Andrew Ritchie.

"The capstone," Anderson said, "was the Fine Arts building, then the student center. We had raised over eight hundred thousand dollars. When I retired in 1984, the funds were there; the plans were there; the site was there."

The large scale work program that had helped to sustain the school and the students from the beginning had declined over the years, due to a number of factors.

And the Farm Family Plan, that had also been so significant in the early days of the school, had lost its relevancy by the 1960s. Fewer people were interested in farming. Families could make a better living in the textile factories that were being built nearby. And with increased mechanization, it took more capital to support the farming industry. The day of the small farm had passed.

"We had the university extension service up here for extended studies concerning the program," Anderson said. "They came to the conclusion that what we were doing was good in its day, but no longer.

"But we had a valuable resource here, we thought – this land. So we increased the dairy, improved the milking parlor, and built a silo. Then, we raised beef cattle.

Later, even the dairy was dismantled. The stringent regulations, such as those enacted by OSHA, combined with the need to hire men, rather than relying on the students for such time-consuming work, put an end to the dairy enterprise.

"But we still looked at the work program as a very vital part of the school," Anderson emphasized. "And our approach to it was that whatever you did was honorable. Whatever you did had learning capacity. The work program, although on a much smaller scale, seemed important to us as a character-building experience."

This aspect of the school, maintaining the fundamental premises of its founder, while providing a modern education, was highlighted in those years by national publications, such as *Time Magazine*, as well as various local and regional newspapers.

When the Andersons first arrived at Rabun Gap, Elizabeth Anderson served as houseparent in one of the dormitories. But foremost in her involvement was the updating of the alumni files, which she and Ruth Ritchie Carter, the daughter of Andrew and Addie Corn Ritchie, began. Although the junior college group had formed its own alumni association, the general alumni group of all students who had attended Rabun Gap-Nacoochee School were not active at that time.

In looking back over his thirty-two years as president of Rabun Gap-Nacoochee School, Dr. Karl Anderson remembers the comment one of the trustees made after the period of transition in the '70s from public to private school again. "Karl, I gotta tell you now. I didn't think you folks were gonna make it."

Karl replied, "I'm glad you didn't tell me that back then.

"George Woodruff and others were wanting to see something happen," he added. "They had been part of the school down through the years, and they wanted to see some shifts. So the Woodruff Foundation and others were gracious to provide the funds.

"And the way the Lord has blessed this school has been fantastic."

In 1983, the Rev. Bruce C. Dodd, Jr, an ordained Presbyterian minister, and director of admissions and former director of the junior school at Stony Brook in New York, came to Rabun Gap-Nacoochee School as president-designate. Succeeding Dr. Anderson in 1984, Dodd became the school's fifth president.

An accomplished athlete and coach, author, musician, and administrator, Dodd began the restructuring of the educational system, ever mindful of the challenges that had changed with each era of the school.

"Make a school where there was none.

Survive a disastrous fire.

Survive the Great Depression.

Provide a junior college.

Stay relevant during national change.

Survive as an independent institution."

A former naval officer, Dodd likened the redesign to a warship experiencing a brief overhaul, and then "proceeding immediately to sea trials. The first year underway was a study in finding everything that leaked, squeaked, and malfunctioned.

"While the mandates of the strong study-work-worship heritage — the what and why of the school's purpose and mission— were to be kept in place, the other aspects of who, when, where, and how were all negotiable," he said.

Realizing its special place as primarily a school for middle-range students, President Dodd took three important steps: to invite a resource person to the campus to assess school performance and potential with the board of trustees and local members of the community, to prepare a case study, and to clarify the school's covenant relationship with the Synod of South Atlantic of the Presbyterian Church, while keeping in mind the pluralistic religious make-up of its students.

And so, while reaffirming its Christian heritage and nurturing environment, changes were made to enhance and upgrade the academic program, to put into place new admissions guidelines, to add outstanding teachers to faculty already in place, and to make major renovations to the physical plant, including new buildings.

Drama, dance, fine arts, and an equestrian program were added. The craft shop was reorganized; summer programs were instituted, and the school advanced into the computer age.

Through some of the more difficult years, the school had gained a reputation as a place to send troubled teenagers. Redesigning the public image, along with new admissions guidelines, Rabun Gap-Nacoochee School once more returned to its heritage of attracting deserving students who needed help in financing an education. But now, the outreach was not only into the community, but into the inner cities and other countries.

New technologies and a flexible curriculum reflected the changes in society; yet "the traditional rudiments of learning" remained in place.

"We find it essential to always keep in touch with the classical elements of education," President Dodd said, when interviewed during his administration. And with the completion of the Fine Arts building, he added, "We want every student's spine to rattle with the finest culture in the world. We certainly don't want our students thinking that Pavarotti is a linebacker for the Colts."

Through the suggestion of then-Chairman of the Board of Trustees, Joel H. Cowan, the school, after three years of study and investigation, adopted Wicat's integrated learning systems courseware, whereby the school's two hundred and fifty students benefited.

At that time, Dodd said, "Using Wicat's learning systems in a classroom means that we can do what amounts to a reinforcing, enriching tutorial program impossible otherwise. A teacher who is computer literate can tutor twenty-four students simultaneously, and seventy-five percent of the time those students are spearheading their own learning process."

Recognized as an outstanding and active member of the Rabun Gap community, Dodd was also called upon to speak on behalf of the one-thousand-member National Association of Independent Schools in hearings in Washington, D.C., on the negative impact of the Tax Reform Act of 1986, governing the alternative minimum tax on charitable gifts.

"Charitable giving enables private resources to be invested for the public good," he said. "If the government is short of money for education and social services, the least it can do is to encourage private sources of support."

Carolyn Dodd, as wife of the president, became an active liaison between the school and the Rabun Gap-Nacoochee Guild, one of the private sources of support for the school. She also served as Alumni Director, computerizing alumni files, and helping to develop a strong alumni association, with class agents, and to encourage a program of giving among alumni.

Bruce Dodd remained as president of Rabun Gap-Nacoochee School until 1992, when he became headmaster of Monroe Academy in Forsyth, Georgia. Currently, he is serving as minister of the First Presbyterian Church in Clarkesville, Georgia.

The Field and Soccer Complex on the Rabun Gap campus is named in his honor.

In his nine years as president of Rabun Gap-Nacoochee School, Bruce C. Dodd, Jr. became the catalyst as the school began to "develop its sense of vision for the future."

MORRIS BROWN BUILDING

Chapter Thirty-One
VISIONS FOR THE FUTURE

In 1992, the board of trustees voted to retire the title of "president" and designate the private school's educational administrator as "headmaster."

So, in effect, Robert D. Johnston, formerly head of Country Day School in Charlotte, North Carolina, became Rabun Gap's first official headmaster.

Serving for four years before retirement in 1996, Johnston affirmed that "students are different today, as are families." Speaking of one-parent homes, or homes in which both parents work, he said, "It is not uncommon to find young people who have spent years in day care. And young people are highly influenced by television."

In defining the school's added responsibilities, Johnston said, "This is an era when we can effect some change of our own in the educational program." While focusing on academics, an emphasis was also placed on behavior—on "the character we want our students to... learn."

More important than ever were the intrinsic values set forth at the beginning, with a strong nurture of character and self-esteem alongside the academic development of the student.

Excelling in sports, the arts, and social consciousness, the students were kept busy during those four years.

The Gap Singers performed in Carnegie Hall, just as thirty-odd years previously, students from the school had exhibited their crafts at Rockefeller Center.

Held on campus was Georgia's first Envirothon, an academic competition on the environment. And the socially and environmentally conscious students helped flood victims in south Georgia to put things in order again, once the Flint River had returned to its banks.

Plays, musical performances, the fortieth-year rededication of the chapel, the completion of the outdoor volley ball court and a replica locomotive made by students in industrial arts were milestones, as were academic and poetry awards by students.

HEADMASTER ROBERT D. JOHNSTON
1992-1996

The school, in keeping with its global commitment, hosted the former Bosnian Junior Olympic Basketball Team in a two-week basketball camp, and barns that had been a part of the Farm Family program were selected for restoration.

Four new endowment funds were created, making Rabun Gap's total endowment $64,271,024—a far cry from the initial $5,000 raised to create the school in the early nineteen hundreds.

Conscious of the importance of gathering significant memorabilia from the past to document the school's centennial history, Bill Stiles, class of '49, was appointed school archivist.

Also appreciating the legacy of the past while recognizing the rapid change in society and the new role of schools keeping up with those changes, Johnston said, "The work force in the next century will involve only one-third of the nation. With each generation having a shorter time to prepare for those changes, we must adapt if we are going to be effective with what we do in education."

Shortly before Headmaster Johnston's retirement in 1996, Mr. Robert L. Rearden, Jr., Chairman of the Board of Trustees, initiated a committee search for his replacement.

HEADMASTER GREGORY D. ZEIGLER
1996 —

On January 4, 1996, Gregory D. Zeigler, assistant headmaster for academic affairs at Wasatch Academy in Utah, was named as Rabun Gap-Nacoochee School's new headmaster.

Prior to Wasatch, Zeigler was headmaster of Sunriver Preparatory School in Oregon. With a bachelor's degree in English from Washington and Jefferson College in Pennsylvania, and a master's degree from the University of Utah, he also did graduate work at Emerson College.

Growing up in Pennsylvania on the campus of a boarding school, where his father taught science, Zeigler is particularly well suited for a mountain school with a strong background of academics combined with faith.

A Presbyterian, he has long been interested in wilderness programs, mountaineering, and outdoor recreation, as well as a strong academic program combined with the arts.

During his thirty-year career as both teacher and administrator, he has taught English, drama, journalism, and has, himself, written fiction and screenplays. Perhaps that is why he is so interested in seeing the school develop in the arts, to enrich not only the students, but the community, as a whole.

Arriving on campus with his wife Dimmie and children, Zeigler said, "As a family, we have sought a community which is safe, caring, and diverse."

He also brought an enthusiasm to the campus, that in the past two years has caught fire with both the students and the alumni, revitalizing commitments to honor the past while building for the future.

In a short period of time, exciting changes in the classroom, the dormitories, campus life and extracurricular activities, and relationships with alumni have been made.

Enrollment at the school has grown forty percent, with all dormitories in use. "Classes and administrative areas are linked campus wide. Through access to the Internet and teaching software on our new laptop computers," Zeigler said, "students and faculty alike have been connected to a universe of educational opportunities."

Citing the endowment and the generous contributions of interested friends and patrons, Zeigler pointed out that "the tuition at Rabun Gap is twenty percent less than at comparable schools."

Consequently, almost two million dollars have gone to merit scholarships, with financial assistance provided to seventy percent of the students, annually.

"The Board of Trustees, under the leadership of Robert L. Rearden, Jr. is in the process of planning for the next century at Rabun Gap-Nacoochee School," Headmaster Zeigler added. Included in these plans are "a new arts and technology building, sports complex, expanded science facility, additional faculty and staff, and educational excellence, supported by the basic beliefs of Judeo-Christian values... with the traditional flagship virtues of work, study, and worship."

Among the staff and faculty playing a significant role in this revitalization of the school, and serving as liaison with alumni, friends, and patrons are Patricia L. Boyd, Assistant Head for Advancement, and Janie Owens, Alumni Secretary.

Boyd, a former director of development for National Museum of Wildlife Art in Jackson Hole, Wyoming, and founder and executive director for Arts in the Parks, is an expert in marketing, public relations, and the development of educational programs.

Today, if visitors walk through the campus of Rabun Gap-Nacoochee School, they will no longer find any mule racing to the barns, with Dr. Ritchie chastising the participants in the dining room. Instead, the school has a bona fide equestrian team, winning ribbons at regional horse shows.

No longer do students sit under the trees and study while

EQUESTRIAN TEAM

watching over the cattle, or provide the meat for the student dining hall. Instead, the prime beef cattle are watched over by a farm manager, and then sold at a premium price to a meat company.

O.C. Skinner, who once stumbled on a pathway in the dark, would be gratified that safety is still a priority at the school. New pathways and bike paths are being built, linking the campus to the town of Dillard.

Yet, as the school builds toward a new millennium, there are also many things that remain unchanged. Among these are the recognition of the uniqueness of the school, combined with the strong ties of friendship, love, and respect that bind its former students to each other.

To celebrate one hundred years of faith and hope, they have come together, with the school, to honor the past.

The Alumni Heritage Center, the life-sized bronze statues of the school's founders, a permanent archives, and the Farm Family restoration project are all a part of that heritage, revisited.

Sharing in the centennial celebration is this story of Rabun Gap-Nacoochee School's fragile beginnings and its struggle for survival in all adversities. But most of all, it is the recording of events that took place in a particular time in the school's history, the junior college years.

The hills and valleys of the Blue Ridge are resonant with voices from the past. Listen to them and remember the dream. Remember the harvest. And remember the mountain legacy that is a gift to future generations.

1934-35 JUNIOR COLLEGE CLASS

First Class, 1934-35

1. Martha Arline (Barham)
2. Woodrow W. Coffee *
3. Cool Arch Jones
4. Ralph Corn
5. Fred Z. Harris
6. Dorothy Hudgins (Shaw)
7. Winifred Hudgins
8. Agnes Jones (Wilcox)
9. Howard Jones *
10. Willie Faith Little (Ginn)
11. Gladys Juette Logan (Hill)
12. Mary Loggans (Church) *
13. Olive McClure
14. Daniel H. Maloy
15. Helen Mason
16. Agnes Moss
17. E. Villa (Bill) Page
18. Fay Pittman
19. Harold Rogers
20. Maude Rogers
21. John W. Sloan *
22. Claude L. Smith
23. George Stewart
24. Velma Webb

*Deceased

1936 JUNIOR COLLEGE CLASS

CLASS OF 1936

1. Alma Davis Abercrombie (Faris)
2. Elsie Lee Ariail (Neal)*
3. Reba Josephine Blackwell (Cameron)
4. Viola Prudence Bleckley*
5. Leona Fostel Bowen (Branch)*
6. Luther G. Bowen, Jr.
7. Marian Catherine Campbell (Hart)
8. Vesta Elizabeth Coleman (Blount)*
9. Lois Elizabeth Cooper*
10. Sarah Merle Copeland (West)
11. Ina Mae Crabb (Gatins)
12. Mildred Carolyn Craig*
13. Laura Lavon Crawford (Butt)
14. Marguerite Elizabeth Davis
15. Darrell Emerson Dollar*
16. Lonor Hobert Durden, Jr.
17. Nina Grace Dykes (Harris)*
18. Clymelia Elrod
19. Helen Thelma Franklin (Stephens)*
20. George Andrew Grist
21. Braxton Seaborn Harrison
22. Mary Lou Head (Hughes)*
23. Ruth Hollifield (Kilby)
24. Herman Edgar Hopper*
25. Oscar Kirkham Jolly, Jr.
26. Fred Martin Kelly*
27. Alice Mae Kitchens (Garren)*
28. Julia Waldroup Lane
29. Charles Edward McRae, Jr.*
30. Georgia Alice Miller*
31. Hazel Ann Moore (Musto)
32. Dakota Mozeley (Lee)*
33. William Kretzer New*
34. Fannie Jane Partain (Carithers)
35. Vera Virginia Peacock
36. Homer Eugene Pennington
37. Frances Ellen Phillips (Varner)
38. Dorothy Sue Pittman (Powell)
39. Truett A. Porter—first president of the Junior College Alumni Assn.
40. J. Paul Raby, Jr. *
41. Martha Kate Rhodes (Smith)
42. Hazel Self (Kelly)
43. Rita Pauline Shields (Stephenson)
44. Roy Clyde Smith
45. George Montel Stamey
46. James Marion Sutton*
47. Inez Swanson (Purcell)
48. Blanche H. Truelove (Bowen)
49. Walter Erman West *

*Deceased

1937 JUNIOR COLLEGE CLASS

Class of 1937

1. William Jackson Adcock
2. Mary Virginia Bailey (Cragg/Nix)
3. Bonnie Lucille Blackwell (Stoffer)
4. Lucille Jean Blalock (Cook)
5. Elsie Aleta Brendle (Sawyer)
6. Lucy Mae Burdette*
7. Mary Jacqueline Cannon (Watrous)
8. Elma E. Carter (Suttle)
9. Frank L. Clark
10. Lige Alston Corbitt
11. Ellen Corley (Hawkins)
12. John Clive Cragg*
13. C. Olan Davis
14. Herschel Davis
15. Floyd Lyman Dellinger
16. Dr. Emmett Urcey Dillard
17. Dr. Albert H.H. Dorsey
18. Bryant Durham
19. Early Frank Ford
20. Lucy Grace Forrester
21. Cora Lee Fowler (Adcock)
22. Clarice Leona Free (King)
23. Wesley Fulgham*
24. Marion Holman Haley
25. Gladys Hazel Hayes
26. Nellie Blanche Higginbotham (Ford)*
27. Robin Vesey Hiscock
28. D. Maurice Wilber Hoover
29. Earl Monroe Irby
30. Ruby J. Jackson (Ruch)
31. Myrtle Katheryn Jones (Stewart)
32. Bessie Mae Jordan (Carrol)
33. Evelyn Ellen Keen (Denton)
34. Sarah Bell Lee
35. Frances Bell Mason
36. Bonnie Evelyn Moore
37. Sarah Thelma Moore
38. George Morrow
39. William A. Newman
40. Claude Augustus Nix*
41. Martin Clinton Nix
42. Luther Duckett Nunnally
43. Naomi Ethel Nunnally (Chambers)*
44. Lillian Lenora Paul
45. George W. Perkins
46. Joseph E. Peterson
47. Fred Edgar Petty
48. Garlan James Richardson
49. J.B. Richards
50. Buford Sanders
51. Florence Alberta Smalley (Robinson)*
52. Pauline Stonecypher
53. Ruby Nell Taylor (Acree)*
54. Tiney Albert Townsend
55. Cassie Frances Wagnon (Crouch)
56. Ruth Waldrup (Ellis)
57. J.D. Ward
58. Norma Kathleen Weber (Hamilton/Haggerty)
59. Gladys Lucille Wells (Morris)
60. Frances M. White*
61. Helen Elizabeth White
62. John W. Young, Jr.

*Deceased

1938 Junior College Class

CLASS OF 1938

1. Frank B. Allgood
2. Marion Arnold
3. Curtis Randolph Ayers*
4. Nancy Helen Barrett (Barker/Petty)
5. Lillian Katherine Blalock (Willis)
6. Elva Boggs (Cordle)
7. Jefferson B. Burdette
8. Mamie Burdette (Deese)
9. Alec Caswell
10. Robert Henry Chandler*
11. Hallie Craig (Suddeth)
12. Eleanor Dalton
13. Arnold W. Darden
14. Nancy Eudora Dawkins (Perry)
15. Margaret Louise Dillard (Coldren)*
16. William Turner Enloe
17. Samuel Fletcher Fant*
18. Fred Z. Greenway*
19. Willie Lee Hammond (Burdette)*
20. Guelda Hay
21. Cosseta Heath (Morrow)
22. Velzie Hicks (Hiscock)
23. Everett High
24. Jack Vernon Hulme
25. Roy E. Jones
26. Virginia Kerr (Arey)
27. Nellie Ruth Liddell (Seay)
28. Maurine Elizabeth Lyle (Ross)
29. Aubrey Mann*
30. Floreed McDaniel (Lazar)*
31. Doris McIntosh
32. Weems R. McIntosh*
33. Rebecca Minor
34. Margaret Amanda Moody
35. Annette Moore (Garber)
36. James Furman Moore
37. John Wesley Morrow
38. William Woodrow Moore*
39. Edwin Norton
40. Irene Norton*
41. Louise Dessie Parker (Hill)
42. Willard Parrott
43. Ora Peacock (Bridges)
44. Martha E. Roberts (Nix/McDowell)
45. Clifford Schuler
46. Kate Stiles (King)
47. Jessie Lee Suddath (Rouse)
48. Jimmy Tripp
49. Alta Turpin
50. Allie Mae Webb (Petty)
51. Virgil Horace Welborn
52. James Millard White*
53. John Boyd Wood

*Deceased

1939 Junior College Class

Class of 1939

1. Bernard Adair*
2. J.T. Alexander, Jr.*
3. Robert Lee Babb*
4. James Vinyard Bailey*
5. William Edwin Bannister *
6. Oertelle "Ted" Barker
7. Otis Wilson Bell*
8. (Miss) Clifford Benton
9. Thomas J. Blair
10. Charles Cecil Bridges*
11. Annie Lou Brown (Holt)*
12. Ray Brown
13. Eugene Bryant
14. Alton Buchanan
15. G. Thomas Calloway
16. Elizabeth Cheek (High)
17. Sudie Frances (Sue) Coleman (Chandler)
18. Charles Boyd Culpepper
19. Nancy Eula Daniels (Holmes)
20. Hugh Franklin Davis
21. Earl John Dillard*
22. Kathryn Eberhart
23. Grace Faircloth (Fuqua)
24. Ernest Farmer
25. Buris Franks (Crowell)
26. Grace Jarrell Fuqua
27. Walter Pierce Fuqua*
28. Anna Marie Gibbs (Futch)
29. Geneva Ginn (Mayfield)
30. Max C. Glymph
31. Mildred Gulley (Powell)
32. Charlie Oxford Gunn
33. Doris Autry Hart*
34. James Franklin Haynes*
35. Mable Johnson (Flarity)
36. Rose Annalee Ledford (Rhodes)
37. Kathleen Lindsey
38. Alice Rebecca Logan (Tate)
39. John Beck Mauldin
40. Eloise Moye
41. Hilton Norton
42. Corrine Philyaw
43. Charles Allen Puette
44. Myra Nell Randall*
45. Randall J. Rice
46. Mary Helen Richardson (Hooper)
47. Edwin Roe*
48. (Miss) Dean Sanders
49. Doris Scales (Wright)
50. Bobby Gertie Lou Sellers (Perry)
51. Martha Nell Sudduth (Childress)
52. (Mr.) Cumbie Talley
53. Andrew Edwin Teasley
54. Zeke Thomas
55. Faye Thompson
56. Denver V. Truelove*
57. Wayne Varner
58. Theron Ward
59. Christine Mildred Warren
60. Montine Warren (Grist)*
61. Louise Webb (Bassinger)
62. Peter M. Williams*
63. Louise Wilson (Haynes)
64. Sherman V. Wilson *

*Deceased

1940 JUNIOR COLLEGE CLASS

Class of 1940

1. Mary Addington (Martin)
2. Carolyn Alexander
3. Georgia Edith Amason (Hintz)
4. Robert L. Ambrose
5. Thomas Earl Arline
6. Earl Dean Bannister*
7. Edith Grace Bannister (Cox)
8. Lila Grace Barrett
9. Mary Marguerite Barton
10. George Bennett*
11. James Ed Bleckley*
12. Thomas Cleon Bleckley*
13. Walter H. Bowen, Jr.
14. Lee Brook
15. George David Brown
16. Martha Louise Brown (Nix)
17. Evelyn Bryant
18. Ralph C. Buchanan*
19. James Harold Buffington
20. Louise Buffington (Keim)
21. Senna Burrell
22. Joseph Harding Cain
23. Iris Carnes (Nelson)
24. Sarah Elizabeth Carnes (Newman)
25. Marjorie Carpenter (Robinson)
26. Richard B. Chandler, Sr.*
27. William Rogers Chandler*
28. Tommie Crawford (Spears)
29. Hubert Davis
30. Floss Darnell (Sitton)
31. Mark E. Deal
32. Dr. Irwin Allen Dyer*
33. Muriel Dykes
34. Dr. Martha Annie Edmunds
    (Beaumont)*
35. James Enloe*
36. Joseph Hansel Farmer*
37. Therron E. Florence
38. Louise Fraser (Rose)
39. Dr. Elmer Lee Fry*
40. Mildred Gardner
41. Virginia Ann Gilbert
42. Eula Mae Glenn (Payne)
43. James Foster Goolsby
44. Garfield Garsden
45. Ethel B. Hamby
46. A. Jack Hayes
47. Jessie A. Hayes
48. Frances Jeannette Hayes (Russell)
49. Viola Elizabeth Hill (Andrews)
50. James Etsel Hopper
51. Kitty Hopper*
52. Mildred Elizabeth (Hutcherson)
53. Thomas Ivy
54. Howard Kaylor
55. Hugh W. Kelly
56. Martha Maybelle Langston (Judd)
57. Watson Ray Lankford
58. Claude E. Lester
59. Delle Elizabeth Lindsey
60. James R. Lyday
61. James Martin*
62. Dr. Joe A. Martin
63. Orlana Maxwell
64. Quentin Hughes May*
65. Dr. Fayette M. McElhannon*
66. Horace McMillan
67. Walter Morris
68. Henry Roy (Rex) Neal
69. Dr. Charles J. Ogletree
70. Louise O'Kelly
71. Kate O'Shields (Ledford)*
72. Robert Ware Oswald, Jr.
73. Dwight L. Owenby, Jr.
74. Henry Franklin Peeples
75. Martha Ellen Phillips (Deming)

*Deceased

CLASS OF 1940 (continued)

76. John Cecil Porter*
77. Ray Porter
78. Radie Sue Pritchett
79. Tabitha Ray (Melton)
80. Byron Rich*
81. Hazel Richardson
82. Jack Barnard Roberts *
83. Weyman E. Roberts
84. Ruth Robinson (Glenn)
85. Owens Robson
86. Carl Rogers
87. Helen Rogers (Nichols)
88. Eloise Elizabeth Boss*
89. Harris Sanders
90. Bartley Jack Sanders
91. Virginia Shephard (Clontz)
92. Norman A. Simonton
93. James M. Smith
94. Herbert M. Spears*
95. Billie Lee Spradlin
96. Locke Craig Stepp, Jr.
97. Leon Stratton
98. Blanche Weeks Suddath (Descani)
99. Reba Orene Swanson (Wall)
100. Liza Jane Thigpen (Alexander)
101. Ray Turpin*
102. Horace Oscar Tyler
103. Ollie Mae Wages (Hayes)
104. Hautelle Warren (Milford)
105. Katie Mae Warren (Burgess)
106. Helen Lucille (Wilder)
107. Henry Marshall Wilson

*Deceased

1941 Junior College Class

CLASS OF 1941

1. Mary Willie Alexander
2. John Henry Askew
3. Josephine Askew (Wheeler)
4. Lanelle Avery (Wyatt)
5. Dr. Charles Edwin Bishop
6. Elbert Earl Bishop
7. Inez Blair
8. Joe B. Braddy, Jr.
9. Russell Bradford*
10. Rachel Fay Brown (Allin)
11. Mary Bruce (Hart)
12. Dorothy Mae Burrell (Church)
13. Doris Roberta Cheek (Thomas)
14. Frances Myra Cobb (Bagwell)
15. Joseph Raleigh Craft*
16. Merle C. Cromer (Brown)
17. Florine C. Crowe (Collins)
18. Paul E. Crowe*
19. Jack Darnell*
20. Hubert Davis
21. Leroy Deaton*
22. Ella Lou Denman
23. Annie M. Dillard (Klar)
24. Frank Hawes Drinkard
25. Dolphus I. Duckett
26. Essie Mae Eller
27. Lila A. Evans (Ogletree)
28. Dollie Exum
29. Eva Nell Franks (Moon)
30. Frances Freeman (Johnson)
31. William O'Gilvey Gosnell
32. Jake Griffin*
33. Dorothy Grindstaff (Blair)
34. Ruth Grist (Moseley)
35. Rev. Curran Thorton Gunn
36. Freddy Hall*
37. Philip W. Harper
38. Roy S. Harper, Jr.
39. Richard M. Hart, Jr.
40. Julia Head (Pope)
41. Roberta Henson (Grant)
42. Rubye Herringdine (Skelton)
43. Bernice Ledford
44. Morene Holland (Hopper)
45. Mabel Hunter (Bowen)
46. Allene M. Johnson (Johnson)
47. Col. Charles G. Johnson
48. Kenneth L. Johnson*
49. Oscar Lloyd Jollay, Jr.
50. Marshall Jones
51. William E. Kirkland, Jr.
52. Bernice Ledford
53. Raymond Paul Leonard *
54. Walter R. Lloyd, Jr.
55. Margaret McGee (Rodgers)
56. M. Talmadge McNeil*
57. Willie Mize
58. Charles Herman Moon
59. Pauline Moore (Matheson)
60. J.D. Morgan
61. Nadine Nelms (Birdsong)
62. L.C. Nix
63. Victor C. Nix
64. William F. Osborne
65. Gladys Mildred Owens (Potts)
66. Joel Peace
67. Nina Lorine Ferry (Caudell)
68. Geraldine Pittman (Dial)
69. Rev. Morris Jesse Ramey*
70. Sam Ramey*
71. Emmett Louis Rhodes
72. Ouida Roberts (Craft)
73. Willa Sanders
74. Robert Sangster*
75. Duard Segars
76. Naomi Ruth Singleton (Osburn)

*Deceased

CLASS OF 1941 (continued)

77. Warren S. Slaughter
78. Eric Smith
79. Hugh Smith*
80. Raymond Smith*
81. Susie Smith
82. William T. Smith
83. Winnon Smith*
84. William Clyde Stegall
85. Glenn Southers*
86. Frances Taylor (Goolsby)
87. John Edsell Taylor
88. Leila Blanche Thigpen (Davis)
89. Cady Louise Varner (Roberts)
90. Kathleen Varner (McCoy)
91. Ruchia White (Peterson)
92. Nellie Faye Williams
93. Col. Wesley Benjamin Williams
94. Warner H. Witcher*
95. Betty Mae York (Ray)

*Deceased

1942 JUNIOR COLLEGE CLASS

CLASS OF 1942

1. Col. Henry Strange Addor
2. Louise Allen (Gregory)*
3. Sarah Dean Allen
4. Hubertee Anderson (Vandiver)
5. Richard E. Black
6. Hazel Black (Hare)
7. Doris Bleckley
8. Betty Evelyn Branch (Bond)
9. Neil Brantley*
10. Marlar LaFayette Carpenter
11. Mary Marie Carter (Dean)
12. Edwin Ross Cathey
13. Samuel E. Chambless, Jr.
14. Cecil Compton
15. Lloyd W. Cowan
16. George W. Crews, Jr.
17. Doris Dean Dallis (Adams)
18. James F. Deal
19. Ellis Jaudon Dollar
20. Dorothy Douglas (DeYoung)
21. Rosa Fant
22. Margaret E. Folsom (Taylor)
23. Frances H. Fry (Deal)
24. MaeBeth Galloway
25. Robbie Lou Green (Lovett)*
26. Archie Lamar Gregory
27. James Lester Grist, Jr.
28. Louise Hopper (Enloe)
29. Emily Nankit Horne (Threlkeld)
30. Gladys Mae Hulette (Lowe)
31. Donald J. Johnson
32. McKinley Jones*
33. Lloyd A. King
34. Samuel Hoiwell King*
35. Joseph Loomis Knight
36. William J. Lovett
37. Sybil Malcom (Simmerson)
38. Harold M. Mauldin
39. Dr. Charles P. McDaniel*
40. Ruth Belle McPherson (Yates)
41. Lois Wander Miller (Romanczyk)
42. Christine Minor (Williams)
43. Mary Sue Morgan
44. John Naglich*
45. Marvin Rex Neal
46. Ralph Nelms
47. Dr. Walter E. Neville, Jr.
48. B. Ralph Nicholson*
49. W. Goodwin Nix
50. Eschol Owensby
51. Mildred Parkins (Johnson)
52. Russell Greene Perkins
53. J.S. Perry
54. Jean Phillips
55. Mary Ruth Powers (Carter)
56. Helen Pratchard (Harper)*
57. Samuel Carithers Pursley
58. Charlie Jo Queen
60. Carl Marion Rooks
61. Myles Wilson Scoggins
62. John Singleton
63. Bessie Smith
64. Joe Smith
65. Guy Taylor*
66. Tommie Lee Taylor (Gaines)
67. Ruby Nell Teat (Haffner)
68. Cardyn Ann Ussery (Weatherly)
69. Sybil Varner (Taylor)
70. Miriam Watts (Wheeler)*
71. Hilda Vernelle White
    (Darlington)
72. James L. Whitfield
73. Col. Albert M. Willoughby
74. Lynda Wilson (Ramey/Hasty)

*Deceased

1943 Junior College Class

CLASS OF 1943

1. Beaman Allen*
2. Chloe Allred Jarrow
3. Martha Virginia Bickley (Derrick)
4. Edna Bruce (Bienvenue)
5. Erna Bruce (Deal)
6. Florence M. Brundage (Pursley)
7. Geneva Burton (Pelfrey)
8. Lt. Col. Joseph L. Clark
9. Mary Clinkscales
10. Hulda Compton (Petty)
11. Ollie Mae Crenshaw
12. Mary Frances Dunson (Boswell)
13. Wylene Forrester (Smith)
14. Ruth Gibby (Faulkner)
15. Nancy Jean Glymph (Spearman)
16. Emma Ruth Gunnin (Stronigan)
17. Mary Frances Hair (Wilson)
18. Kathleen Harris
19. Mary Frances Hayes (Sarzoni)
20. Glenn Hopper
21. Margie Venette Hudson (Flarsey)
22. Luther Gentry Johnson
23. Mary Louise Jones
24. Grace Kendrix (Corbett)
25. Juanita Kendrix (Oates)
26. Doris Kimsey
27. Dr. William R. Ledford
28. Alma Aldine Logan
29. Lucy Mashburn (Blackwell)
30. Hazel Irene Miller (Pocher)
31. Doyle Mitchell
32. Carolyn Mize
33. Delia Mize (Whitaker)
34. Maude Mize (Griffeth)
35. Evelyn Mae Moore
36. Mildred Evangeline Owenby (Simandle)
37. Evelyn Phillips (Maxwell)
38. Johnny Phillips
39. Lamar Pickens*
40. Vernice Mozelle Quarles (Wald)
41. Jean Roberts (Briggs)
42. Elura Belle Sanders
43. Ruth Sisk (Williams)
44. Ronella Skinner
45. Alline Smith (Jones)
46. Paul Smith
47. Mary Louise Sparks (Lanceford)*
48. Johnnie Sue Taylor (Dean)
49. David Henry Tinius
50. Edith Verner (Copeland)
51. Eliza Jane Watts
52. James H. Williams, Jr.

*Deceased

1944 JUNIOR COLLEGE CLASS

CLASS OF 1944

1. Susie Lee Bailey (Lancaster)
2. Frances Blalock (Windham)
3. Robbie Jo Brown
4. Ida Mae Bryant (Beacham)
5. Angie Josephine Carithers
6. Mable Carter
7. Mildred Carter (Parham)
8. Robert Shirley Dickerson
9. Elloise Douglas (Artime)
10. Ouida Fry
11. Mildred Harding
12. Adelaide Louise Harwell
13. Julian Nelson Hayes
14. Willie Mae Hembree*
15. Homer Reba Hill
16. Annie James
17. Patricia Ann Knight (Peck)
18. Otho Maxwell*
19. James Delma McAfee
20. Mildred M. McClain (Chlupacek)
21. Eleanor McMurray
22. Rose Marie Moore
23. Vesta Eloise Mundy (Hunt)
24. Martha Perteet (Ayers)
25. Jessie Mae Porter
26. Frances Jean Queen (Jackson)
27. Nina Richardson (Bradford)
28. Sarah Rucker (Haley)
29. Lorena Tanksley (Powell)
30. Nellie Thompson (Brown)
31. Warren Thornton
32. Lamar Vandiver
33. Evelyn Mae Watts (Mobley)

*Deceased

1945 Junior College Class

CLASS OF 1945

1. Emily Ruth Adams (Cabe)
2. Willie Jo Addison (Scott)
3. Jimmie Sue Addor (Buffkin)
4. Alice Bass (Horne)
5. Prudence Darnell Bass
6. Mary Wynne Berrong
7. Mary Jewel Blalock (Kelly)
8. Sarah Frances Bleckley (Fisk)
9. Lois Kate Butler (Cooper)
10. Addie Sue Carnes (Smith)
11. Edna Julia Collins (Dills)
12. Marilyn H. Cothran
13. Miriam Johnette Ertzberger (McAfee)
14. Terry Jane Franks (Duffy)
15. Mildred Gilstrap (Senn)
16. Doris Grist (Rogers)
17. Ruth Hill
18. Mary Elizabeth Hunt
19. Mabel Ruth Kelly (Hulsey) 20. Matie English Kendrick
21. Merle Kesler (Adams)*
22. Audrey Willene Kimsey (Herring)
23. Angieline Kirkland (Crum)
24. Wymna R. Kirkland
25. Dewey Edwin Lovin
26. Stella McGuire (Smith)
27. Virginia McPherson
28. Julian Wylie Neville
29. Awa Irene Nix (Smith)
30. Lois O'Shields (Turner)
31. Henrietta Reed (Barrett)
32. Hilda Rhodes (Dumesil)
33. Marialice Rickman (Wynn)
34. Arthur A. Schlock
35. Iris Jean Smith (East)
36. William Jefferson Terrell
37. Clara Belie Turpin (Bearden)
38. Floy Z. Underwood
39. Bertha Mae Watts
40. Ellen Watts (Clevenger)
41. Verna Ruth Wilson (King)

*Deceased

About The Author

PHOTOGRAPH BY HERBERT KUPER

Frances Patton Statham is the author of fourteen historical works of fiction, including *The Roswell Women*, and numerous magazine feature articles. She received her B.S. degree, magna cum laude, from Winthrop University, her MFA degree from the University of Georgia, and was awarded an honorary doctorate from World University.

She is the recipient of numerous state, regional, and national awards in music, art, and literature, and was selected Georgia Author of the Year in Fiction for three successive years.

Listed in various biographical reference books, such as *International Authors and Writers Who's Who*, *World Who's Who of Women*, and *Personalities of the South*, Frances Patton Statham resides in metro-Atlanta, Georgia.

ACKNOWLEDGMENTS

To all those who had a part in bringing this book from idea to reality, please accept my heartfelt appreciation and gratitude.

Foremost in their wonderful support were the members of the Rabun Gap-Nacoochee Junior College Alumni Book Committee: Marlar L. Carpenter and Wesley B. Williams, co-chairmen, and committee members, L.G. and Blanche Truelove Bowen; Harding Cain; Sue Coleman Chandler; Jimmy Deal; Foster Goolsby, President of the JC Alumni Association; Geneva Ginn Mayfield; Rex Neal; Jack Acree, advisor and consultant; and the two direct descendants of Andrew Jackson and Addie Corn Ritchie– Nannette Carter Curran and John Carter.

To Patricia L. Boyd, Assistant Head for Advancement and liaison between Rabun Gap-Nacoochee School and the book project committee, I wish to convey a very special appreciation, along with Bill Stiles, school archivist, whose foresight in preserving the pictures of the past has made the book more meaningful.

To former presidents of the school, Dr. Karl Anderson and Mrs. Anderson, the Reverend Bruce Dodd, and the present headmaster, Mr. Greg Zeigler, who supplied information of the school, past and present, and to John Knox Coit, Jr. Ph.D, whose memories of his father and mother, Dr. and Mrs. John Knox Coit, recreated the earlier days of the Nacoochee Institute, I wish to thank for weaving the major events in the lives of the two schools into whole cloth.

My thanks also go to Viola Hill Andrews, 1985-87 president of the Junior College Alumni, whose idea to send out questionnaires became the first step in accumulating information on the lives of former students, and to Guy B. Arthur for supplying information on his business partner, the late James Haynes.

To the junior college men and women who consented to be interviewed and to have their stories told, so that those special years from 1934 to 1945 could claim their rightful place in the centennial history of Rabun Gap-Nacoochee School, I wish to express my gratitude. And to all the others who continue to be the keepers of the mountain legacy envisioned by the school's founders, Addie and Andrew Jackson Ritchie, I say, well done.

Frances Patton Statham

BIBLIOGRAPHY

BOOKS:

1. Adams, James Truslow. Copyright: *The March of Democracy*, Vol. 5. New York: Charles Scribner and Sons, 1945(revised)
2. Blackwell, Lucy M. Copyright: *Little Earthling*. Privately published, 1976
3. Parrish, Thomas, editor. Copyright: *Encyclopedia of World War II*. New York: Simon and Schuster, 1978.
4. Ritchie, Andrew Jackson, Copyright: *Sketches of Rabun County History*. 1959 Reprint
5. United States. *The People Left Behind:* A Report by the President's National Advisory Commission on Rural Poverty. Washington, D.C. 1967
6. United States. *Urban America in the Eighties*. President's Commission for a National Agenda for the Eighties. Panel on Policies and Prospects for Metropolitan and Nonmetropolitan America. Washington, D.C. 1980

PERIODICALS AND PRIVATE PAPERS:

1. Anonymous. "All Things Saved." Personal memories of Dr. Ritchie's dining room talks. Rabun Gap-Nacoochee School Archives
2. Coit, John Knox, Jr., Ph.D. Unpublished personal recollections of Dr. and Mrs. Coit at Nacoochee Institute
3. Kontz, Ernest C. "A Story of Beginnings." Unpublished paper concerning the merger of Rabun Gap Industrial School and Nacoochee Institute
4. Miller, Charles W. *An Educational Survey of the Rabun Gap-Nacoochee School*. For the Carnegie Corporation of New York, submitted June 12, 1933. School Archives
5. *Presbyterian Survey*, 1926
6. Rabun Gap-Nacoochee School
——Catalogue, 1937-38
——Catalogue, 1939-40
——*Indian Chief*, Vol. 11, Number 4, May 23, 1842
——Junior College Alumni Questionnaires
——*Nantahalian*, 1936
——Quarterly Periodical, Spring 1995
——Quarterly Periodical, Winter 1996
——Quarterly Periodical, Spring 1997
——Southern Association of College and Schools Ten-Year Self-Study, 1988
7. Ritchie, Andrew Jackson. "The Hungry Mind." From the private collection of Ritchie papers. School Vault
8. Transcripts of personal interviews

Index